The Day Is Short

Morris B. Abram

The Day Is Short

AN AUTOBIOGRAPHY

Harcourt Brace Jovanovich, Publishers
New York and London

Requests for permission to make copies of
any part of the work should be mailed to:
Permissions, Harcourt Brace Jovanovich, Publishers,
757 Third Avenue, New York, N.Y. 10017.

Material in Chapter 12 was published in different form
in the 1979 *Medical and Health Annual,*
published by Encyclopaedia Britannica, Inc.

Library of Congress Cataloging in Publication Data

Abram, Morris B.
The day is short.

Includes index.
1. Abram, Morris B.
2. Lawyers—United States—Biography.
I. Title.
KF373.A27A327   349.73′092′4[B]   80-8738
ISBN 0-15-123982-7   347.300924[B]   AACR2

Printed in the United States of America

B C D E

Illustrations

With Joshua Abram, 1975
Joshua and Adam Abram, 1973
With Carlyn Abram, 1975
With Irene Abram, 1976
With Carlyn, 1977
In 1978

Preface

AUTOBIOGRAPHY is a very treacherous undertaking. A good case could be made that it should be written only for the family and the historical record, for candor opens the pains of the past. A cautious memoir, on the other hand, is not worth the effort of either the writer or the reader. This book would never have been conceived had I not fallen victim to a fatal disease in 1973. The oral history on which it is based was expected to be a posthumous record in the archives of the American Jewish Committee. When the tapes were transcribed, I was then under aggressive chemotherapy treatment but felt the impulse to impose an order and cohesion on the chronicle by organizing its segments in writing.

While I was doing this, I had acquired a large audience because the story of my unusually long remission from the most malignant form of leukemia appeared on the front page of the *New York Times* on August 15, 1977. Letters and phone calls from a wide circle of cancer patients and their families poured in from this country and abroad.

This account covers events long before and a few years after I fell ill. Many people contributed to the life which I have described. Some are named, as seem to befit my story. Others who played significant roles are not.

I acknowledge and thank my partners and associates, past and present, in Atlanta and New York, for their support, personal and professional, and also that of colleagues in many organizations mentioned in the text.

Families are so often acknowledged by authors. I now better appreciate the reasons.

The Day Is Short

1

ON AN EVENING in June 1973, I sat alone in a fashionable New York restaurant and waited for a beautiful woman. A few hours before, the meeting had promised to be one I had longed for in the weeks since my wife and I had separated. Not that I was expecting to run wild in my fifties—in fact, I deeply hoped for a reunion with a woman who was my first love, and whom I had rediscovered, recently divorced, after thirty years. Still, I wanted to breathe free for a while—to explore old friends anew and begin the whole process of forging new relationships. I craved the unpredictable.

But now the rendezvous seemed the cruelest joke. I had come there straight from my doctor's office. I had just been told that I was fatally ill.

Under the circumstances, the fuss and ceremony of the fancy French restaurant seemed bizarre. I stared miserably at the maître d' and the waiters, darting about me as if it really mattered.

Until that moment I thought I was in the best of health. Since there's nothing so rosy, so cavalier, as having a complete checkup when you're enjoying perfect health, I nailed down our elusive family physician, Hyman Ashman, for an appointment. We hit on my fifty-fifth birthday, June 19. I even managed a bid for serious attention: yes, I *was* experiencing a slight dizziness when I rose from a long sit in my office rocking chair and I was slightly concerned by blackish marks around the nails of both big toes. I knew of a genetic circulatory disease peculiar to Jews. I asked Ashman if the marks might be the beginning of that. "Shoe polish," he had said, and banished the black with spirits of turpentine.

But following a thorough examination, Dr. Ashman said that he'd call me after the lab had given him the results of my blood tests. That had never happened before. It was only later that it occurred to me what a tough year I had had with incessant colds that lingered on through the winter. Still I attributed these colds, really, to the immoderate number of cigars I was smoking, as well as to increased alienation from my wife, Jane, and the unavoidable pain that resulted for both of us.

When Dr. Ashman called two days later, I was astounded by his cautious phrasing: my hemoglobin was down to 11.6 from 16.8. Something was wrong, he told me; either the lab had made a mistake or I was ill. He wanted me to have a new blood count, and since I was on my way to Atlanta, I agreed to take the tests there.

In Atlanta I was relieved to learn that the hemoglobin was up to 12. I sent the report to Dr. Ashman as soon as I returned to New York. He called at once to see if I could keep an appointment with a hematologist the next morning at nine. After some impatient waiting in that gentleman's offices, I finally found myself on his examining table. He explained that he was going to do a bone marrow, and pointed two needles, one large and the other small, toward my sternum. It would only take ten minutes, he said.

Those ten minutes were the beginning of an excruciating journey through hospitals and treatments, through endless medical inquisitions, debates, experimental studies, and new therapies. I vaguely knew even that morning that the hematologist suspected something was radically wrong with me, a fact he could only have learned from Ashman. When the test was over, I rose from the table and went to my office—distraught for all my outward calm. My relative fortitude may have been due to a kind of spiritual anesthesia, for the next day I realized that I had already guessed the actual nature of my affliction.

4

When Ashman called, his anguish was manifest.

"Six o'clock tonight?"

"Sure, what's wrong?"

"We'll discuss it when you get here."

"Do I have leukemia?"

The word resonates even today, nine years later, with the sound of death.

"We'll discuss the matter at six o'clock," Ashman said.

It was only then, sitting across from me in a windowless office lit by a desk lamp, that he verified my suspicion.

"There is very little that can be done about it," he said. "I don't know that. . . . I just don't know." There was a brief silence. "I think you'd better take your advice now from a hematologist. I don't know. . . ."

I began to sympathize with my physician, not because I'm saintly or stoic but because I felt disassociated, estranged from myself—my flesh, my future. I was sorry that he had had to pronounce such a sentence.

Prodded, he began to discuss chemotherapy, the most commonly applied treatment. He abhorred it; at best, it could be a palliative. At worst, it could corrode the precious, painless days which were left and eradicate whatever joy I might salvage before the end. He kept repeating, "These chemicals are dreadful poisons, these chemicals are dreadful poisons." I respected him for refusing to lie to me or mouth some middling words of comfort.

One more bone marrow and biopsy later, I learned that I had the worst form of the disease: acute myelocytic leukemia. Not lymphocytic leukemia of childhood, where some progress had been made, nor a chronic leukemia, which sometimes smolders for years. Mine—I now possessed it, or it me—was a killer ravaging the bone marrow, bringing death by infection or hemorrhage within weeks. Four of my friends had recently perished from myelocytic leukemia, two in the previous year. None had lasted sixty days after diagnosis. Now I would not, I mourned, live the three score and ten years I had assumed a certainty, but would be cut down much earlier than anyone in my immediate family. Why?

Now the real meaning of my new freedom came home to me. I foresaw horrible, lonely weeks leading up to an inexorable death. I was not prepared to pay the price for solace from Jane, from whom

5

I had separated six weeks before. I was not even sure there was anything I wanted from her. And from Carlyn, the long-lost love I had recently found, what could I expect of her now but the most natural and healthy process of kindly disengagement? Even to call her now seemed a prologue to death; the end of a beginning.

But I couldn't resist. I called Carlyn in Atlanta. At first it seemed she did not understand the mortal seriousness of my condition, though she is an immensely informed woman. Was she masking her feelings in order to shield me? I decided I must see her, to know what she thought, by speaking with her face to face.

By the time I got to Georgia, she had already researched the hard facts of my illness with the help of a physician she had known since childhood. By doing that, I thought, she was telling me I could count on her to help me with that dark area where the physical and the psychic converge. She was actually confident that I would survive!

I suddenly felt then that if there were any chance of a miracle, if the spirit could in some way surmount my cellular catastrophe, Carlyn held the key. Forty years before, when she was only a teenager and in love with someone else, I had written her sententiously, "Go and marry Ted. If not him, it will be another, but some day I shall marry you."

But let me turn back to my story.

It was just after Dr. Ashman had given me the dreadful news and I watched apprehensively as the maître d' escorted my "blind date" to the table. She was magnificent; clearly a master of the difficult art of walking across a room. I started to crumble. As I rose to greet her, I wanted to say, "Go on home, this is a swindle. I'm a married man in love with another woman, and to top it all off I'm going to die in two or three weeks."

"I'm sorry I'm late," she said. "But I've really had a horrible, horrible day."

"Tell me about it," I said, trying to hide my resentment. I summoned the waiter, but her clear eyes had detected something in my manner.

"No," she said quietly, "First tell me about yours."

I did. I told her everything, starting with the death sentence. On the loneliest day of my life, I brashly solicited that rarest of gifts, the kindness of a stranger.

6

I have known personally scores of cancer victims. Most have treated the diagnosis as a secret, as dread as the disease. After sharing the news with a stranger on this first night, I felt relieved, and in the next days and weeks I hid Dr. Ashman's death sentence from no one. Among the first to hear were colleagues at the American Jewish Committee. I told Bert Gold, the executive vice president, at breakfast the very next morning.

To my declaration, "I'll lick this thing," he nodded in agreement, but within a week he called to ask whether I would promptly begin recording my oral history as a former president of the organization. He assigned Eli Evans, author of *The Provincials,* a history of southern Jewry, to help me. We would begin soon after I came out of the hospital—assuming I *would* come out, after the drastic initial treatments.

Eli lost no time. His dispatch in getting the taping under way when I was hairless, haggard, and anemic, and his prodding for continuing sessions, alarmed me. Did he know something I didn't? I wondered. Eli is a very bright man; he knew members of my family. . . .

In the gloom of my rented apartment, heavily draped with brown on brown on brown, where we met for our taping, I felt him out:

"Eli, I have a disease which is supposed to return and kill me in a few months or at most in a year. I intend to beat the odds."

"I know the usual prognosis."

"Well, you fit into my survival plan."

"How so?"

"Because I'm determined to finish this oral history, so I shall survive until the next taping, and the next, and the next. . . ."

For weeks we worked, Evans probing me with questions to which I gave eager and open responses. I withheld nothing. Self revelation, at a time when I was separated from my family and under sentence of death, brought a remarkable psychic release.

At first, I thought mainly of making a record for my five children, especially those who were still so young, like Josh, then only eleven. I was determined to be relentlessly truthful. I wanted my children to know me as I had longed, but failed, to know my own father.

But as I worked on, I understood that it was I who was learning about myself. In the face of extinction, I was seeking the meaning

7

of my life, adding up achievements and failures, attempting to strike a balance, unveiling motivations.

By the time the oral history was completed, I wanted to unite the disconnected fragments of my life in the form of a book. I still felt that my days were numbered and that whatever I managed to put down would be published, if ever, after my death.

It has been said that the prospect of the hangman's scaffold concentrates the mind. So, also, does imminent death loosen the tongue, removing the constraints that shape most autobiographies. It is usually left to the novelist to write the true autobiography, disguised as fiction.

I told Eli on that cold morning in 1974 that I wanted to leave a candid record, the truth as far as I knew it. He said, "Very well, let's begin."

"Where?"

"At the beginning."

2

FITZGERALD, GEORGIA, where I was born, is situated in Ben Hill County, a piny mass of some 255 square miles near the southerly tip of the Ocmulgee River. It has been the county seat, in some ways a unique country town, ever since it found itself at the juncture of three railroad lines. Though Fitzgerald never really boomed, it maintained a small steady rate of growth through the years. Despite the red clay soil and the inescapable summer heat that visibly shimmers off brick streets, the responsible citizen can live a comfortable life.

Fitzgerald was founded by Northerners, many of whom were sixty-five-year-old Civil War veterans, lured from their homes in the Midwest by the climate and through the efforts of an editor from Indianapolis named P. H. Fitzgerald, the town's official founder. Their move to the South was one of those long forgotten migrations that collectively comprise a nation's history. By the time they arrived, there was little reason for friction between them and neighboring Georgians, for the war was thirty years in the past.

The possibility that regional passions might rise to the surface was reduced by well-thought out civic tributes to the heroes of both North and South. On opposite sides of the town there's a Lee Street and a Grant Street. There's also a Jackson Street and, extraordinarily enough for Georgia, a Sherman Street. An enormous public works hotel, built to supply jobs during the depression of the late 1890s, was called the Lee-Grant.

We had two Methodist churches in Fitzgerald because the parent church had long since been divided on the subject of slavery. And we had two Memorial Days, one on April 26 for the Confederacy and the other on May 30, when Northern delegations would crank up their cars and carry wreaths to Andersonville Prison near Americus, Georgia, sixty miles away, and decorate the tombs of their dead, victims of a Confederate cruelty which matched Sherman's.

Due to the efforts of Isadore Gelders—more about him later—Fitzgerald had free school books long before there was a free school book program in the state. Schools, of course, were segregated in those days.

There never was a lynching in Ben Hill County, though in most other respects my home town, and its Northern veterans, had adopted all the traditions embraced in the highly touted "Southern way of life." The Grand Army of the Republic had occupied the territory, but by 1900 their Confederate foes had won the battle for their minds and hearts.

There were about six thousand people in Fitzgerald when I was growing up. Looking back I take a certain pride in the town. It incorporates a profound aspect of the American experience, and it gave shape to much of what I am.

When I think about the first sixteen years of my life, I recall painful scenes of estrangement, awkwardness, and confusion. I deeply resented my Roumanian father's humble circumstances, lack of education, and unmistakably foreign ways. I hated, then, his heavily accented and ungrammatical speech. Yet I eventually emulated his sociopolitical convictions and his historical heroes.

I felt more comfortable with my mother—particularly with Gentiles present—and even emulated her prideful disdain of East European Jews, a form of snobbery I would later deplore and come to resent. Mother was not trying to deny her Jewish inheritance. It was just that she regarded Judaism as a religion, she said, and not a social code, and as far as religious practice was concerned, she preferred the Reform wing, which clearly resembled the Protestant churches and was less likely to elicit anti-Semitic prejudice.

As young children, we were indoctrinated with the idea that our form of Judaism was observed in Rabbi Landau's temple in Albany, Georgia, and was quite different from the "foreign" practices of East European Jews. We never went to any services, however. Albany was ninety miles away, too far to travel on dirt roads when we had an automobile, and by the time the roads were better, our 1926 Buick was on jacks in the garage because we could not afford to operate it.

Mother's and Rabbi Landau's brand of Judaism blurred the outward distinctions between Jews and Gentiles. It used little Hebrew in the liturgy and discarded Yiddish, the language of the people, in the home. Thus, I was cut away from my father's roots.

I still envy my friends who can speak Yiddish and can communicate with gestures and Old World idioms. I held mother responsible for my disinheritance even as I strove to live up to her dreams. My confusion was heightened by a paradox: friends, even my Gentile friends, clearly favored my greenhorn father over my American mother. Why? How? Couldn't they see? Weren't they impressed by the fact that mother reserved and read every new title acquired by the Carnegie Library?

The extended burdens of my Jewish name and my father's foreignness and failures might have been more tolerable had peace reigned in our home. Mother was a frustrated woman. She never discussed the circumstances of her marriage, though she frequently mentioned that she had very much wanted to be a doctor like her father. Grandpa had quashed that, pleading lack of money, but when she said she'd settle for becoming a nurse, he forbade that too as socially unacceptable.

Grandpa might have been able to pay her tuition at a medical college had his doctor-sister, Sarah, taken her into her Philadelphia home. But grandpa had broken off all contact with Sarah after she turned down his request for financial help during the panic of 1893.

Perhaps also, in suppressing my mother's ambitions, grandpa was reflecting the rural Georgia definition of a woman's role, in which a profession had no place. Whatever his reasons, a striking and intelligent woman, who could still help me with Latin when she was in her forties, was left stranded in Fitzgerald, Georgia, teaching in a one-room school. In 1909 it was rare for Gentile men or Jewish women to marry outside their faith. The pickings for mother in Fitzgerald were very slim. There was daddy, apprenticed to his uncle, who ran a dry goods store, and an occasional traveling salesman. That was it.

My father could not have seemed a good match from the viewpoint of either of her parents. To grandpa he was an uneducated salesman; to grandma, he was not of the same breed as her German Jewish family. To all, probably including mother, he was a compromise candidate in a field of one.

Whatever pride my father had in his own family, and at one point it must have been considerable, it was eroded, subtly, through the years. I remember his talking about his two brothers in the Roumanian army, who were killed in the same year in World War I. One, he claimed, had been an officer. Also, he used to show us proudly his sister's wedding photograph, and point out the elegance of the dress. His family, he seemed to be protesting, *was* well-bred. I doubt that mother ever refuted this, but there are other ways of expressing disdain. As the years wore on, my father, too, denied his Yiddish tongue. Was he ashamed of it? Until his second financial collapse, he rarely associated with the Eastern Europeans in Ben Hill County though they comprised the overwhelming majority of the twelve families of Jews. For the most part Sam Abram shuttled between Gentiles and loneliness.

Born in Vaslui in Roumania, thirty miles from Kishinev Russia, the site of a 1903 pogrom in which scores of Jews were massacred, my father had emigrated in 1904 and arrived in New York City on St. Patrick's Day. He was twenty-one. He had been trained as a harness-maker and probably intended to make his living as one in New York. It was, however, a profession with rapidly diminishing customers. So the following year he came to Fitzgerald, where his maternal uncle was running a store.

My father's foreign origins pressed heavily on me in the mid-twenties when immigration of non-Anglo-Saxons became a hot national issue. In 1927, the Redpath Chattauqua pitched its tent at the corner of Lee and Pine Streets for a six-day stand offering plays and lectures. The lecturers were florid elocutionists who played the audience with their baritone voices, dramatic gestures, and fervent exhortations. One day I was transfixed by the afternoon speaker who outlined the menace of the foreign immigrant tide from southern Europe. I, the nine-year-old, fourth-grade south Georgia kid, could find no fault in the lecturer's logic, but I was tortured and pained by the sudden realization that the enemy he named included my own father.

As for my mother's family, her mother, Daisy, was the daughter of Rabbi Elias Eppstein, born in Alsace-Lorraine and educated at the University of Bonn. Eppstein came to the United States for some reason vaguely connected with the European revolutions of 1848, and, as one of America's first Reform rabbis, had lived and preached in Philadelphia, Milwaukee, Kansas City, Detroit, and finally, Quincy, Illinois, where he died. Along the way, in Philadelphia, Daisy had met and married Morris Cohen. His history is a bit more obscure. How he had come to Philadelphia is not known, except that there were intervening stops in London and Rochester, New York. But, irony of ironies, I have lately become convinced that he was originally a Roumanian like my father, whose antecedents he disparaged.

As a youth in Philadelphia, Morris Cohen plied the trade of watchmaker in order to send his sister Sarah to the Women's Medical College of Pennsylvania. She graduated in 1879, a pioneer woman physician. Not until then did grandpa decide to take a whack at medicine himself. He entered Jefferson Medical College, one of the premier schools of the day. Upon graduation he started to practice in a Jewish charitable institution in Philadelphia. By the late 1880s he had moved to the coal-mining town of Cataract, Pennsylvania. Restless, he soon moved on to Dubuque, Iowa, and a succession of towns including Pine Bluff, Arkansas, and, finally, Fitzgerald.

I suspect that grandpa's outspokenness made it difficult for him to remain too long in any one spot. His colleagues hated his candor, his religion, and, perhaps most of all, his monumental talent. Here was a country doctor in 1900 who performed radical surgery in his office, who taught himself optometry and prescribed glasses. Not trusting the lens grinders—they were "dummkopfs"—he made the lenses himself.

I was seven when grandpa left Fitzgerald for Cleveland, and it was the first great loss of my life. The man had delivered me at birth; he could never have entrusted his daughter to local doctors. One morning before he was due to leave, I awoke to find I could not move my legs. My mother feared it was polio and called grandpa in panic. "Irene," he said, "crank up your car." When we arrived he picked me up in his arms—he was then seventy—and carried me into his office, which was still full of diathermies and all kinds of whirling electrical instruments. He placed me gently on his table and made a few meaningless sparks ignite over my body. Then he said, "You can walk." And I walked. I walked because Morris Cohen had known instinctively that my affliction, far from being polio, was simple hysteria at his leaving. But even grandpa didn't know all the reasons I dreaded our impending separation. Three years before, I first heard of death when my parents spoke of a friend's dying. I was startled and frightened, but only for an instant, as I heard mother say "but he suffered so much." Immediately, I connected death with suffering which, I reasoned, would give time for grandpa to be summoned and to save me.

I remember him as being around 6'6" but mother later told me he stood a mere 5'8". I see him now as a kind of magician whose tricks were culled from the lore of scientific knowledge, and who combined in his person all the traits of master technician and tribal shaman. Perhaps those are the very greatest doctors, the ones who make it seem as if the cures spring newborn from their hands, as if the healing potions are grown fresh from their minds. If so, they are a scarce breed.

Like all shamans, grandpa has left a legacy of mythic images and legend: I see him sitting on his chair roaring with delight as he reads his beloved Dickens, collecting scrap from harness shops to build braces for kids, audibly calling Cleveland's most prominent orthopedic surgeon a "dummkopf" to his masked face at the critical moment of the reduction of a severe compound fracture. My physician Uncle Milton, also in attendance, was horrified at this insult to the venerable orthopedist. Grandpa would not retreat: "The mechanics won't work. The patient will never walk again." Six weeks later the surgeon, who was too honest to deny his mistake, told Milton to tell grandpa that a second operation was necessary! Grandpa replied, "So, what else is new?"

Years after grandpa's death a black man, Tom Williams, in Fitzgerald told me, "Your granddaddy, Dr. Cohen, was my man." I had to know every detail: Williams had once consulted him for terrible stomach cramps. Grandpa questioned him and learned they occurred only in the summer and pinned down (this was before allergies were known about in our section) that the pain came after eating watermelon. "Tom, don't you ever eat another slice."

One night, in agony, Williams rang up grandpa. Grandpa asked, "Have you eaten watermelon?" Williams confessed that he had. Grandpa grumped, "I told you not to," and hung up.

It would have been difficult for Tom Williams and grandpa to get together that night, anyway. When automobiles replaced horse and carriage, Dr. Cohen gave up owning a vehicle and never learned to drive a car. He'd walk to a patient's house or be sent for by car. Grandpa claimed that if he owned such a machine, given his enchantment with mechanics, he'd be forever tinkering with it. I believe he was really afraid he was too aggressive to trust himself at the wheel of so much power.

As my memory whizzes from this galvanic figure back to the scorned humanity of Sam Abram and the bitter power of Irene, my mother, I can still remember constant bickering between them. As a Jewish child in a Gentile community, I was not immune to insults in the street. I would rush home for comfort, only to find a quarrel, or a stony hostility between those two utterly mismatched people, and my hurt would remain unsalved. Once, in the years after grandpa died, when my gentle and utterly loving Grandma Daisy visited, there was an awful set-to between mother and daddy, and I heard grandma, biting her lips, utter the most uncharitable words ever heard from her: "That's what happens to girls who marry against their parents' advice."

The battles between my mother and father were especially protracted on Sundays when the store was closed. The only thing for me to do was to get out of the house. Daddy must have felt the same way. He and I usually took to the road, first in our Chalmers, then in our Chevrolet, and finally in our 1926 Buick, until the Depression grounded it. We no longer could afford the thirty-two-dollar license plate. One of the funnier footnotes of history is that the popularity of Governor Eugene Talmadge, the first in my father's catalogue of political villains, was originally based on the promise he made (and later kept) in his 1932 gubernatorial campaign to bring in the three-dollar license plate. Of course the Cadil-

15

lac owners got off cheap, too, but such are the twists of populism.

Those drives with my father were pure escape, but I had another in books. They were borrowed from the Carnegie Library, where I spent hours, and I brought them home two at a time, the allowed limit. In the summer I usually read lying on the porch swing; in the winter, on the floor, on my stomach, beside the fireplace. I accumulated knowledge from which I have ever after drawn and ideas which lifted me from my restricted environment. Still I was very much a part of Fitzgerald's social conventions.

My mother was a victim of one of its conventions, that housekeeping was strictly women's work. It would not have occurred to my father (or any other man in Fitzgerald) to pitch in and help. It is true that he cut the firewood to keep the stoves, hot water heater, and fireplaces going. This was man's work. But he did not help in other ways except to carve the Sunday fowl. This might have been a fair division of labor in the traditions then prevailing, except that mother did as much in the store as daddy. She did the banking, the correspondence (except when the children pitched in), and much of the buying and selling.

She must have felt frustrated by the denial of her chosen occupation, depreciated by a marriage beneath her status, and encumbered by four children. She was assigned total responsibility for running the house while working in a store which provided bare support and thrice went broke. Neither she nor daddy, to my knowledge, once took a vacation during my entire childhood.

I was four years old in 1922 when bad times first came to stay, with the bankruptcy of dad's store on Grant Street.

That spring daddy had gone with my brother, Lewis, then ten, to the market in Nashville, Tennessee. There, the wholesalers, who foresaw the impending crash, cajoled Sam Abram into heavy purchases on credit.

On his way back from Nashville, daddy and Lewis passed through Atlanta, where they went to take a look at the Georgia legislature, then in session. A farmer friend of dad's, Marcus Fletcher from Irwin, the adjacent county, had told him some time before that he wanted a "poleetical" job. Since Marcus could read and write no better than he, daddy had been unable to figure out a job for which Marcus was qualified. When he and Lewis saw the legislature in action, talking, laughing, chewing, spitting, generally enjoying themselves, he turned to Lewis and said, "Now there's a poleetical job Marcus can do." He so advised Marcus, who ran in the next election, won, and served with average distinction for many terms.

By the time the Atlanta, Birmingham, and Atlantic train arrived back in Fitzgerald, the panic had swept the country, and daddy was ruined. The merchandise he had bought, not yet delivered, was worth a fraction of the agreed price. He never again would be a Grant Street (the better section) merchant, and his downs and ups— the latter occurring only during World War II—would be limited to East Pine Street, where the blacks and poor whites traded.

His next venture, a store called the "Red Star," was financed by an illiterate farmer named Henry Land. For every rebuff by more sophisticated Gentiles, I can count the almost incongruous kindness to my father of some such man as Land. He, Sheriff Dorminey, Rufus Horton (a county probate judge), Marcus Fletcher, and three farmer brothers, the Stokeses, had a combined education of perhaps a dozen years. But they loved Sam Abram, and the three who held public office never made a move without consulting him. The lesson I garnered from observing my father's good relations with people of modest means and the snubs of those above caused me to trust the underdog more than the overlord.

When the Red Star store flopped, dad moved up two doors and started a shoe shop, since he had heard that people who fixed shoes never went broke. But because he was a harness-maker, not a shoe repairer, he had to hire one. Within a few months, however, he started buying used uppers from New York, mainly from Division Street, at twenty-five to forty cents each, which he repaired and then sold for a dollar, sometimes two dollars.

He never got enough large sizes and widths to match the feet of a sharecropper clientele. Feet in the Bowery simply didn't match well with those of our farmers. Soon dad was able to add other merchandise to his store, and by World War II he had added a range of dry goods to a stock of secondhand shoes.

Growing up in Fitzgerald, I was wholly at odds with the life around me. To fill the vacuum, I retreated to an imagined world. Four years before my departure for the University of Georgia at Athens, I conjured up a masterful alter ego. I named him Stanley Withers, and there was little he neglected to dare, nothing he failed to achieve. His academic prowess was on a par with my own, but

17

his physical power was titanic. Mr. Withers was able to attain high political office and simultaneously hurl a shutout in the seventh game of the World Series. Here was a figure who could harness space and conquer time.

Morris Abram was another story. He was a diminutive, studious chap, then a bit under 115 pounds, embarrassed to be a Jew, and humiliated that his father could not earn a comfortable living in a second-hand shoe and clothing store in the poorest part of town. When boys, and especially girls from the high school, rode by, I'd scurry from the front to the rear of the store if I sighted them before they saw me.

But what bothered the flesh and blood of me most was my inability to fight. That particular skill was crucial for an adolescent south of the Mason-Dixon line, where physical valor was highly prized and defeat seldom acknowledged. The results of the "late" war were frequently cast in terms of "we wore ourselves out, beating the Yankees." Yet, even if all scrawny 5'6" of me had learned to fight, I would have had to leave home, for my parents forbade it. My course, therefore, was to avoid confrontation, to placate, to arbitrate. If my arbitration failed, my penalty was to take a licking.

The incidents that led to the confrontations were difficult to avoid. Since I attended no Sunday school, in a community where no Christian child escaped, I was marked an outsider. In those church schools and from the pulpits, too, the story of the crucifixion and the role of the wicked Jews were more enthusiastically taught than Jesus' lessons of love. The "public" schools were properly designated if by that one meant tax-supported and open to whites. In all other respects they were white Protestant establishments, which began with prayer, featured New Testament scriptures, including (and how I held my breath on those occasions) the most offensive tirades against the Jews in the Gospel of John. I can still feel my recoil as the teachers—or preachers, at public school services—read from John, Chapter 7: "After these things Jesus walked in Galilee: for he would not walk in Jewry, because the Jews sought to kill him."

My grandpa had told me early and often that the Romans and not the Jews had killed Jesus, pointing out that only the Romans had civil power in Judea in 30 A.D., plus the fact that crucifixion was a Roman punishment; and the clincher was that Jews did not do legal business that might extend to the Sabbath.

18

Even as a child I insisted on setting the record straight, a course that would later lead me to Rome and a frank talk with Pope Paul VI.

But this habit of contradicting established myth did not endear me to my schoolmates, nor did my noticeable abstention from the refrains of "Onward Christan Soldiers," which was a lot easier to sing than the National Anthem.

I was further estranged by my almost obsessive desire for learning. When I won the approval of good teachers, I found myself envied by my peers, whose paths I crossed on the way home, no longer protected by the discipline of the classroom.

As the separation grew between me and other children, I retreated increasingly into my world of books. When I was eight, mother bought the twenty-volume *Book of Knowledge,* and I set out to devour one subject after another; the *Book of Wonder,* about science; the *Book of Famous Men and Women,* about history. I provoked an intense quarrel with some of my classmates by bragging that "my parents had bought me a book that knew everything." Of course, my adversaries were correct—even the *Book of Knowledge* had its gaps—but it was painful to learn my error from the fists of those who had not even seen a single precious volume.

From the fifth grade on, that *Book of Knowledge* provided the source material for additions to class discussions on every subject. Mrs. Mathis, a fierce redheaded disciplinarian would have preferred, I suspect, to teach only me and a few others rather than a bored mass of thirty. As a result, I was called "teacher's pet," an epithet which stirred long resentment where school learning was not especially valued. Of my high school class of over fifty, only a handful would go off even to junior college.

Until 1930, when I was twelve, I believed two things: First, that when I grew up and became a man I would not have to fight every time someone started an argument. Even my alter ego, Stanley Withers, although of superhuman strength, abhorred violence. Next, I thought that no educated person could be prejudiced against Jews. Negroes were another matter, a different species, and I did not immediately relate society's treatment of them to the problems I, as a Jew, had encountered.

The first belief was confirmed for me during my college years, when, despite disagreements, I was never once even on the verge of a fist fight. But the second of my two verities crumbled in 1930, in my first year of high school. An algebra teacher from Mercer University showed his anti-Semitic prejudice openly. I could not believe it. Here was a college graduate giving me lower grades because I was a Jew. Later, under pressure, the teacher admitted he was wrong in deliberately depressing my grades and making slurs against Jews. The grades were corrected, but his animus continued to be evident and my illusion, that anti-Semitism was a manifestation of the uneducated mind, departed. In tears, I brought the problem home. It was mother, of course, not daddy, who took it up with the school, made the teacher confess, and righted the wrong so far as it could be.

About this time we were assigned the *Merchant of Venice* in our English class. Mother was distressed by the caricature of Shylock, the Jew, but wisely she made no effort to ban a Shakespearean masterpiece from my curriculum. Instead, she pointed out that readers tended to see Shylock's flagrant faults rather than the whole character the author had painted. She had me read the words in Act III in which Shakespeare makes the case for the Jews' sufferings and his common humanity:

Hath not a Jew eyes? Hath not a Jew hands, organs, dimensions, senses, affections, passions? Fed with the same food, hurt with the same weapons, subject to the same diseases, healed by the same means, warmed and cooled by the same winter and summer as a Christian is? If you prick us do we not bleed? If you tickle us do we not laugh? If you poison us do we not die? And if you wrong us shall we not revenge?

Even before my high school years I had heard of the case of Leo M. Frank, a young Jew who, about fifteen years earlier, was lynched and hacked up in Marietta, twenty miles from Atlanta. Frank had been tried for the rape/murder of a fourteen-year-old girl employed in the pencil factory he managed. Entangled in a web of circumstantial evidence, prejudice, and rumor fed by Tom Watson, the frustrated Populist crusader against "the typical young libertine Jew," Frank was found guilty in a trial punctuated by open expressions of hostility in the courtroom and threatening cries of the mob outside.

Sentenced to death, Frank was denied a new trial by the United

States Supreme Court over the dissents of Mr. Justices Holmes and Hughes. Governor John M. Slaton, correctly judging Frank innocent, commuted his sentence, which brought the mob to the governor's mansion, and forced him to flee behind a screen of the state militia. Frank was then abducted from prison by the mob and lynched. In terror, 3,000 Jews left the state.

From whispered accounts of the story, I could tell that in the 1920s my parents and their Jewish friends were still unnerved by the fate of Leo Frank. I suspected that daddy clung to Sheriff Elisha Dorminey and other elected officials for added protection for himself and his brood. As a young man I felt the intense need to tread cautiously where Southern passions might be aroused.

My warmest memories of Fitzgerald feature two subsidiary figures. One was an exquisite history teacher named Lucy Goodrich Henry, with whom I fell in love, and who broke my heart by marrying in midyear. The other was a football coach named Bill Alderman, who encouraged me and respected me no less than he did his prize running backs.

Lucy Goodrich Henry. She was a tall, big-boned, striking woman, fresh from Agnes Scott, a good woman's college in Decatur, Georgia. I was thirteen, a ninth grader, and, because she was the coach of my debating team, our relationship extended beyond the confines of history class. I elicited every opportunity to talk with and impress her. "Morris, did you know that in the Dark Ages, the Church, through its scholarly priests, kept alive the classical tradition until it could be rediscovered and appreciated by the Renaissance?" No, I didn't know that, but I went to the Carnegie Library, and pursued the idea, gathered the details so we could talk on yet another subject. In Miss Henry were combined every feminine element I would forever enshrine and seek—all, incidentally, embodied in some ways in my mother—statuesque good looks, quiet sensuality, intelligence, and high purpose.

The relationship was, however, full of anguish. I was pitifully ashamed of my heavy-duty woolen pants, so seldom dry cleaned, and my Depression overcoat, a hand-me-down from my brother Lewis. In 1932, she married, and those long, good legs and full breasts were lost to me forever. She went to live in Decatur. Years later, after I had made a name for myself at the University of Georgia, I visited her. Her husband was a traveling state auditor. How small he seemed next to her. I was disappointed; she seemed so cheated, her potential so unrealized.

I don't remember how I met Coach Alderman. Lord knows, my own family thought nothing of sports, particularly football. But he had arrived in town to revitalize our Purple Hurricanes, and the spirit was contagious. When the team's manager, Joe Jones, asked me to be his assistant—really a kind of waterboy—I dutifully accepted. I found myself keeping the uniforms in order, filling the water buckets, helping the players strap on their boots, and spending long hours in the locker rooms at the Blue and Gray Park, oppressed by the lingering stench of sweat. It could only have been my need for Alderman's company which allowed me to stick out the season.

Also, while my body was fulfilling this ordinary job, in my imagination Stanley Withers carried on extraordinary feats on a national gridiron. Still, the job gave me some footing in the adolescent power structure of Fitzgerald. I wasn't quarterback, but I had my niche, and that knowledge was the beginning of security. When some players accused me of doing well in school only because I studied all the time, I overheard Alderman answer, "How can that be? He's here when you start every day and leaves after you do." That a golden warrior like Bill Alderman would speak of me with respect even when he thought I was out of earshot afforded me one of the sweetest thrills of my childhood.

My brother Lewis was off to college at fifteen, removed from high school by my parents because they had learned that though the judges had voted him a school prize, the principal had deceitfully awarded it to a Gentile favorite. I, then a runty eight-year-old, was thus deprived of the manly figure of my older brother, who had partially filled the void when grandpa left. More intimidated than ever now by childish taunts, I took refuge in the fact that Lewis would return on periodic vacations and could then redress the wrongs inflicted on me. For Lewis, as I seized every occasion to tell those who didn't know, "was 6 feet tall and weighed 190 pounds." Moreover, he was off learning to be a doctor, and I was preparing myself to do the same, in lonely but diligent surgery practiced on frogs anesthetized by ether. I would cut open the hapless amphibians with razor blades, extract nonvital organs, and stitch them up with needle and thread.

Home with me were my two sisters, Ruthanne and Jeanette, two and six years younger than I. Ruthanne was a born lady, obedient, dependable, cautious, and ever so beautiful. Half a century later I would meet her genetic template in Roumania—Similca, the daughter of my father's brother. On the same trip to Roumania, I would see Jeanette's double, Dad's sister, Rifka, then in her seventies, but even so, a dark bubbly daredevil of that family. Jeanette was spontaneous, unpredictable.

There may have been rivalry between Ruthanne and me. I especially resented her cautious, totally responsible approach even to play. But with Jeanette my role was paternal. Even now I can recollect the sensuous pleasure in holding Jeanette's baby hand as she learned to walk on the unpaved alley next to our yard. Ever since, I have found gratification in the soft, warm touch of children. Good and intelligent persons, these sisters, but they got the heel of a meager loaf of family opportunity. Not that a college education was not offered, and, in the case of Ruthanne, completed, but unquestionably they had lower expectations. Ruthanne, a conscientious student, and Jeanette, possessed of a steel-trap mind, were expected to be wives and mothers. I later realized I suffered, too, as this idea became ingrained in my future relations with women.

As I neared graduation, Lewis returned to Fitzgerald to practice medicine. He, too, grew friendly with Bill Alderman, and became the team's volunteer physician. I was in my glory, utterly protected by two strong male figures.

The security did not last. Bill Alderman fell ill with abdominal pain, fever, and an elevated blood count. It turned out to be a ruptured appendix. Only Alderman's natural resistance was left to fight the raging peritonitis. Antibiotics were still three or four years away. Within a few hours Bill Alderman was dead.

I was devastated. To the loss of Grandpa Cohen and Lucy Goodrich Henry was now added the demise of the one male who respected me and whose opinion really counted. Lewis was the best available substitute. He loved me and I now bonded with him closer than before.

I worked in Lewis' office, accompanied him on his rounds, saw the miseries to which he was exposed, suffered his anxieties as he waited for nature to help him rescue the sick from incurable illness. I assisted when he treated a white farm youth for syphilis with the only available medicine, arsenic and mercury, sitting out the hours while Lewis worried if these crude drugs were going to kill the lad, who went into shock.

I saw, with Lewis, the rawest example of racial discrimination as he tried to save a black field hand whose infected toe had become a gangrenous leg because his white employer had waited too long to call a doctor. In addition to the leg, the man was lost.

Lewis' practice consisted at first of the poor and of close family friends. The other local doctors had not improved on their knowledge or skill since our grandfather had first labeled them "dummkopfs" as far back as 1924. In the ten years since then, these physicians still mistrusted a newly trained doctor. Of course, much of Lewis' proficiency came from nothing more remarkable than that he was just out of an accredited medical school and kept up-to-date by reading the journals of the American Medical Association.

Summer was the deadliest time of all. Often the heat brought the summer colic. Infants were particularly vulnerable, and they died like flies from nothing more than dehydration and the disorderings of their chemical balance. Lewis, simply by dripping salt water and sugar into the cavity between the stomach and belly wall, could quickly reestablish the vital balance. Within twenty-four hours they were playing as usual, and Lewis would shake his head in disgust and mutter, "There's no reason for these children to die." His "miracle" cure was already old hat in other parts of the country.

By the time I was ready to go to college, I was acutely aware of one fact—Lewis was practicing medicine in Fitzgerald so that the family would have enough money to underwrite my tuition in Athens. Lewis himself would probably deny it to this day, but I know that he sacrificed promising internships and postgraduate specialization for my education. The dramatic events of his practice in those days, saving babies from colic, of sorrow over the death of Bill Alderman, are inextricably woven into the texture of my life. At times I feel as if our prospective careers were merely different extensions of a single struggle.

When Lewis came down with double pneumonia in the winter of

1933, I was forced to realize how closely my fate was tied to his. Penicillin had not yet been discovered, so Lewis gasped for breath in the local hospital. It was not that my ticket to college rode on his life that most concerned me as I waited anxiously for every report of his condition. Lewis was more than a brother; he was father and protector as well, and now I was about to lose him.

In desperation I made a trade with whatever powers there were outside of this world: I'd give up my sins, become even more ascetic than I was, if he were spared. Well, no sooner was Lewis up and back to his practice than I was back to mine.

Whatever the influence of my brother, or Bill Alderman, whatever variations they played on the theme of my childhood, the basic divisions in my character, formed years earlier, were now as distinct as an open wound. I felt torn between opposing loyalties, and irreconcilable ways of viewing myself. Was I really a Jew? Why then had I never had a bar mitzvah, never even been pressured to it by my family? If, on the other hand, my Jewishness was merely a quirky encumbrance, and the Protestant culture around me the historically and spiritually justified one, why was I so uncomfortable when the time came to recite hymns in public school? Why did the very name "Jesus" seem to stick in my throat even as I felt the power of the rhythms and melodies that celebrated his mission? Why could I never think of Jesus except as a historic personage, while simultaneously denying myself emotional communion with the Jews around me, avoiding their daughters in favor of Gentile girls (who, I felt, looked down on me) or an occasional Jewish girl whose antecedents were ostentatiously American?

3

ELI REMARKED that he was not a stranger to the tensions that I was describing. "But I wonder how it happened, then, that Jewish affairs came to play such a dominant role in your public life? When did it all take shape for you?"

An image sprang into my mind—that of a man, a bantam-sized man with a bald head and a droopy, tobacco-stained moustache. "Let me tell you about Gelders," I said. "Isadore Gelders—one of the few Jews in Fitzgerald who read books from the Carnegie Library."

Gelders was a Dutch-born Jewish socialist, the editor and publisher of the less prosperous newspaper in town, the *Fitzgerald Leader, Enterprise, and Press*. My earliest awareness of his existence came with my father's vehement railings against him and his "sheet" for supporting the union in the bitter railroad strike of 1921.

Unlike the other Jews in town—Uncle Toms, each and every one—Gelders never stopped to court the "other" or to appease the powerful. Quite the contrary. It was from Isadore Gelders that I

26

first heard it proclaimed that the destiny of the Jews was clearly to formulate the great forward steps of humankind, to enunciate and illumine the most advanced concepts of Western civilization. What was he saying? That I, as a Jew, was inescapably avant-garde?

It was all very confusing—hard to reconcile with the lowly estate of all the Jews I knew in Georgia. Except for grandpa and my legendary great-grandfather, Rabbi Eppstein—neither of whom was available—heroes, particularly Jewish ones, were nowhere in evidence.

Except for Isadore Gelders.

As I entered my teens Gelders became a kind of proxy father, a romantic stand-in for that very prosaic parent of my own. I had found, at last, a man like my mother—a literate man, a strong man, a man of Western European origins.

Perhaps it was because his own five sons were baptized in the Northern Methodist Church by his wife, the daughter of a Union Army veteran, that I was chosen to personify his titanic belief in the history and destiny of the Jews.

His accented voice was a coarse whisper, but what he had to say was vehemently stated in absolutely grammatical English. A feisty man, he capitulated to none of the economic pressures to which he was subjected and would stand his own ground in occasional fist fights with political enemies who towered over him physically.

In the twenties, dad and Gelders weren't on speaking terms, so bitter had been their disagreements over the railroad strike. Nevertheless, I got to know him because his wife and mother were members of a women's club of which mother was president, and Mrs. Gelders ran the women's side of the paper, *Leader,* as we called it.

When I entered high school in 1930 Gelders made me a proposition. "Why should the *Herald* publish in its pages the high school newspaper? Why don't you start a rival which we'll publish in the *Leader*?"

Dad instantly decided that Gelders' judgment had improved, and contacts between the Gelders and Abram households were reestablished. They even survived Gelders' support of Eugene Talmadge for governor in 1932 and in every other campaign that redoubtable racist entered. Although my dad thought this another example of Gelders' rascality, he forgave him because the editor was the friend

27

and patron of his prodigy son. I generally regarded Gelders' political stands as brave and admirable and his support of Talmadge merely quirky, justifiable in contexts I would only later comprehend.

Gelders fought for and won free school books for Fitzgerald decades before the State provided them elsewhere. He defended the municipal power plant against take-over by Georgia Power and when that company took over distribution, he won the fight to keep the old steam plant in place—"just in case."

The opinion of the community was always arrayed against him. The political crowd annually awarded the public and legal advertising contracts to the *Herald*. Gelders never yielded an inch. He ferreted out public evil wherever he could find it and railed against every injustice he saw. But like many other good people of his time, he either didn't see the evil of racial discrimination or decided to overlook it.

As a high school kid, I fought with him over Talmadge's race baiting and chided him for his support of the Georgia Populist Tom Watson. Gelders, blinded by his hatred of economic injustice, simply couldn't see Watson as an anti-Catholic, anti-Negro, anti-Jewish demagogue, but only as the author of rural free delivery for the farmer and the advocate of the poor farmer/worker. Incredibly, Gelders even saw Talmadge in this mold.

Though I baited Gelders mercilessly on these matters, he never treated me as less than an equal. Only once, in 1934, when I asked him whether he was actually going to vote for Talmadge, who was bitterly opposing our shared hero, Franklin D. Roosevelt, did he speak to me with irritation: "How I vote is a private matter." It hurt.

We talked together incessantly. During school time I carried my "copy" to him at his office, where the chattering linotypes made it difficult to hear his whispery voice. On Saturdays he would come to my father's store where the dialogue was resumed. In winter he would draw me over to the stove, in summer he would lure me outside.

I sensed that just as he had turned the paper into an extension of himself, he wanted his views, particularly on Jewish values, to be extended through me. He knew well enough, though he carefully avoided mentioning them, that his Methodist sons could hardly implement his Jewish ideals.

I fitted his agenda for the future; he fitted my need for a Jew to emulate.

One day he walked in the store and said, "I've got to talk to you about a plan. Morris, there's a book that's got to be written about the contribution of Jews to civilization. You've got to do it. I even have the title: 'Stepping Stones of Civilization.' " Then he outlined the steps: The inherent morality of monotheism, the prohibition of slavery, the ethical standards of the Torah, the literature of the Bible, and, in modern times, the contributions of Freud, Marx, and Einstein. I liked Gelders' idea so much that afterward whenever I picked up a book on history, politics, or philosophy, I turned to the index to locate the material under "Jews."

These were matters of which my father knew nothing, but unlike Gelders, he was consistent in supporting FDR and in opposing the president's arch foe, Eugene Talmadge. Daddy, whose business was always teetering on the brink of bankruptcy and whose house was constantly but unsuccessfully on the market to provide working capital, was counting on Roosevelt to get the banks out of failure and farm prices up to a level at which his impoverished customers could buy his goods.

It is true that after my grandfather and then Lewis left, my father failed to fill the void, but I did enter his world when I joined him on visits to the railroad shops of the Atlantic, Birmingham, and Atlanta Railroad (later Atlanta, Birmingham, and Coast Line) some four miles from town. My father was always warmly received there by the now permanent scab labor who had replaced their predecessors after the 1922 strike. What I saw in these outings was a part of American life that has now passed, though I will forever have railroads in my blood.

During the heyday of the AB&A, a dozen locomotives could be seen poking their noses out of the roundhouse. In the erection shops pieces of other trains were being stripped down and reassembled. Huge boilers protruded, and what seemed a legion of men hammered, soldered, and welded, while a quarter of a mile away trains were being stoked and steamed up in readiness for the eight-hour trip to Atlanta or to Waycross, Brunswick, or Tifton. Some were passenger locomotives with high wheels like the long legs of a fast thoroughbred. Others were bulkier and rested lower on the rails, with wheels built for power rather than speed. They all breathed side by side with some of the strongest and bravest men in Georgia.

There was, for example, the heroic Bill Morris, engineer extraordinary, who lived just down Pine Street and whose boys taunted me daily. This did not diminish my image of this gallant man who drove the AB&A's great Pacific type locomotives at seventy miles per hour over a crowded single track between Atlanta and Fitzgerald without the benefit of block signals or any communication system, except for a written order which was lifted en route from a dispatcher's hook while the train was in motion. Once, a lesser engineer failed to sidetrack his train on such an order, and Morris' locomotive collided with it after he had thrown his fireman to safety. Scalded but undaunted, he continued his career until he retired in disgust when he was offered a demeaning diesel.

My memories of Fitzgerald also go back to the picnics, the fish fries, and the swimming in Ossewiche Springs. The fish fries were particularly memorable. The railroad people organized them. They were run by burly Nate Manley, one of the scab foremen, along with our sheriff, Elisha Dorminey, and the Abram family was always included. We gathered at a cleared site on the Ocmulgee River. There the fishermen brought in tens of pounds of channel catfish. Dominating the scene was an extraordinary skillet, the front plate of a steam locomotive boiler measuring at least ten feet in diameter with a depth of perhaps a foot. When operational, this monster could hold about twenty pounds of bubbling lard. Like a minotaur it swallowed up the breaded catfish and cornmeal dough for hush puppies.

This joyous community was extinguished in 1928, however, when Al Smith decided to run for President. For Nate Manley, the catalyst in these outings, a Catholic in the White House was totally unacceptable. My father was equally impassioned in Smith's favor. Who knows but that Manley's hidden feelings about Jews may also have been stirred up by the situation. In any case, he and my father disagreed and went their separate ways. I was devastated by the break with this strong male whom I intuitively considered another protector of my vulnerable family. And worst of all, Nate Manley was a potential and powerful enemy. I tried many times to wheedle my father into a friendly overture to Manley. But the rupture did not mend.

Sheriff Elisha Dorminey, a foot-washing, primitive Baptist with less than a third-grade education, was another kind of man. He supported Smith, and if he and my father ever quarreled except over their weekly setback card game, I do not recall. Their friendship was tested and sealed, I suspect, when in 1922 a Ku Klux Klan organizer from Indiana arrived in town and, as was the custom, called on the sheriff for support, offering him gratis the number one membership card. Dorminey asked, "What do you stand for?" "Americanism," said the organizer, who bore the credentials of a preacher.

"What does that mean?" asked Dorminey.

"We're against niggers, Catholics, and Jews," was the reply.

"Well, that's not what it means to me," said the sheriff, adding, "I am not joining."

"Then we'll run you out of office," said the divine.

"No," said the ponderous, bald, and quietly determined law officer. "If you try any funny business here, I'll run you out of town."

Dorminey looked up the man's record and found he was wanted in another state. The organizer departed, just ahead of the warrant for his arrest.

As far as my father was concerned, Dorminey was the main cog in the machinery of good, and anyone who opposed him—like the one citizen who perennially ran for Dorminey's office—was, by definition, evil.

Still, Dorminey's support for Smith was remarkable. In those times devout fundamentalist Protestants would sometimes grasp a Jew to their bosom, seeing him as a member of the original biblical race. But they viewed the Catholic Church as the Antichrist, or the whore that sits on the seven waters. I don't really understand how Dorminey could have been so tough and gracious of mind as to have supported Al Smith, but the fine fact remains.

After the Red Bluff fish fries came to an end, my family had private outings at frigid Ossewiche Springs, fifteen miles from town. These "boils," as they were called, bubbled amid swamps where water moccasins infested the overflow pools and a rattlesnake or two slept under the thick leaves and moss. But the waters gave the only relief from the vicious Georgia heat of August. There were, in fact, two swimming pools nearer our home, but they were not filtered or chlorinated. No daughter of Morris Cohen would let her children near them. We balked at this. Most of the other kids swam there, and the sad fact is that a fair percentage of them were dead by mid-puberty, whereas all the Abrams survived.

In retrospect, mother did more than just facilitate my survival. Her drive and her values dominated me. I grew obsessed with grades, with becoming valedictorian of my class, with being first. If she and my father were at war for my soul, it was she who seemed to be shaping it.

Divided as they were on almost all else, mother and dad were united on the value of learning and education. Sam Abram would leave his store to watch the Class B Fitzgerald baseball team play afternoon home games, but he never once showed the slightest interest in his own son's athletic abilities. School work and grades were another matter. He would listen to every composition and he encouraged me to commit some to memory so that I could recite them to his railroad cronies, who bribed me with "railroad passes," which I was too young to realize were out of date and would take me nowhere. But still it was then that I developed a sense of the beauty and rhythm of words, the power of rhetoric that seemed to take me anywhere I cared to go.

The skill I developed and the approval it gained encouraged me to take an interest in public issues, which was later to impel me into law and politics. Lacking wise adult guidance in my reading, I became far too oriented toward finding immediate material for oratory. Fiction was neglected in my eagerness for history, politics, and biography. I was forty before a wise older friend convinced me that the real truths of life are found not in recorded facts but in the store of the creative imagination.

I was growing up, very precocious in some ways, and wrote tiresome, moralizing pieces in the school newspaper. I never dated, and the one girl I did ask to the junior prom was an awkward child whom no one else would ask. I knew she wouldn't turn me down.

It almost seems denigrating to my family to describe their absurd evasions of the subject of sex. I was six when grandpa delivered Jeanette and I dogged him to tell me where she came from. Finally, he was on the verge of relating the biological facts. He had even removed his obstetric forceps from his bag and was demonstrating its fit around the infant's head. I can still clearly remember grand-mother's sudden appearance and her stern interruption. Embar-rassed, grandpa retreated into the most ridiculous story imaginable. "You see, Morris, I go down to the creek on Pine Street between Sherman and Lee Streets and in the gully there I find a rock and on it I smear this red stuff [showing me a tincture, probably of iodine], then the baby is attracted to the color." Putting away the forceps, he continued, "I use this thing to pick up the baby, whom I then bring to the house." As I remember my dainty and merry grand-mother, it is hard for me now to fathom how she could instill enough fear in grandpa to force him to back off from the truth.

It was from black domestics and from the streets that I learned what little I knew. If anyone in my family could have taught me more, it would have been my father. I say this because there was a prostitute in the town named Mrs. Davis for whom he had much sympathy. Her home and place of business was above his Red Star store. His sympathy for her derived, I think, from his fondness for her children, whom he called "the little roosters."

Dad adored these kids and was ever buying them clothes, candy, and ice cream. Jake Stone, Mrs. Davis's sometime lover, was also the county crook, a burglar, and a grizzled veteran of many a chain gang. But Stone appreciated the way my father treated his "fam-ily" and gave his word he would never break into our store.

1933 was a year of hope; like everyone else who listened to Roosevelt's inaugural address, I sensed new times coming. For a high school declamation contest, I memorized his famous first in-augural speech in which he so eloquently declared that Americans had nothing to fear but fear itself. I'm afraid I even tried to emulate the Hyde Park modulations. Of course, conditions were still de-plorable. The three banks in town were losers after Roosevelt shut them down, while cotton dropped to under seven cents a pound.

Tobacco was a catch-as-catch-can proposition. No one knew what price the bright leaf grown in our area would bring until the annual midsummer auctions. No one could predict if the expenses of seed, fertilizer, and labor would be redeemed. Merchants would await the news from the auction warehouses as people darted around town spreading the first bidding results. It would all boil down to a thumbs-up or thumbs-down from the Caesars of Winston-Salem.

Meanwhile, I was becoming something of a local public figure.

I achieved minor distinction as an occasional speaker at local churches and Bar Mitzvahs. The Christian ministers were glad to have a Jewish lad through whom they might cavalierly acknowledge the Judaic roots of their religious traditions and better enforce the theme of the triumph of Christianity over the Jewish relic. I didn't dare argue for the distinctive ethical principles of Judaism, even where I understood and believed in them.

Reverend Berry, pastor of the Christian church, asked me to speak one Sunday on the Jewish view of Jesus Christ. I boned up on the subject from every book I could lay my hands on. I had a dreadful dilemma. I had to be honest, but at the same time it would not do to offend my host.

The church auditorium was packed, the air stifling as I faced not only Berry's congregation but several of the town's Jews, who were invited guests.

"Jesus was born a Jew in a land ruled by pagan Rome," I began. "It was a time of terrible troubles. The Jews could scarcely endure their sufferings and looked desperately for relief. The people craved a Savior just as we craved for Roosevelt to put us out of our miseries. Some saw in Jesus the promised Messiah because he was a man who spoke in the best tradition of his Jewish faith. Rome saw him as a threat; so did certain Jews who made form more important than substance. The fate of Jesus was that of too many leaders who are ahead of their times. His moral teachings are true for all times. You Christians believe he was divine; we believe that only his teachings are."

Brother Berry thanked me graciously, but he could not refrain from emphasizing "Christianity's dominant theme of love," as if Judaism somehow lacked that. No doubt Brother Berry thought I was yet a prime candidate for that greatest of all evangelical achievements—the conversion of a living, breathing Jew.

One Christian preacher was very different. He was Brother Winn of the Presbyterian church, a minor denomination in our overwhelmingly Baptist and Methodist town. Winn was a tall, gaunt, silver-thatched man whose relatively small flock and curious background marked him too as somewhat an outsider. He'd started off as a bank teller and moved into the ministry because it challenged his homespun philosophical bent. He'd talk to me and Gelders separately or together—not in a preachy or goody-goody manner—but as equals, examining ethical and religious propositions. Jewish merchants felt he was anchored to a practical world beyond theology, for as a side line he did some of their income tax returns.

My role in Bar Mitzvahs arose because there was no local rabbi, and it was a big expense to import one in those hard times. Besides, since the thirteen-year-old candidates had received no religious instructions, the event was celebrated socially. An adolescent local boy who spoke with callow eloquence was more exotic than an unknown bearded import who might drone on at length to justify his journey and his fee. My prowess, first developed in the debating classes of Lucy Goodrich Henry, continued to expand. Other kids had athletic skills. I had no competition in the area I had staked out. There was little humor in my style. At the time, wit, like fiction, seemed a waste. I was not only capable of forgetting a joke, but what is worse, forgetting the punch line.

As class valedictorian, I delivered a graduation speech, though I was so short that I had to stand on a stool so I could peer over the podium. By then I had become the mascot of the adult Jewish community, speaking in Ben Hill and surrounding counties in connection with communal efforts to stem the tide of Jewish business failures. The core of the effort was a cooperative loan company named the Hebrew Commercial Alliance. It was headquartered in Fitzgerald, and soon our town became the focus of other common efforts, which culminated in the formation of a congregation in the 1940s. It was housed in the abandoned Northern Methodist Church. My discourses, fashioned to fit the occasion, were regurgitations of oddly thrown together material I had picked up, largely from the *Book of Knowledge*. When I did expand on a theme, it was usually a moralizing essay on what, for example, I had been writing for the school newspaper. At times I could almost, in the manner of the local preacher, breathe fire and brimstone.

Indeed, I had absorbed a great deal of the Baptist sensibility that surrounded me and that left its mark as tellingly as Jewish characteristics from my family. Alcohol and gambling were favorite targets. Mrs. Walter Stancil, my seventh grade teacher, flatly asserted that all card games were immoral, as they might lead to gambling. The self-destructiveness of gambling, the indolence of the hand which dealt the cards or spun the roulette wheel inspired me to heights of indignation. Almost fifty years later I found myself prejudiced toward Howard Samuels' gubernatorial efforts in New York because of his having been the first head of the off-track betting system. The Southern Baptist lives within me. Even as I contemplated this, I found myself calling up the head of the organized crime division of the Department of Justice to ask why Meyer Lansky, reputed to be the chief of organized crime in America, was not brought to trial on an old indictment.

During my adolescence I often flailed against the demon rum, but I didn't feel its sinfulness quite so intensely. My family abhorred excessive drinking, though my mother would make home brew for Sheriff Dorminey. I remember a Jewish alcoholic my father used to bring home, ashamed that he would be tottering around Fitzgerald dishonoring his tradition and making an ass of himself.

I sermonized a number of times in a black church presided over by a preacher called Slop Jackson. He had come by his nickname honestly. For six days a week Jackson, a roly-poly, jovial man, earned his livelihood picking up garbage for his hogs with his horse and cart. But on the seventh day he mounted the pulpit of his big stone Baptist church on the outskirts of town. When I was the guest speaker he'd intone, "My brothers and sisters, please welcome my fine young Jewish friend." Reverend Jackson also gave me my first lesson in fund-raising. I asked him why he never passed around a collection plate. "If I did that," he told me, "I could pass it around forever without picking up a thing. But if I let people come to the altar and give where everybody can see them and provide the opportunity to show off their finery, why, that's another matter."

I am not so sure that I provided Reverend Jackson's congregation with lessons of equal validity. On one occasion in 1932 (I was fourteen) my theme was "the South, a Friend of the Negro." Repeating the philosophy of Booker T. Washington, expressed thirty-eight years earlier, I said, "In all things purely social the Negro can be as separate as the fingers, yet one as the hand in all things essential to mutual progress." I continued, "One man cannot saw a big log, but two can; one race cannot break old man depression's neck, but two can. You and your friend, the southern white man." So far, conventional enough, but then I topped it with an outrageous peroration: "Stay by the South! Develop with the South! If you were crossing a stream on the back of a horse and it was swimming well, you would be a fool to leave it. Don't be fooled by promises.

Always remember that your best friend is your mother, your next is the South.''

I just knew somehow that I was different and destined for higher things than the other kids around. Yet I did not know how to lift myself out of Fitzgerald. I had never been outside the state or ridden a railroad train except to go to Cleveland to see grandpa before he died, when I was seven. I kept hoping I'd be "discovered" by some prominent man, especially one with enough to pay my way to college. I was exuberant when I heard that Harold Hirsch, Coca-Cola's Atlanta counsel, would be in the neighboring Valdosta synagogue one Sunday when I would be speaking. I was devastated when he did not show up.

My greatest public triumph was directly inspired by my father's railroad friends. I had written an essay for school called "Our Shackled Railroads,'' demonstrating how badly the railroads were treated in the United States. Daddy showed it to some local members of the railroad association. I was soon invited to speak at a big convention they were holding in Savannah. So, after years of hanging out with my father at the roundhouse, I took my first actual train ride. By the time I was to perform, I had perfected my timing on each word, each syllable. In fact, I had had no choice but to practice it repeatedly for undistracted hours. The night before the convention I had accidentally locked myself in the bathroom of a Savannah hotel while the conventioneers who had accompanied me went out for a night on the town. There was nothing else for me to do but to rehearse until they came to release me from my prison.

I was a ninety-pound orator who succeeded in inciting the burly workers, joined for the occasion with management, to loud huzzahs and a standing ovation. I used standard gestures and intonations, and I don't think my voice cracked. What I said was gospel truth. The railroads were, indeed, overregulated and could reap none of the benefits of free enterprise. They were able to transport goods cheaper than the trucks, but the I.C.C. made it impossible. It was unfair that the lines had to pay right-of-way taxes on the tracks they themselves built and maintained. I voiced these hard facts with an oratorical flourish possibly unrivaled since William Jennings Bryan's fiery "Cross of Gold" speech.

Although I could share some of Bryan's political populism, the comforts of his religious certainty were beyond my grasp. At most,

I could visit the temples of my people and give an edifying discourse on some topic of Jewish history or morality as I saw it through my naive eyes. On Rosh Hashanah in 1934, in the Masonic hall, rented as a synagogue, I demonstrated my enthusiasm for the new president in a sermon in which I asked for a New Deal for Jews. I warned my elders not to expect it, however, as long as we insisted on "measuring ability by how much a man can make." Then, possibly referring to my own father, for the description would have fit, I chided the congregation for having "cast the poor businessman aside as insensible and ignorant. We have balanced man on the scales, weighing him in gold." Not only was I aching to reconcile myself to my Jewish identity, I was also beginning to hunger for an irrefutable proof of God's existence. I was living in a Baptist culture which, carrying Luther's protest against axiomatic theology to an extreme, took the world on blind faith.

A "rabbi" had come from Atlanta to lead the davening. For the great occasion it was not unusual to employ one of these itinerant holy men. Some of them were textual scholars, others intoners of words detached from meaning. They had their counterparts in Jerusalem or Warsaw. Their articles of faith—the tefillin, the menorahs—filled cumbersome satchels. Some of the brood had questionable credentials. Little towns like Fitzgerald were sometimes so desperate for someone to lead them in prayer that a Yiddish-speaking cop might have passed as a talmudic scholar.

It happened that I was to leave for the University of Georgia immediately after the service. I wanted to travel by train to Atlanta and transfer there for the remaining seventy miles to Athens. My family decided, however, that at least six dollars could be saved if I hitched a ride with the car carrying the "rabbi" back to the capital. For reasons which I still don't understand, I protested vehemently. As I look back, I can surmise that it was my first great adolescent rebellion, but I did not prevail.

I consoled myself with the thought that I would have five hours to extract from the spiritual leader the Jewish evidence of God's existence. The car was small, the Indian summer air stifling.

"How do we know God exists?" I asked the rabbi.

"It says in the Torah!" he replied impatiently.

"But how do you know the Torah is right?"

"Because it comes from God."

I was already seething about my mode of travel, but now I was ready to go through the roof. When we got to Atlanta we parted quickly. Thus I slammed the door on the house of my father and set out into the world.

4

In February 1975 my doctors returned me to the hospital, and I had to cancel a taping with Eli. I was wracked by hiccups and on top of that the doctors believed I was bleeding internally. Leukemics suffer loss of the clotting element of blood, or platelets, and the chemotherapy reduces all blood components, including platelets. Nothing would stop the hiccups, not even sedation with various mood modifiers, such as the powerful thorazine. No specific treatment seemed to work, but finally the hiccups subsided and the symptoms of bleeding disappeared.

When we were finally able to meet again, Eli asked, "Whatever happened to that alter ego of yours, Stanley Withers?"

Stanley Withers died, I told him, in 1934 at the University of Georgia. I suppose it could be claimed I let him die of neglect, as I no longer needed him. I remember when I first became aware of his demise. I was traveling by bus from Atlanta to Fitzgerald on my first Christmas vacation. Seated next to a beautiful freshman, the daughter of a Fitzgerald eye, ear, and nose doctor, I was surprised to find myself acting in an expansive, animated manner with her. I was suddenly happy, and then it occurred to me that Stanley had withered away.

The university had given me an exhilarating sense of freedom. My days were no longer darkened by the shadow of my father's failure or my mother's awesome strength. Now I could do what I wanted with neither approval nor censure. I wasn't tempted by drinking or gambling. For one thing I couldn't afford them any more than the ten-cent bus fares from the campus to my room two miles away. Still, I began an active social life, and as if my freedom needed more space to accommodate it, I suddenly began to grow. Within a year and a half I was five inches taller and forty-five pounds heavier than when I had arrived at Athens.

Not once did I question my purpose in coming there or the relevance of the curriculum. I wanted to be educated and trained, and it never occurred to me, as if did to so many students in the 1960s, that "training" was an authoritarian procedure by which society molds the individual into fodder for the system. This was the Depression, and survival was the name of the game. We were all hungry in one way or another, and there was nothing we craved more than a comfortable slot.

Athens attracted some of the best and brightest people in Georgia, and served as a forum for diverse men and women whose interests tended toward law, politics, and business. Except for those who chose Georgia Tech, the wealthier Georgia families still sent their scions to Athens. A shy young man from a small town like Fitzgerald could find himself rubbing shoulders with rich kids like Bobby Troutman, whose father was counsel to the Coca-Cola magnates, or the sons of Governor Talmadge. There was also a group of non-Georgians who had chosen, for one reason or another, to attend or teach classes at Athens. Some of them were to have an enormous influence on me. There were those who came there to socialize and savor the experience of being in the Deep South. A few young men from eastern prep schools drifted through. There was a pace-setting coterie from Episcopal High in Washington, D.C., whose very presence was a challenge. I found the competition bracing and made the discovery that classical music and the visual arts were fit subjects for academic consideration. I learned, too, that some gentiles hardly noticed, much less weighed, the fact of my Jewishness.

Like everyone else at the university, the Jews were divided into fraternity/sorority or campus men and women. I was one of only a handful who remained in the latter group. There were three Jewish fraternities. The most prestigious was Phi Epsilon, an assimilated crowd, mainly from Atlanta. Their house was known for its spirited parties and high-stakes poker games. Beneath them in the pecking order was Tau Epsilon, somewhat less assimilated Eastern European Jews, and last was Alpha Epsilon Pi, who expected the least of their new social environment and were perhaps the most comfortable of all Jewish groups at the university.

I was immediately asked to join the Tau Eps and the AE Pis, but declined both. The Phi Eps didn't rush me. I was too rural and too gauche. To them I was Sam Abram's son, not Dr. Cohen's grandson. It was only after I made a name for myself on campus that they invited me to join, but caught somewhere between principle and pique, I rejected them, saying I did not believe in religiously or racially determined social groups. I did believe that Jews were doing themselves a disservice by evolving "separate but equal" associations. I failed to add, however, that I did not have enough money to pay the Phi Ep dues or to play their poker and games, which offended the puritan principles I had brought from Fitzgerald.

The image of myself in that time, following the demise of Stanley Withers, is one of triple exposure—I was far too proud to assimilate with Gentiles, far too anti-semitic to associate with exclusionary Jews, and far too socially inept to fit in with the assimilated German Jewish Phi Eps.

The issue became especially complex where women were concerned. I dreaded being put down by non-Jewish women but self-consciously avoided women who were palpably Jewish. The quirky Baptist in me complicated matters further by directing me away from overtly lusty women, but secretly I dreamed of a torrid affair with a buxom blond.

More important to my future than the Phi Eps could ever have been were the loud, seemingly street-wise New York Jews who had come to the inexpensive campus in Athens because their grades did not qualify them for free tuition in the city college system. I loathed them for being so ostentatiously Jewish and for their public scorn of Georgia and all it stood for. They were blind to the extraordinary southern culture which had survived, somewhat adulterated, from plantation South to the present. It was this boisterous bunch that had set up picket lines in front of the Palace Theatre protesting the exorbitant thirty-five cent admission charge to first-run movies. They were reinforcing the two standard caricatures of the Jew, as radical troublemakers and as penny pinchers.

But I was also drawn to them. Their world was big, foreign, full of new ideas. They discussed for hours on end the relative virtues of museums or of orchestras of which I had only the vaguest knowledge. I'd hear them talk about the New Deal as if all intelligent men and women were born either voting for Roosevelt or hating him because he was too conservative. Here were Jews who nonchalantly assumed superiority to me. I, whose great-grandfather had been one of the first Reform rabbis in America and whose grandpa was a fine physician!

Then there were our political differences. In 1934 I thought it would be a great idea to send the fleet up the Thames to London to collect the British war debt from World War I. Their derisive dismissal of such chauvinism infuriated me.

While I wrestled with their kind of Jewishness, I found myself exploring my religious dilemma in yet another way—by attending Sabbath services every Friday evening at the Athens Reform Temple. I felt an immediate kinship between this synagogue and the tradition espoused by my mother's side of the family, and hoped I'd be noticed by the German Jewish community and adopted as one of theirs.

I began a flirtation with the rabbinate. Though this was short-lived, it was a significant indication of my need for a platform. Twice a week I went to the home of Rabbi Abraham Shulman, an intelligent man whom I respected. I was still looking for the proof of the existence of God and I thought he might have the answer. Alas, he did not, and though I struggled with Hebrew lessons, a requirement for admission to Hebrew Union College, the seminary of Reform Judaism, a strange breach developed between me and the ancient language. Its intonations were too similar to Yiddish, and psychologically I was too blocked to learn it. Meanwhile I was a star in the French class.

Eventually the idea of being a rabbi grew less alluring. Not only did I have to reconcile myself to the heavy fact of Jewishness, but I would be at the beck and call of my congregation. I noticed that Shulman's time was not his own. The pastoral visits, the ceremonial rites—circumcision, marriage, eulogies for the dead—I knew they were not for me.

At the time my attraction to the rabbinate ended and my feelings about those shrill, yet fascinating carpetbaggers from Jewish New York grew increasingly ambiguous, I was living with the Boleys. They were German Jews who had fallen on hard times and were now taking in boarders. Their daughter, Evelyn, brought to the house two of the New York contingent, Joe and Naomi Gittler. These two were striking variations of my stereotypical urban Jewish image. They held the same alien, threatening ideas as the others but possessed none of the harping arrogance that I despised. They had good minds, finely honed by the CCNY of the 1920s and 1930s. In the following months I would thrill to a parade of fascinating ideas—from Montesquieu to Marx, from aesthetic criteria to fundamental questions of physical science.

Joe and Naomi had a lot to do with the maturation of my political outlook, as it was developed and expressed in the university literary clubs, which were really debating societies. I joined Phi Kappa, founded in 1831, and housed in a stately building of that vintage. Its competitor was Demosthenon, thirty years older, which had been my first and natural choice, as a nonfraternity freshman, until I saw that Herman Talmadge had a place of honor on its dais. I refused to be associated with any organization that would so honor the son of the anti-labor, anti-Roosevelt demagogue governor. By my junior year, I was Phi Kappa president.

My disgust of Demosthenon cooled, but a friendly rivalry persisted. It was to take a swipe at Demosthenon that I decided to enlist Franklin Roosevelt as a member of Phi Kappa. I sat down and wrote to the president and invited him to join, but I could hardly believe it when he replied accepting the offer.

I remember the emotion that welled up in me as I read his letter. I simply couldn't believe my eyes, though the reply was doubtless authentic. I walked lightheaded across a park in Athens, my mind savoring the idea that the son of an immigrant father would preside over a ceremony in which the president of the United States would participate.

Considerable correspondence ensued about where to hold the initiation. The debating hall of Phi Kappa was on the second floor, and the Secret Service decided that as Roosevelt could not manage the stairs, we should be invited to Warm Springs, the little White House. It was 1937, the year Roosevelt was trying to pack the Supreme Court. I was nineteen. Our group included three other officers as well as the oldest member of Phi Kappa on the campus, the University Registrar, T. W. Reed, a striking man who sported a white moustache and stiff celluloid collar. I had also invited my father to come with me to Warm Springs though, of course, he would have to remain outside the compound. As we entered the small house, we literally had to step over Jimmy Roosevelt who was lying on the floor between the front door and the unroofed porch where the president was sitting relaxed in the sun. He offered us cigarettes, Camels. I nervously refused, and later regretted having given up an invaluable souvenir.

"Did you see Jimmy when you came in?" he asked, grinning.

"Yes," I said, "he was on the floor with a telephone in his hand."

"Ah yes," said the president. "He has been talking to Washington about the Supreme Court."

"Mr. President," volunteered Mr. Reed, relishing the moment, "you are looking at the most unreconstructed old-line Democrat you ever saw in your life. Now, as far as I am concerned, the weakest man the Democrats can nominate is always stronger than the strongest Republican. But I want to tell you, Mr. President, that I don't like your packing the Supreme Court. Not one bit."

I gulped, expecting a scowl on FDR's face. But no. He threw back his leonine head and roared with laughter. "Mr. Reed," he said, "you are not in a class by yourself. There are multitudes who share it with you."

We performed the induction and chatted with the president while my father waited outside the gate. Part of me needed him to enjoy my triumph, but another was embarrassed by his presence. Still, it had been my father, not my mother, I had wanted to bring. Something in me rejoiced that Sam Abram would have the chance to be

45

close to the one person who was so important to all the Sam Abrams of the world. And I, his son, would have brought it about.

When we left the little White House, my father's eyes were shining with tears. Years later I would recall the image of him standing at the gate and wonder how much fulfillment my own public life had brought him. He seemed out of place, so shy, so hesitant, as if he felt it an absurdity being here. I, too, have felt that awkwardness in the glare of celebrity and high places.

I was accumulating a string of minor honors and society presidencies. Eventually (in Fitzgerald this would have been unthinkable), I would be elected president of my freshman law class. Finally, I was admitted as one of six in my senior year to the holy of holies, the secret Sphinx Society, whose traditional claim that it was "the highest nonacademic honor in the university" was never disputed.

As my confidence increased, I dared to advance the boundaries of my ideas. I was, without knowing it, developing the underpinnings of the political and social man I was to become. I was absolutely transported, not by Eliot's *The Waste Land* or by Joyce's *Ulysses,* as was the literary elite, but by the majestic prose of the United States Constitution. I committed lengthy passages to memory. The words of the Fourteenth Amendment grip me as much now as they did then:

> No state shall deprive any person of life, liberty or property without due process of law, nor deny to any person within its jurisdiction the equal protection of the law.

Once, in the mid-1930s, when I was on the Georgia debating team, I was assigned the negative side of the resolution "that Negroes should be admitted to all state universities." Unlike my colleague, I could not bring myself to deny the force of the constitutional argument made by the opposition. So I advanced a theme we would hear thirty years later from black leaders—that predominantly white colleges ". . . teach from the viewpoint of the dominant race. . . . Racial pride must be stimulated in the Negro. . . . [At Harvard a student] would never realize that the Negro had any history aside from being the frequent source of internal disruption in the United States."

I was further conflicted by the clash of values of urban-centered people such as the Gittlers and the southern "Agrarians," of whom Professor John Donald Wade was the chief Georgia apostle. The latter were a distinguished group of southern literary figures who celebrated the economy and culture of the pre-Civil War South, claiming it much superior to that of the industrial North. Wade invited me for a weekend to his charming antebellum home in Marshallville, Georgia, to sample the ambience for myself. For three days I was transported into a world of white columns, magnolia trees, and smiling servants. I was captivated by the pastoral beauty, the gracious life style, and the facile flow of conversation, but I knew that only a few could live like Professor Wade and that his respectful but patronizing relationship with his black "staff" was not the general southern custom I had observed.

At the point at which I was recapitulating these racial and political dilemmas, Eli suggested we go to Fitzgerald to retrace the steps by which I first became aware of the discrepancy between the Constitution I loved and the practices of segregation.

We visited my mother, living still in that house of concrete block made to resemble stones into which we moved when I was only six months old. We saw the grade school, now abandoned, where Mrs. Mathis had taught that magical fifth grade. We visited the Fitzgerald high school, an old red brick building with Corinthian columns still surrounded by a dusty playground on which blacks now, as well as whites, romped. We toured the still-segregated churches, saw the public swimming pool drained and empty since the fateful time when such facilities were ordered integrated. We took in the whole scene in one afternoon, the community in which I was almost totally encapsulated for sixteen years.

I began to recall the conflict I saw, as a student of nineteen, between the principles of the Constitution and southern practices and institutions. Strangely, no professor ever made this point. Segregation was simply an accepted fact and even the softest opposition, usually from some New York Jewish quarter on campus, was dismissed as a subversive and foreign idea.

I was not only offended but made anxious by the implicit anti-Semitism in the charge that the only northerners on campus who challenged segregation were Jews.

I can now pinpoint the time and place when the creed of segregation crumbled for me. I was home from college, tending my father's store on a Saturday evening. Pine Street was thronged with tenant farmers, sharecroppers, and field hands adrift on the town, to frolic and shop after a day of harvest. I looked over the sea of ragged, unwashed, illiterate folk and found myself testing the idea of desegregation with a silent question: "With how many of these ragged, dirty, illiterate blacks do I have enough in common to ask them into my house?" The answer was a resounding "None." This might have disposed of the issue if something hadn't prompted another query: "With how many of these ragged, dirty, illiterate whites do I have enough in common to ask them into my house?" The answer was the same. My musings progressed toward a conundrum: "Why is it that I do not ask that all members of the white community be acceptable before any are accepted? Why are such demands, on the other hand, made of the minority or black community?"

I probably realized at the time that I was identifying with the blacks, the implicit thrust of my question also being: "Why should all Jews be acceptable before any are accepted—or even more to the point, why are all Jews held responsible for the conduct of some?"

From that time on, segregation became an abomination to me and irreconcilable with the American tradition. Certain past experiences which I had long accepted as not only right but very charitable, now became illuminated. In the third grade I remember having felt very good—indeed noble—when the teacher had us gather up our worn, out-of-date textbooks, provided at public expense, for shipment over to the colored school.

Until I left a still-segregated Georgia in 1962 I was out of step with the principal political and social fundament of the society. Although I was cautious and did not frontally challenge the system, I never lied about my feelings and few doubted what they were.

The political structure of Georgia was such that it was possible to attack the manifold denials of "equal protection of the laws," of which segregation was certainly the principal example, without attacking segregation itself. Since 1917, when the primary election rules of the reigning Democratic Party in this one-party state were incorporated into law, any primary was required to be conducted under the so-called county unit rule. This was an electoral vote system in which the eight largest Georgia counties were each assigned six votes; the thirty next largest, four, and the remainder of Georgia's 159 counties, two. The unit vote of the county was conferred upon whomever carried a plurality of the popular vote. All statewide offices, including the governor, United States senators, and appellate judges, were elected in county unit Democratic primaries, general elections being mere formalities. Congressional districts could and usually did adopt the same rules and ratios in contests for the United States House of Representatives. Before the United States Supreme Court finally declared the county unit law invalid in a case I argued in 1963, Atlanta's principal county, Fulton, contained 550,000 people sharing six votes as contrasted with the two votes assigned to the less than 1,900 people of Echols County.

I do not recall when I was not offended by the rank inequity of the unit system, though my home county, Ben Hill, benefited from the disproportionate power of its two unit votes. Eugene Talmadge, and later his son Herman, were staunch defenders of the unit rule. Eugene boasted in the 1930s, when it was not anachronistic to say so, "I never want to carry a county that has a street car." Indeed, it was to the politician's advantage to pitch his campaign to the small, manageable, and relatively homogenous white electorate in the 121 counties with two votes, which possessed a clear majority of the unit voting power.

While the Democratic white primary stood, racist campaigns characterized the entire tier of southern states, and traditional politicians felt secure. In 1944, the Supreme Court declared the Texas white primary unconstitutional, and southern legislatures scurried to find new devices to protect their primaries or otherwise exclude blacks from the electoral process. Even after the Georgia white primary was invalidated in 1945, the effect was modified by the county unit system.

Herman Talmadge, when he became governor in 1948, proclaimed, "The county unit system and Governor Herman Talmadge are the only bulwark protecting us against federal courts race-mixing in our grade schools and colleges in Georgia." The system, which was largely neutral on the surface, systematically disenfranchised blacks because black registrations were low (and in some cases nonexistent) in counties which had disproportionate voting power under the unit rule. In rural counties in the plantation belt, black populations had few registered voters, of whom only a fraction might dare go to the polls.

Despite the fact that the unit system stripped the white electorate of equal voting rights randomly, such victims had been relatively docile prior to 1946, reminded as they were by politicians that the unit system was their protection against urban vice, mob rule, union tyranny, and concentration of black political power in the cities. Educated, influential whites in Atlanta, particularly some bankers and utility and textile magnates, were surprisingly willing to have their votes diluted so long as the candidates they favored were elected by rural whites. They opted for real political power over mere form. The persons who lost in this charade of democracy were not only blacks and union labor but, of course, every person who wished to participate genuinely and equally in the democratic process.

In early 1935 I began to speak out against the county unit system and for the principle for which I later coined a slogan, "one man, one vote." I was, without expressly saying so, putting in my licks against a whole edifice, of which the county unit ruse and segregation were a part.

I was now spending nine months a year in Athens, honing my mind with books and exchanging ideas with such visionary people as the Gittlers. Very little was induced by contact with most professors, who studiously avoided the overriding moral and political issue of the time. But slowly I began to separate the imported ideas from the complex and overwhelming people who seemed to hold them. In the case of Naomi and Joe Gittler, I even began to like the people. Their ideas grew more and more seductive.

I was beginning to grasp the fact that so long as a central issue lay outside the realm of permissible discourse—race, specifically— the academic atmosphere was stultified. Though it would be ten years before I would read Freud, the parallel in psychoanalysis is clear: When there is a personal resistance in one area, the psychoanalytic discovery and learning process cannot proceed unimpaired in any other.

The South, and this included almost all southern universities, lay under a suffocating blanket. The Gittlers had lifted one corner and

I began to yearn for more, and for a scholarship to some distinguished university.

By the time I left Athens I was a practicing liberal. In 1938, E. D. Rivers, an FDR Democrat, ran for governor against Eugene Talmadge's candidate, Hugh Howell. Since I was known as an anti-Talmadge man and as a good speaker, the Rivers campaign assigned me fifteen minutes on WSB in Atlanta, the state's most powerful radio station, to make the young people's case for Rivers. I was astonished afterwards to be chided by Bobby Troutman's father. "Morris," he said, "it isn't wise to stake out so early a flat political position, particularly on the liberal side." As Ed Rivers was in every sense a conventional Georgia politician, except for his support of the New Deal, I could not understand how my act could be construed as risky. Much later I would learn that to the conventional, conservative southern family, the political walls were a solid phalanx, all parts of which had to be defended lest any weakness be exploited.

In addition to growing out of small-town conservatism and parochial interests, there were other developments in my political views during my five years at Athens. One was my strange relationship with Herman Talmadge which, as I have said, began almost the moment I arrived at school, and revealed, I felt, the unique character of political and personal loyalties in a South that hovered on the precipice of change. Another was my friendship with Bobby Troutman, whose family, as I said also, was connected to the Coca-Cola establishment.

My walking out of Demosthenon in disgust at Herman Talmadge's sinister presence there was soon a piece of university lore. Our mutual enmity became, in fact, such legend that the debating coach from the English Department decided to set up a debate between Talmadge and Abram. The subject: *Should Eugene Talmadge be reelected governor of Georgia?* The campus chapel would be the site, and the Associated Press would be there.

Herman was in his early twenties. The son of a superb politician, he was anything but convivial—a closed-off man, tall, good-looking, and saturnine. Coal black hair fell over a face of sallow complexion. I always felt he forced himself to be the successful political figure he became, using his razor sharp mind to shape a

51

career to which he was born. He would, I thought, have preferred the streams and woods of rural Georgia to the streets and sidewalks where for thirty years he stalked for votes.

The gala evening arrived and with it a violent thunderstorm. Herman had stacked the audience with men in workclothes who were probably seeing a college campus for the first time. He began his part of the debate with the customary call-and-response rhetoric. He would shout, "Who reduced your utility rates?" And his boys would scream, "Gene Talmadge." That went on for some moments and covered the catalogue of his father's accomplishments, including the reduction of the automobile license tag to three dollars across the board, from flivver to Cadillac.

Then it was my turn. "You know," I said, "I've never liked Eugene Talmadge, that's for sure. On the other hand I do say that I've always thought he was original. Therefore, I don't believe he would be very proud of his son tonight, for his son is not original. He copied his father's techniques without improving on them. This time instead of having his chorus shouting from their perches in the trees, they are in the front row of this chapel." Herman's supporters couldn't help him, however, as the outcome of the debate was in the hands of neutral judges. They decided that I was the winner. Herman was a sore loser. We never again shook hands on campus.

If Herman represented the Georgia redneck, though he came from an old and distinguished family, which for political purpose obscured its origins, Bobby Troutman personified the cool, conservative aristocrat. Bobby, a devout Catholic, could ally himself with Herman Talmadge and make friends with Morris Abram, but he remained what he was: a patrician, born to command. He was a stocky, very solid fellow—not good looking, ill-dressed in expensive clothes. A superb athlete, he would have been a varsity star had he dared to risk in contact sports his one kidney remaining after an automobile accident.

My relationship with Troutman was my first real experience in mutual exploitation. We were useful to each other, and I say that now without denying the very real affection that existed between us. I spent many weekends at his parents' elegant Atlanta home, and by the time I returned to Atlanta after the war, I had a fund of Troutman-based contacts on which to draw. His friendship was the key to the city. By the same token I was valuable to him; particularly after I was made a member of Sphinx. Bobby wanted to get in; his father had been a member. While he was one of the most talented young men on the campus, his goals were still unfocused. He tended to scoff at the academic status symbols that others needed.

Bobby came from a family already accredited in every sense. His father had been an editor of the Columbia Law Review and was a leader of the Georgia Bar. Still, in his senior year at Georgia, Bobby was up against a hard fact. He might well not be admitted to the Sphinx Society. (He eventually was, as Sphinx No. 317; his father had been No. 122.)

I did everything I could to help him, although he did not ask for my help nor did I ever speak of it. My efforts were rewarded by the most welcome favors—the best of all, the use of his car. Though he was honestly disturbed by my radicalism, this devout Catholic aristocrat was one of the first people I ever met who, it seemed, genuinely didn't give a damn whether or not I was Jewish.

Bobby and I were introduced to each other and to Gus Cleveland, a Baptist, by a campus administrator named Ernest Segrest. Segrest ran both a voluntary religious association and the campus YMCA. Out of our conversations grew a project in which we three—Catholic, Protestant, and Jew—spoke around the state, telling people that there were no unbreachable differences between the three great religious traditions: We all worshiped the same God, and didn't much worry about the Trinitarian Godhead, which neither Bobby nor Gus understood anyway; we shared the same Old Testament; and we all adhered to the same ethical principles. All true believers love each other anyway! Our act caught on and met with thunderous applause wherever we went, for we were telling people what they wanted to hear. I was speaking the verities of my mother's Judaism; and I was gaining plaudits and acceptance from audiences which wanted, at the least cost, to experience universalistic sentiments.

I had begun at Georgia in a premed program with the models of my grandfather and brother in my mind. During my freshman year I couldn't help being struck by how mundane it seemed. A respectable doctor's practice in a sophisticated town would mean contusions and tonsilectomies, deliveries, making the rounds. I found myself abandoning medicine in the same way I had abandoned the rabbinate: by observing it and considering its wear and drudgery insufficiently rewarding.

Or was it something else?

I have never suffered failure gladly and consequently tended to eschew whatever I intuitively feared I could not master. While I succeeded in all the textual and analytical materials connected with the premed courses, I had great difficulty drawing representations of what I had seen in anatomical classes or under the microscope. My spacial senses are faulty, something I had noted when I thought of electing a high school course in solid geometry. I found plane geometry a delight, majestic, elegant, and stimulating. I always turned in a perfect examination paper. However, the simplest structures of solid geometry were complex mysteries.

Premed classmates were turning in beautiful replicas of comparative skeletal structures of vertebrate animals. Mine were not worthy of a first grade school child. If I should have to depend on good grades and scholarships for the long road through medicine, I feared I might not make it. It never occurred to me to ask a medical academician if I would really be disadvantaged by this weakness.

Beyond these negative aspects of medicine was the powerful magnet of the law. I was by now a very political man and politics was more closely associated with the law than with any other discipline. Also, I knew how much I enjoyed public speaking, especially debating, activities closely identified with the law. Why not then go into law?

This would indeed be strange, for my brother, Lewis, had begun studies at Athens to become a lawyer but had switched to medicine. Now I was contemplating exactly the reverse. Was I trying to avoid some collision course of which I was unaware?

I decided to see the dean of the Law School, and pose the one question that still troubled me: Can a lawyer be an honest person? My parents had bemoaned mistreatment by the lawyers representing the creditors in daddy's bankruptcy in 1926, and my head was filled with descriptions of lawyers as tricksters or worse. Dean Harmon Caldwell satisfied me with his answer, saying that he had practiced in Atlanta and had never found it necessary to surrender his conscience because of the tugs of his clients' interests.

I knew there would be a lot of romance in the law, for I remember the courtroom I used to visit in Fitzgerald; I thought it such a majestic place. In fact, it was the only good drama staged in the town except when the Redpath Chautauqua pitched its tent at the corner of Pine and Lee streets.

From my earliest memories education loomed as the highest good, not only in my mother's hierarchy of values, but in my father's as well. When I first heard of the Rhodes scholarships, while I was still in high school, I set my heart upon receiving one. The first opportunity to compete for it came in 1937. I got past the state competition, but failed in the regional. I shared my disappointment with Bobby Troutman, who put it to me bluntly: "How in hell do you expect anybody to give you a Rhodes scholarship when you talk as you do?" I replied, "What do you mean?" "I'll give you an example," said Troutman. "You talk like a hick. Here's the way you sound: 'Ah lak whait ice cream.' " I was crushed by his criticism and became determined to remedy my handicap. For the next year I practiced pronunciation of the letter "i" as in "Ike." By the time the Rhodes scholarship competition rolled around again a year later, I was pronouncing my words as clearly as any Yankee, but with the soft intonations of my region. I could not, however, paper over all the gaps in my cultural development. I thought I was doomed when a member of the committee on final selection said he would like to talk about music. The question he posed happened to be one which I, as a Jew, had pondered.

"Hitler likes Wagnerian music," I replied, "probably because its themes and moody romanticism strike a German nationalistic chord. Also Wagner is thought to have been anti-Semitic."

When I found I had won a scholarship, I was ecstatic. I clutched another winner, Harvey Poe, from Virginia—a descendant of Edgar Allan Poe—whom I impulsively invited to go with me to Fitzgerald for the weekend. As Harvey and my family met I was sobered by the vast disparity between the Abrams and the Poes, but I was also proud that I had come from further than he.

I was scheduled to sail for England in October 1939 to take up my scholarship at Pembroke College, associated with Samuel Johnson and with Blackstone of the venerable legal commentaries. All during the summer of 1939 the air waves crackled with news out of Berlin, Warsaw, Danzig, Paris, London, and Moscow. On the one hand I felt passionately that Hitler must be stopped. I felt so as an American, as an Anglophile, and as a Jew. On the other hand, I knew that if Hitler were faced down it meant war and the end of my dreams of Oxford—probably forever.

The die was cast for me one night when I was attending a movie, *The Wizard of Oz,* in Macon, Georgia. Emerging from the theatre, I learned that Hitler was in Poland. Within days the Rhodes Trustees sent word that our class was not to sail.

5

SOMETIMES the most caring of friends, in trying to comfort someone who is mortally ill, only succeed in assaulting his intricate defenses against rational fear. When I was undergoing the radical initial treatment in the fall of 1973, a former partner from Atlanta, whose wife had died of my disease three years before, sent me a poem which was intended to deflect my concern about oblivion and provide one view of the mystery and meaning of death. I was infuriated, and I resolved more than ever to survive. Even spite can be a spur!

Now in 1975 as I was pouring out my story to Eli something similar happened. I received in the mail, from a close psychiatrist friend, an article published in the British medical journal *Lancet,* which reported that immunotherapy (which I was receiving) had little, if any, statistically measurable effects in maintaining the remission in my type of leukemia. My friend added: "You must not translate the material too directly. . . ." "I'm going to do more than that," I said to Eli: "I'm going to ignore it." And I proceeded to tell him about the first time I left Georgia, in September 1939.

The University of Chicago offered tuition scholarships to all Rhodes men frustrated by the war. I was short by hundreds of dollars of the funds required for board, room, and other necessities. Bobby Troutman's father then volunteered to give me the money, which provided the way up from the provincialism against which I was struggling with even greater intensity now that Oxford had disappeared.

I rode by train from Fitzgerald to Chicago, two entirely different worlds connected by track. The final leg of the journey ended at Twelfth Street Station. I hit the pavement, picked up my steamer trunk, and headed for the campus on Chicago's South Side. In my bones I felt the transition was really too great and too fast, from the rolling hills and slow pace of Athens to this bustling city and the imposing Gothic buildings of a university celebrated for its rigorous academics. I was frightened not of failure but that I would not excel here. I took refuge in the sole accreditation I possessed: I was a Rhodes Scholar. I was admitted to the third-year class with full credit for my two years at the Law School of the University of Georgia.

The first class I attended, Anti-Trust Regulations, was taught by William Crosskey. He was a bear of a man who prowled about the classroom growling questions and chewing up the answers. He was writing a book called *Politics and the Constitution,* which set out to prove that the New Deal laws recently invalidated by the Supreme Court were valid under the proper interpretation of the commerce clause of the Constitution. Whatever the merits of his conclusions, his methods were spellbinding to me.

The case under discussion—or rather, under attack—was the celebrated Baseball Case in which Mr. Justice Holmes, writing for the Supreme Court, held that baseball reserve clauses were not antitrust violations as baseball was not, according to the Court, commerce regulated under the Sherman Antitrust Act. Crosskey probed one member of the class after another about a question related to the decision, with which he was in furious disagreement. He was very frustrated by the responses from the familiar faces in the room, and suddenly he sighted me, new prey.

"What's your name?"

"Abram, sir."

58

"You're a southerner."

"Yes."

"Then you can surely supply the answer I seek."

"But Professor, I haven't read the case."

"Makes no difference; you see, my question might just as easily be 'Why was the Civil War fought?' It's the answer I'm after."

"Well," I replied, "I do know the answer to that."

"So let's have it."

"The War Between the States," I said, supplying the correct, southerners' nomenclature, "was fought over states' rights."

"Poppycock," Crosskey exploded, "everybody knows it was fought over slavery."

It was a terrifying beginning, but I developed a marvelous relationship to this brilliant, skeptical, cynical man—my first intimate contact with a first-class legal scholar.

Thereafter I was in the position to measure intellect against a yardstick I had never had before. As a transfer student, I was disadvantaged by my relatively poor preparation. I was also handicapped because I held two part-time jobs, as associate director of the Hillel Foundation at the University and Sunday school teacher at Sinai Temple. Still I made academic progress. In Crosskey's classes, once I recovered from the shock of total immersion, I performed as well as any.

In Professor Charles Gregory's class in Labor Law, I led the pack in the intense competition for grades. In other courses such as Mortgages, Bills and Notes, and Legal Philosophy, I found myself struggling. I was not interested in or particularly well grounded in the grubby subjects of commercial law. Legal Philosophy was another matter. But my command was restricted by the novelty of the conceptual materials. No matter how Professor Ed Levi, subsequently United States Attorney General, tried to teach me, I could not then grasp the idea of "the natural law," uncodified, unwritten, existing in nature, perhaps ruling it, and discoverable by reason and conscience. Never having been exposed to a primer in philosophy, I wallowed my way through to a passing grade. It would be six years later, at the Nuremberg trials, that I would first understand that the Nazi leadership had violated, by a transcendental arrogance, a system of right and justice binding on all humanity. I then understood what Levi had never been able to get through my head.

In one year the University of Chicago stretched me in many directions. One of the most profound influences on me was a wizened hunchback rabbi, Maurice Pekarsky, director of the Hillel Foundation at Northwestern University, thirty miles away. Now he had been charged with establishing a Hillel unit in Chicago as well.

Somehow Pekarsky and I found each other. He needed a student assistant for his newly added responsibility. I needed money. Soon I realized Rabbi Pekarsky paid me in a purer and more valuable coin. He became a Jewish role model when I needed one badly. If I was ill prepared for the senior class at the Law School, I was less prepared to act as Pekarsky's assistant. This kind, gentle, sparkling man was a disciple of Mordecai Kaplan, the founder of the Reconstructionist Movement in Jewish life. Reconstructionism had examined the liturgy, the literature, and the practices of Orthodox Judaism, not to see what could be discarded but what could be preserved and validated in modern practice. Pekarsky for the first time made me feel that Jewishness could be quite different from Protestant practice without being incomprehensible to me personally and out of phase with the American social setting.

I must have seemed very silly, if not absurd, in the constant reiteration of my experience in the Catholic-Protestant-Jewish trialogues which Troutman, Cleveland, and I had developed in Georgia. But Rabbi Pekarsky never consciously made anyone feel silly. He taught by example, and subtly. Through this shining man, I began to restore my diminished identity.

The contrast between Maurice Pekarsky and my other employer, Rabbi Louis Mann of Sinai Temple, defined my struggle with Jewishness. Mann was a pillar of the ultra-Reform Movement. He had discarded Friday night sermons for services on Sunday. His reputation in the community and nation was established. Pekarsky, beside Mann's lofty bulk, was a dwarf, but Pekarsky's influence on me and on thousands of students whom he touched was towering and enduring.

In June 1940, I received my J.D. degree from the university, and returned to Georgia to take the Bar examination with the expectation of practicing law in Atlanta with the firm of Howell & Post. The Post in the firm was Allen, a former Rhodes Scholar who had sat on the committee that selected me to enter his college, Pembroke.

I did not, like others who sat for the examination, take a Bar review course or even work with other candidates in private "skull practice." I simply assumed that having passed successfully through a distinguished national law school, the Georgia Bar examination would be a snap. When the results were published I was shocked and incredulous to find that I had failed. I had never failed *any* assignment! How was I to face Allen Post who expected me to come to work the following month as a qualified lawyer? I could not even face myself. I was sure there had been some mistake. My handwriting—that was it—my illegible handwriting had either put off the examiner or was misread. I could neither sleep nor eat nor enjoy anything at all until this disgrace was erased. I petitioned, pleaded, and petulantly demanded a review and reconsideration, all to no avail.

My flailing about to correct the "mistake" put me in touch with former Governor John M. Slaton, who had commuted the sentence of Leo Frank. Slaton in 1940 was chairman of the Board of Georgia Bar Examiners, and at the request of Governor Rivers he agreed to hear my petition. Slaton then was an aged man, no longer a controversial figure, but a veritable patriarch. He also served as chairman of the governing body of the Atlanta Public Library, which enforced total segregation in the main facility and carefully screened the terms on which books were made available to Negroes. During my interview Slaton courteously but peremptorily refused to consider my petition, so I switched the subject to the Frank case. I was very curious to plumb this paradox of a man who adamantly kept black professors out of the reading rooms of the Carnegie Library in 1940, but who risked his life and destroyed his political career in 1915 by saving Leo Frank from the legal gallows.

"What led you to do it?" I asked.

"I don't deserve a bit of credit," he replied. "I was married to a remarkable woman, Sarah Grant. She knew I was troubled as the date of execution neared. 'John, do you think he's guilty?' 'No,' I told her, 'but if I act I shall risk my life.' 'You must, John, for I'd rather be the widow of an honest man than live with a man who, having the power to stop it, let an innocent man be killed.' "

Slaton's refusal to open my case left me with nothing to do but wait until December, when I took the Bar exam again. I trembled as I phrased each answer succinctly, and what was just as important, legibly. I found I had passed and with high marks—this time there was no "mistake" about it.

Meanwhile, waiting for the results of the examinations, I went to work for Howell & Post for the standard salary—wage, it really was—of seventy dollars per month. I even got to perform in the courtroom before I was admitted to the Bar. The senior partner, Hugh Howell, who was once again running for governor, decided to have me attend to some of his incidental court matters, and he possessed enough influence to have the rules waived.

But I had a problem at Howell & Post with a senior associate there named Sam Green, a lawyer ten years older than I but a legal hack. Just as I was the choice of Post, Green had been selected by Howell. Green was invariably kind, considerate, and even effusively friendly. He did me the favor of showing me his complex, expensive toy railroad system which covered the entire attic of his home. The problem was Green's affiliation with his father's organization. Sam Green, Sr., a physician, was the Grand Dragon of the Knights of the Ku Klux Klan. It is worth noting that while in 1940 Dr. Green was the medical "expert" of the three examiners who sat to pass on the sanity of persons whose mental competence was challenged in the probate court of Fulton County, thirty-two years later the mayor and congressman from the district were both black.

I was not happy at Howell & Post even after I had passed the Bar. Apart from Green, Post was far too busy to supervise and instruct me, and Howell was incapable of it. I longed to join up with the Troutman firm, but no one had asked me. If Troutman, Sr. thought me worthy of support in law school, what held him back? I wouldn't permit myself to think through to the awful and inescapable reality that no Jew had ever been employed by that firm, now the renowned King & Spalding of Griffin Bell and Charles Kirbo.

About this time I met Carlyn Feldman, whom I would not marry until thirty-five years had passed. She was then seventeen, and an overwhelmingly beautiful young woman, tall and slim; her eyes an unforgettable blue-gray, the color usually associated with blond hair, though hers was raven black; her face replete with angles, a photographer's dream; her smile, full and natural. For three years, off and on, I courted her, but she would not then think of marrying me. I was a man of law and politics; she was far more interested in life's mysteries. She saw me as a rising star, but she did not wish to be drawn into any such field of gravity. She told me: "You are verbal and I am visual. You like exciting people, but I would just as soon be with rocks, trees, and tides."

Meanwhile, the war: FDR, reelected to an unprecedented third term in 1940, was by the beginning of 1941 pressing for lendlease, which would unequivocally commit him to the Allied cause. I was a second lieutenant in the reserves, some of which were being called up. My sister Jeanette was soon to be ready for college, and I felt morally obliged to help foot her bills, as my brother had helped with mine. The second lieutenant salary was not much, but with lodging and fringe benefits it beat seventy dollars a month. Moreover, if I would be called up soon anyway, I could, by volunteering in January 1941, choose Fort McPherson, outside Atlanta, as my first post.

My part in the military drama began poorly at the classification center at Fort McPherson. God knows why, except to save money, but instead of buying a proper officer's cap, I chose to wear a peaked campaign hat, which I had left from ROTC days, with its wide, round brim reminiscent of World War I. My commanding officer, a Lieutenant Colonel named Brokaw, took one look at me and said something so painful that I have utterly blocked it out of memory.

I was rebellious. Senseless regulations angered me, and only my conviction that Hitler had to be destroyed came between me and probable dismissal. Yet these years of the military were not entirely wasted after my inauspicious beginning.

I am sure Lieutenant Colonel Brokaw, if he had not perished in the Phillipines, would have shared my own astonishment when by 1945 I adjusted sufficiently and widened my activities enough to advance to the rank of major and to win the coveted Legion of Merit at the age of twenty-six.

Or did Gus Tyler (then Tilove) win it for me? Sergeant Tilove, 32, of the ILGWU, former editor of the *Call*, the right-wing socialist newspaper of New York, became my principal tutor.

In December 1944, when I expected to be ordered overseas, my commander said, "Abram, you're going to Santa Ana Army Base in California to head up the public relations office."

Astonished, I asked, "Why?"

"Because this is the largest Air Force facility in the country, cheek by jowl with the West Coast media outlets, the place where *Winged Victory* was recently filmed, and it has a lousy public image, which is growing worse."

"What's the problem?"

"Well," the Colonel answered, "the Commanding General."

I couldn't see how the job had anything to do with me, so I pointed out that I had no experience for the position.

The Colonel grew a little testy. "Major, you're an Air Force officer. You're supposed to do any job within your grade. This post is important, your staff will be large; report to Santa Ana within two weeks."

When I entered the Public Relations office at this huge sprawling base, then a reclassification and reassignment center, I found a collection of soldiers who seemed no more fitted than I for the task of refurbishing the reputation of this Command. At a total loss, I asked for the personnel files of my staff.

As I thumbed through each card, I grew more pessimistic. Finally, I came to the file on Sergeant Gus Tilove, as he then was known: "Graduated NYU, educational director-political director, ILGWU, Editor, etc." I called for Tilove and when he walked in, he handed me the sloppiest salute I had seen even at this most relaxed post.

"Sergeant," I asked, "what do you do here?"

"I'm a clerk/typist," he replied.

"Why, with this background, are you merely a clerk/typist?" I asked, suspecting a drinking or personality problem.

Tilove's answer was delivered with a chuckle I've grown accustomed to in succeeding years, "Because, Sir, the Air Force trained me as an aerial gunner."

I said to myself: There's a smart guy, who's going to be able to help me out of this pickle. Gus, it turned out, would also continue my political education at the point at which Joe Gittler had stopped, and in a far more practical and worldly way.

In January 1944, I had only the vaguest conceptions of the theories of socialism, right and left, and of communism, Stalinists, Trotskyites, Mensheviks, and Bukharinites. I knew nothing of the passionately debated twists and turns of shifting alliances, embraces, exoduses, and exclusions of New York ideologies, including the then recent break of the Liberal Party from the American Labor Party over the latter's tolerance of communists. I had never once attended any meeting at which one caucus attempted to sit out another, or called a quick vote when the room was temporarily short of opposition. Gus was not only grounded in the theories of the various brands of left-wing politics, he was accomplished in practice. He also knew about strong-arm tactics, goon squads, and the role of organized crime in the labor movement. Gus, who later wrote a book on it, thought organized crime could not be tamed within the framework of constitutional due process. My lawyer's instinct rebelled at the suggestion that only by wiretaps and other dirty business could the cities be freed from crime's daily ransom.

We were no doubt a curious sight, a major who seldom whiled away time at the officers' club, and his friend the sergeant, who was opening vistas of incomparable dimensions and interest. Gus's wife, Marie, and my wife, Jane, also became close friends. Jane was pregnant when we arrived at Santa Ana and when our first child, Ruth, was delivered there, Gus and Marie attended to the expectant father. When mother and child were due to come home, Gus and I formed a two-man germicide squad to wash down our apartment with rubbing alcohol, lest the baby be exposed to disease. My mother's fierce sanitation regime, inspired by Grandpa Cohen, lived on in me. Now I had co-opted my sergeant, who on hands and knees with me swabbed the kitchen, bathroom, and nursery.

Gus and I had our hands full with the general and the Air Base image. But through the months there were no problems for which Sergeant Tilove did not have a uniquely creative solution.

Finally, as the war was drawing to a close, Gus and I planned a conference on the returning serviceman. The general was delighted with the idea that our base, his staff, and particularly he himself would be the focus of the nation's attention. The official purpose of the conference was to address the emotional, economic, and physical needs of the fighting men—to prevent and treat the "shell shock" syndrome, which was expected to be a much larger problem than in 1918, because of the unprecedented scale of the war and its duration.

The meeting brought together the giants of various disciplines:

65

Dr. Roy Grinker, in psychiatry; Dr. Howard A. Rusk, in physical rehabilitation; and Donald Nelson, Chief of the War Production Board, in reemployment. The Air Force brass was very nervous about the involvement of psychiatrists in discussions of "Men Under Stress." I received a peremptory letter a few weeks before the conference warning me that "psychiatrists are a little too enthusiastic about their opportunities in this war." I knew next to nothing of psychoanalysis and I was being asked to find out what Grinker, one of the nation's top Freudians, "expects to say." Traveling on the bucket seat of a DC-3 to headquarters East to explain myself, I read through the night Freud's *Introductory Lectures in Psychoanalysis,* which opened a new world of ideas to me. The conference was a huge success, and the general was now hailed as a visionary as well as the most humane of generals. He pushed for and obtained for me the Legion of Merit—for outstanding service, which had "reflected great credit upon the Army Air Forces."

Though I valued the stunningly beautiful medal and the ribbon I received from the Secretary of War, I valued more the education that had led to it.

It was in 1943 that I first saw the woman who was to become my first wife and the mother of my five children. I was still a captain in the Air Force, and Jane Maguire was a reporter for the Orlando *Sentinel,* preparing to be a maid of honor in the Orange Bowl festivities. I met her through a mutual friend, Keith McKeon, a Ph.D. student at the University of Chicago. Keith had once been Jane's beau, but now she was going with a regular naval captain some twenty years her senior. As Keith put it, "Somebody has to rescue her; she is, after all, in imminent danger of either spinsterhood at twenty-three or marriage to a senior citizen." Three years earlier Keith had shown me Jane's picture and read me some of her letters. I had been haunted by the face in the photograph—its great beauty was enhanced for me by an appealing wistfulness.

I went to Orlando to meet her and drove so fast I burned the rubber of my tires. I was racing to meet an ideal, not a woman, for the image had been in my head for many years and I yearned for its incarnation. When I met her, I fantasized the fulfillment of a dream and at once resolved to marry her.

She had confused me with another friend of Keith's named Monrad Paulsen, an orange-haired Dane, 6'4", with hands as large as hams. Well, if she didn't know the difference between a Paulsen and an Abram, I would not have to worry about the Jewish thing. That was an immediate load off my shoulders, which could only serve to encourage my intention. Within a week, I blurted out a proposal of marriage, and after a few days, Jane accepted. We were married by Reform Rabbi Landau in Albany. We never told her parents, recently separated, about that first ceremony. Neither was happy about our marrying, and a clandestine nuptial could well be the last straw.

Two weeks later the Maguires arranged a traditional wedding, performed by a Methodist minister, who was sensitive enough to quote the passage from Ruth: "For whither thou goest, I will go; and where thou lodgest, I will lodge: thy people shall be my people, and thy God my God."

After the ceremony, Raymer Maguire, Jane's father, walked us to our car. As we climbed in, he said, "I'll give this marriage ninety days." I would never forget those words. I think both Jane and I relished proving this superb advocate, the former president of the Florida Bar Association, wrong. There were times years later when we'd say to each other, "We aren't doing so badly, are we, considering we weren't supposed to last ninety days?"

I liked the idea of a wife with wide interests, particularly one who worked on a newspaper, the place where politics, economics, social issues, and society intersected. Jane was not a run-of-the-mill cub reporter. She and her family were socially connected with the publisher, who ran not only the Orlando papers but an influential newspaper chain in the South. Here was a partner who could live and work in my world, and who had all the social graces besides. She was intelligent, beautiful, and far more literary than I. What *I* saw in her was not hard to decipher. What had she seen in me? If I wanted access into her world, she wanted one foot out of it. Orlando's upper crust was a stultifying place for a bright, creative woman. For Jane, the young Jew from nowhere must have seemed an invigorating breath of fresh air. I suspect she also saw in me some of her father's quality of aggression, though I was otherwise most unlike Raymer Maguire, whose magnetic smile concealed a cold rigidity.

Perhaps I saw in Jane reflections of my own mother's drive and intelligence, though Jane worked at what she enjoyed, while Irene

Abram worked for her family's survival. Jane invested much energy in the perfection of our home. She saw gracious entertaining as a woman's natural role, and a constant procession of visitors were welcomed to our hearth, from our first humble rooms to the palatial quarters in Atlanta and New York.

Our first residence was a charming suburban house in Montgomery, Alabama. There we became the center of a circle of friends, husbands and wives whom we had known for years. Compared to my wife other southern wives seemed provincial, insipid, and sometimes thoroughly giddy. I was so proud of my Jane, who was a charming hostess, and beautiful to boot. I thought, how marvelously suited to me she was and how snug and contented we were. Suddenly she announced that she was going back to Orlando; she needed to be with her mother for awhile. But instead of insisting that she wait and give us a chance to talk about whatever she was escaping, I ignored the symptoms of her discontent and cheerily insisted on accompanying her.

In a hundred later episodes in which either Jane or I was hurting, we failed to come to grips with the true issues, but concealed them instead, and thus, over the years, built a wall of impenetrable defenses.

After Montgomery, we were transferred to Washington, D.C., where Jane seemed happier, working now as an investigator for the United States Department of Labor, and in the summer of 1944 we were moved to Fort Sam Houston, San Antonio, Texas.

Instead of getting another job, Jane turned to the passionate preoccupation of her life, writing fiction. But she made the mistake of enrolling in a correspondence course, one of those self-improvement exercises for second-class minds with time and money enough to invest. Neither Jane's mind nor her talent was second rate. Each week would bring a different verdict from a reader in Oklahoma or Arkansas. A word of praise would brighten an evening; criticism would douse it, and the criticism didn't even come from a worthwhile source. (In 1975, two years after Jane and I separated, W. W. Norton published her book *On Shares,* which related with great fidelity the story of Ed Brown, a black sharecropper who moved north with us.)

By September 1945 we were in Santa Ana, and the birth of our first child tied us closer together. I was delighted to be a father. I had wanted a child since I was six, when my sister Jeanette was born. I cherished the times Jeanette and I were together, and they were blessedly frequent. When my daughter Ruthie came along, it was as if I were rediscovering an earlier sweetness.

A month earlier Hiroshima reshaped the fears and hopes of this world forever; but for me, at the time, it signaled the end of the war, release from military duty, and the prospect of Oxford. Not more than a dozen of my Rhodes class of 1939 ever took up residence in England. Some, like Charles Collingwood of CBS, had already carved out significant careers. There was no question of what I wanted, or Jane as well. I wrote off to Dr. C. K. Allen, the Warden of Rhodes House, saying that I would like to commence studies at Hilary Term, January 1946, bringing along my wife and infant daughter. Allen, a brilliant legal scholar and a thorough misanthrope who believed England would lose the war after Dunkirk, replied at once:

"Come, bring your wife if you insist—she and you will probably freeze and starve, but on no account bring that infant."

I was demolished. As much as Oxford meant to me, I could never leave Jane behind, and neither of us could think of abandoning Ruth to any grandparent. We wanted every day of her for ourselves.

The Warden of Rhodes House was the chief executive of the Rhodes Trust. His word was law and he wrote the stipend checks. He had absolutely forbade me to come under the only conditions I would consider. Nevertheless I felt impelled to pick up the telephone and discuss my predicament with Dr. Frank Aydelotte, President of Swarthmore College, and the American Secretary to the Rhodes Trust. Dr. Aydelotte crisply advised: "Take passage on the Queen Mary in January with your wife and child. Get off the ship at Southampton. Go immediately by boat train to London. Get rooms in London. Then—but only then—call C. K. Allen and tell him that you, your wife, and child have arrived and see what he can do about it."

I followed Aydelotte's instructions to the letter. When I called, Allen sputtered into the telephone but invited me to come at once to see him. We met at breakfast. He predicted serious troubles for me and my family—disease, at least, which would be a very proper desert for one so foolish and disobedient. My first great tribulation would be, he said, the total impossibility of finding housing for this unmonkish family. I allowed that I would set about doing so that morning. He invited me to join him at lunch, and when I returned I announced I had suitable rooms in a sixteenth-century dwelling, a "private hotel" known as the Old Parsonage.

Months later I learned why Aydelotte had so quickly and positively responded to my plea for help. He had lost his scholarship by marrying when Rhodes scholars were strictly forbidden to do so.

Jane and I eventually found a mews flat, really a loft over an Edwardian stable in North Oxford. The entrance to the premises was up a stairs and through a trap door in the floor of the kitchen area. Up these came a succession of students and professors, through whom I learned as much as through reading.

One night, Arthur Lehman Goodhardt, Regius Professor of Jurisprudence, emerged from the trap door in the company of Professor Harold Laski of the London School of Economics. Goodhardt, scion of the Lehmans and the Morgenthaus, was a strict constructionist lawyer; Laski, a peppery intellectual pillar of the Labor Party, which had recently knocked Winston Churchill from office. The talk turned to Labor's nationalization of steel.

Goodhardt observed that Churchill was out but certainly not down:

"Harold, what if you people nationalize steel and Winston returns and Parliament denationalizes it?"

"That would be unconstitutional," Laski heatedly replied, astonishing every lawyer in the room, because the word of Parliament is supreme in a country which has no written constitution.

"How so," asked Goodhardt, a distinguished academic politician who knew British institutional theory as well as anyone.

"Because," said Laski, now very shrill, "no Parliament has the right to undo a condition when it knows its action will be militantly resisted by a large and powerful minority."

Goodhardt began to toy with Laski, known on both sides of the Atlantic for his vigorous support of an anti-lynch law in the United States:

"Harold," he said, "I suppose those politicians in the South of the United States would be pleased to cite your novel theory in their opposition to all civil rights laws."

Laski must have been glad the hour was late so that he could retreat in haste to his lodgings.

An Oxford education, under the auspices of the Rhodes Trust, was a milestone in my career. After a few false starts toward a Ph.D., I took the good advice of the senior tutor of my college and read for the Oxford B.A. in the Honors School of Politics, Philosophy, and Economics. He had said to me, "A Ph.D. is a very fine degree for Americans and Canadians. However, if you want an education, do the Oxford B.A. in some worthwhile subject." Never did a man give better advice.

My tutors varied in age. In Economics I had Neville Ward-Perkins, one year older, with whom I was to form an intellectual and personal friendship that would endure until his death of leukemia in 1959. Neville's father, whom he called "the Master," had been a British civil servant, a District Officer in India. I constantly challenged father and son on the morality of British Imperialism, always receiving a reasoned response in which "the Master" showed his deep affection and respect for the Indians in his territory and his dedication to their economic and social advancement. On holiday and at home Neville and I, together with our wives, shared happy times even as he unlocked for me the mysteries of Keynes. When I finally "got it"—the Keynesian explanation of the Depression—I felt I had received a revelation of transcendent importance. I naively, it turns out, assumed that just as streptococci were controlled by penicillin, the business cycle that had caused such sorrow in my family would be straightened out by Keynesians.

Mr. McCallum, my much older Politics tutor, instructed while blowing smoke at me from his ever-present pipe. He loved Americans and allayed my frustrations over the peculiarities and the hardships of life in those meager times. For his incomparable knowledge of European history and institutions, in many a pub session after hours, I traded my more limited understanding of American politics.

The magisterial beauty of the university, the knowledge of its continuous contribution to the intellectual life of the West since the thirteenth century, instilled in me a respect bordering on awe. Once when I went with a friend, Ralph Gibson, now a judge of the High Court, to a debate at a fine "red brick" university (as all except

Oxford and Cambridge are called) he said, and I understood: "How can men be inspired in surroundings as ordinary as these?"

I had relished being in the antebellum buildings at the University of Georgia—the Chapel (1801), Phi Kappa (1831), Old College (1800). The sense of continuity of history and tradition excited me in Athens, even though I was repelled by the knowledge that its cornerstone was slavery. At Oxford and Cambridge, too, I spent hours savoring the beauty and replaying in my mind the historic personalities and events with which they were connected. Standing in the Chapel of Trinity College, Cambridge, I was overcome with more reverence than I had felt in any ecclesiastical building, by contemplating the statues of Newton, Bacon, and Rutherford, founders of modern science, and memorials to a collection of other greats, including Byron and Tennyson. I felt similar feelings of awe as I contemplated that William Blackstone and Samuel Johnson had attended my own college.

No place in England affected me more than a flat, still meadow near Windsor Castle, where no structure stands to remind that this is Runnymede, the place where individual liberty had its hard birth. I stood there in silence, conjuring the scene in 1215 as King John met his barons and conceded what became the palladium of English liberty.

I had hoped a drastically new environment would eradicate any ambiguities in our marriage. However, when the novelty of our parenting was past, the environment of Oxford only served, understandably, to intensify Jane's frustrations. Here I was, a student at one of the world's most prestigious universities, and Jane, though equally qualified, was not. Probably she felt inhibited about proposing her own matriculation and I was too preoccupied or too selfish to encourage her to pursue it. I should add that few, if any, of my colleagues at Oxford encouraged their wives to become scholars. Although some of us had wives planning future careers, most of my generation found it perfectly natural that a wife should be primarily a homemaker and a mother—in other words, a satellite to a star. Thus, Jane's life and the life of the marriage fell victim to a cultural conditioning that was even then on the verge of explosion.

In the spring of 1946, the Nuremberg trials of the principal Nazis—Goering, Speer, von Ribbentrop, and Hess—took place

72

amidst considerable debate in western legal circles. Distinguished lawyers, including Senator Robert A. Taft, condemned the proceedings as an extralegal process by which the victors exercised their powers over the vanquished. Obviously, the allied powers could not have conducted the trials had they lost. In that event, instead of a dock of nineteen Nazis in the Grand Palace at Nuremberg, Churchill, Roosevelt, DeGaulle, and Stalin might have been dealt with as Hitler saw fit, and not likely by trial with the forms of due process.

In June 1946, I discussed these issues with Professor Goodhardt, after he had returned from a visit to Nuremberg as a guest of Justice Robert Jackson, the American Chief Prosecutor of Nazi war criminals. Goodhardt was euphoric about what he had just witnessed: The trials were proceeding with scrupulous regard to due process. The defendants were accorded every opportunity to confront their accusers, and, indeed, most of the evidence consisted of documents of uncontested authenticity. The defendants were also given every opportunity to present a full defense and had been furnished able counsel for that purpose.

I realized that these trials were a legal landmark and was delighted when Goodhardt offered to call Jackson with a suggestion that I be placed on his staff at the Oxford summer recess. When I reached Nuremberg, I was assigned to look through the trial record of Goering and the others, for evidence to be used in the subsequent trials of the Nazi industrialists.

As I observed the defendants in the dock each day in the courtroom, I was struck that these defendants—Goering, Hess, von Ribbentrop, Keitel, Frank—did not look different from other men. Yet they, with Hitler, Himmler, and Goebbels, had planned and perpetrated atrocities on a scale hitherto undreamed of. The evidence lay in written orders no defendant could contest and in films taken by the Nazis themselves. The incongruity of it astounded me. Sophisticated men, some even handsome, none cretins or palpably deranged, had in the twentieth century led one of the most civilized states in the brutal ravage of European society.

As a young lawyer, I was fascinated to compare the relative skills of the various prosecutors and learned a lesson I have never forgotten. Justice Jackson took on the cross-examination of Goering, the most prominent and least difficult case to prove. Jackson made the

73

mistake of examining the Reichs Marshal on the evils of Nazi philosophy rather than on specific deeds. Goering knew the ground Jackson had chosen better than his inquisitor and the first day of his cross-examination was embarrassing to the American team.

The British prosecution staff was less prestigious than Jackson, but was more experienced in the ways of the courtroom.

Julius Streicher, the Jew-baiting publisher of *Der Sturmer*, was as loathsome as any person in the dock. Yet the case against him seemed thin, for he had been a mouthpiece for the Nazi regime rather than a leader. He had not been in the military, so he had not committed war crimes. Therefore, he had to be caught in the dragnet charge of a crime against humanity, and it fell to British counsel Lt. Col. Griffith-Jones to cross-examine him.

Griffith-Jones did not deal in generalities but focused on the destruction of the great synagogue in Nuremberg, which Streicher had instigated and now defended. It had been carried out on August 10, 1938, under the statute which authorized the renovation of German cities. Streicher claimed that his only motivation was to rid this "beautiful medieval city of an 'architectural monstrosity.' "

Griffith-Jones read from the *Frankische Tageszeitung* of August 11, 1938: "In Nuremberg the synagogue is being demolished by a huge mob. Julius Streicher himself inaugurated this work with a speech lasting one hour and a half." Then Griffith-Jones turned to Streicher and said: "I ask you, were you talking for an hour and a half on the architectural beauties of Nuremberg and not against the Jews? Is that what you are telling us?" Streicher never recovered his composure.

My experiences at Nuremberg convinced me that Goodhardt was right, that the trials advanced the rule of law. Those who took the contrary position ignored several factors. The contention that these defendants were being tried under law established after the fact just did not take into account the binding treaties which the defendants knowingly violated, including the international conventions relating to the rules of warfare. Though it had not been customary for violators to be tried in international tribunals, it did not mean there was no law to be breached. The law was known to all. I am afraid that too many people confuse the matter of punishment where there is no law with the quite different situation where there has been law but no punishment. The legal maxim that states there shall be no punishment without law has no corollary holding that because no punishment was inflicted in the past, there was no law.

The Nuremberg trials were a great advance, not so much in establishing precedents but in giving meaning and effect to existing law. There are those who complain that since the court at Nuremberg was created for the purpose of trying the Nazi leaders, the principle of natural law was violated. However, I have never met a critic of Nuremberg who had a better legal solution.

Having captured the Nazi murderers alive, what should the Allied powers have done? Would it have been acceptable to execute them without trial? Would it have been conscionable to set them free?

Lawyers and statesmen debated the Nuremberg charter and trials from reference points in international law. My own experience at Nuremberg affected me at a very personal level. The Nazi decision to exterminate European Jewry, the Final Solution, was taken and carried forth despite its drain on German war resources and regardless of cost—military, moral, or political. The evidence was incontrovertible that the most modern state in Central Europe had decided to destroy systematically every last Jew it could find. Indeed, there is a museum in Prague for which Adolf Eichmann planned a perpetual exhibit of the artifacts of a people totally wiped off Europe's surface.

Faced by the calamity which had befallen Jews, not only of my father's ancestry but of my mother's as well, I began to ponder the links that bind all Jews to some common fate. Moreover, the bond was not, as formerly, based on religious grounds, so that the Jew could escape by religious conversion. Now, the anti-Semite had refined the definition—genes of one Jewish grandparent marked their bearer for extermination.

Jane had joined me in Nuremberg. Together we saw the photographs, films, and files that recorded the fate of the millions of Jews Hitler had destroyed. Occasionally we would see some living remnants of the death camps passing, hollow-eyed, through German towns. At the climax of the trial, on the day Goering and his colleagues were sentenced, there were hundreds and thousands of Jewish victims of Nazism who were unwanted anywhere except by their own people in Palestine, which the British, in 1917, had promised as a Jewish homeland. Now the British authorities in Palestine barred them from entering. As we looked at these heartbreaking refugees we were outraged by the additional pain for wracked bodies and grieving souls. It was Jane, however, who voiced the stark and simple truth: "A Jew is either a Zionist or without a heart."

Her words shook me, the self-proclaimed "anti-Zionist," as Joe Gittler's intellectual arguments never had. But where had she, a Christian, upper-crust Orlando girl, gotten it, this remarkable empathy for Jews—and for blacks? She was no classroom liberal. It all sprang from something deep within her, a compassionate identification with the victim.

My role in the Nuremberg proceedings was very minor; but the experience was a major turning point in my life. The Holocaust became for me, and for Jane, a personal experience. As the captured Nazi films rolled in a darkened courtroom, showing SS extermination squads holding Jewish children by their feet, bashing their heads against walls, I had to think of Ruthie, then a rosy-cheeked two-year-old, who would have been a candidate for extinction had she lived in this city only three years before—and despite the fact that her mother was Scotch-Irish.

I would never be the same after Nuremberg for I now understood that the veneer of civilization is thin, and that when it cracks, even in the twentieth century, the Jew is a first victim.

I was no longer the Jewish boy of Fitzgerald struggling to be accepted. I was one Jew of the half remaining after the Holocaust, now determined that nothing like this would occur again—ever. And Jane, emblematic of millions of non-Jews, was totally committed with me in this determination.

6

When I returned from Oxford in January 1948, I was uncertain of what I would do or where I would do it. I sought the advice of Supreme Court Justice Hugo Black, who told me about the beginnings of his practice in Birmingham. "I'd not gone to a distinguished law school nor did I have a well-connected family. Hence no big firm wanted me. So I struck out on my own to build a plaintiff's negligence and criminal practice. I joined every organization I could to meet potential clients and jurors." And somewhat defensively, perhaps to explain his early membership in the Klan, he added, "I'd have certainly joined the B'nai Brith if I could have."

As we discussed my political views, now very close to his, Black warned: "If you practice in the South, and I urge you to, expect to get your head bloodied." The justice reminded me of Isadore Gelders' nephew, Joe Gelders, a brave labor lawyer who had been brutally assaulted in Birmingham.

My uncertainty as to how I might support my family in the totally foreign environments of New York or Washington led me in 1948 to return to Atlanta to practice law. It was a decision that by

77

no means precluded political ambitions. I had no roots except in Georgia, and I hoped that my old college associations might give me some access to political support in Atlanta. Within six years after my return I was off and running—for the United States Congress from the Fifth District. Part of me must have known that the sights were too high, but I considered the state legislature or any lesser position too unchallenging. I was always torn when I thought of running for public office.

My father felt that a Jew would do well to avoid the exposure of public campaigning. Though he was intensely politicized, I could not expect his blessing; in fact, he withdrew into silence whenever I approached the subject of my running for office. I soon reestablished contact with former Governor Ed Rivers and with Governor M. E. Thompson, and I went out of my way to become known to a host of others in the circumscribed liberal political spectrum.

They hadn't forgotten those old debates; Herman certainly hadn't. I, for one, still thought that the Talmadges sat at the center of everything that was wrong in Georgia, and at the center of the Talmadge machine sat the county unit system. I had started speaking out against this antediluvian arrangement the day I came back to town, and I didn't stop until I left in 1962.

I have described the system as I saw it in my college years. Now, ten years later, it discriminated with even greater force. The urban areas had gained population in the intervening years. The decline of cotton culture and the advance of the tractor, plus the dislocations occasioned by two wars, had left vast stretches of farmland depopulated. The disproportions reflected in the unit rule were thus magnified.

The results of the 1946 gubernatorial election had highlighted the injustice. Lockheed industrialist James Carmichael had actually carried the popular vote, but old Gene Talmadge, running for another term, had bested him in the unit count, which made Gene the winner. A lawsuit was filed to prevent determination of the winner according to unit votes. But the Supreme Court of the United States, in *Turman* v. *Duckworth,* denied jurisdiction on the ground that by the time the case reached Washington the question was "moot," meaning that the election results had already been certified. It was to take sixteen years, and at least six more cases, in which I was the leading counsel, to reverse the Supreme Court's reluctance to come to grips with the massive injustice of this voting system.

In 1948, the battle lines between those favoring and opposing the system were more defined than ever. The Carmichael/Talmadge contest had demonstrated that even in a democratic primary, limited almost entirely to whites, the more liberal candidate could win the popular vote.

Greatly feared was the prospect of a fully enfranchised black electorate in the urban centers now that the grandfather clauses and white primary rules were no longer legal barriers to black registration and voting.

The Talmadge political weekly paper, *The Statesman,* baldly trumpeted that the county unit system was the remaining bulwark against the ''bloc vote'' and ''race mixing,'' and the guarantee of the ''Southern way of life.''

The Statesman had a point, for by 1960 a considerable portion of Georgia's urban communities were blacks. While they comprised 29 percent of the voting-age population of the state, in 1960 they accounted for only 12 percent of the total voter registration. This was not the full story, however, because the 12 percent was heavily concentrated in the urban centers. True, many rural counties with disproportionate voting power also contained large numbers of blacks, but before Vernon Jordan's leadership, through the Voter Education Project in the early 1960s, these blacks were largely unregistered and even if registered frequently did not dare to vote.

The black tenant-farmer had good reason to be in fear of an encounter with the local registrar or precinct voting clerk, who would very likely bark at him, ''John, what the hell you think you'all doin' here?'' Conditioned by the past, beholden to the economic realities of the present, black voters avoided trouble by simply not voting. Yet Georgia would not change politically until its urban centers got a fair share of political power.

The congressional seat I ran for in 1954 comprised three counties with 14 unit votes. Fulton and DeKalb each had 6, though DeKalb had only half of Fulton's 550,000 people. Rockdale had 2 units for its 13,000 souls, each of whom was as politically potent as 13 of Fulton's. Had there been something akin to fair apportionment, Fulton, in which Atlanta principally lay, would have been itself a congressional district.

I declared my candidacy in early 1954. In May the Supreme

Court announced its epoch-making decision in *Brown* v. *Board of Education of Topeka*, which was the end of the "separate but equal" doctrine that had been the law since *Plessy* v. *Ferguson*, decided in 1896. The timing could not have been worse for my campaign. My opponent was the sitting Congressman and a former State Superior Court Judge from DeKalb County, James C. Davis, in reality a fitting incarnation of one of Nat Turner's most fearsome nightmares. Notoriously unfair to blacks while on the bench, he was closely associated with ultra-right-wing organizations. He was supported by "the money boys," as we called them, and his votes in Congress were fitted to their interests as a shoe to a foot.

As I have often said, the people who put Jim Davis into Congress—the power brokers of Atlanta—would not have dreamed of inviting him to dinner. Yet, in 1946 they had helped him defeat a great feminist, the incumbent Helen Douglas Mankin, and they kept him there in 1952 against a serious challenge by a brilliant young establishment lawyer, Baxter Jones. Mankin and Jones were two more Georgians who lost their bid for office despite victory in the popular vote.

In 1950 Helen Mankin approached me and asked if I would bring a new suit against the county unit system. I pondered the history of the failed attack in *Turman* v. *Duckworth* in 1946. I knew the auguries had not improved. Mr. Justice Frankfurter still sat on the court, adamant in the conviction, expressed in *Colgrove* v. *Green* in 1945, that the political heavens would descend on the Supreme Court if it entered the "political thicket" in which voting power in election districts was challenged. The political and social climate in Georgia was more tense than before. Legal battles to preserve white political dominance and segregation were erupting all over the South.

Helen Mankin had probably sought me out because in 1949 I had gratuitously inserted myself as a "friend of the court" in a Georgia Supreme Court contest challenging the constitutionality of the effort of Herman Talmadge, then the governor, to curb blacks from voting. Four years earlier the federal courts had struck down the existing Georgia Democratic white primary. Gene Talmadge, the winner of the Democratic nomination though now fatally ill, pledged that blacks, nevertheless, would somehow be barred from voting in that primary.

In 1949, Herman proceeded to honor his father's pledge. But the federal courts were knocking down subterfuges fashioned in other states; those devised in South Carolina and Alabama, to turn the public Democratic nomination into a private activity beyond constitutional challenge, had been declared invalid. Herman Talmadge, in his winning gubernatorial campaign of 1948 ranted, "If we can't have an all-white primary in Georgia, then we want one just as white as we can get it."

Herman's device, the New Voter Registration Act, based the right to vote on either literacy or the ability of the applicant to understand the duties of citizenship, to be determined subjectively by white registrars.

Already qualified voters could be challenged and removed from the franchise list on one day's notice. The whole scheme was designed to derail the few black voters and to exclude as many new black applicants as possible. Herman summed things up, thus: "I believe that 90 to 95 percent of our white citizens should vote. There are many good white people in our own county who cannot read or write. I don't think that more than 10 or 15 percent of our Negroes should vote."

I was in Atlanta for less than a year when the case challenging this outrage reached the Georgia Supreme Court. I asked to intervene and persuaded my firm and Elbert Tuttle, later to become the Chief Judge of the Fifth Circuit Court of Appeals, to join me in my brief. I felt the need to touch all the chords of convention as we appealed to the better natures of the judges and our own peers. We forcefully argued the rights of the blacks as American citizens, but with none of the stridency of civil rights activism in the '60s. Instead, I invoked precedents established by the great Chief Justice White of Louisiana, an ex-confederate soldier, and Federal Judge Waites Waring of South Carolina, whose ancestors lived in that state from the time its native son, Andrew Jackson, was president.

Referring to the new statute's break with previous voter registration acts, I reached into Proverbs 22:28, "Remove not the Ancient Landmark." We were trying desperately to place the principle of equal justice as well as ourselves on the southern side of the Mason-Dixon line. It was all to no avail. The Georgia Supreme Court dodged.

Now, in 1950, Helen Mankin was asking me to mount a new assault on the unit system. The more I studied the 1946 decisions, the more convinced I was that we had a chance, provided we could get a case to Washington before the Democratic primary was held. In that case, we would not be in the position of asking for the reversal of a certified vote. True, Justice Frankfurter was a principled and effective opponent of Federal judicial intervention, but he had kept the court in line by narrow majorities fashioned out of very special circumstances. I reasoned that if I could get a case to Washington in time; if we could defuse some technical arguments against the case; if we could present the stark contradiction between the unit system and Negro rights and democracy itself, maybe we could persuade the necessary five justices.

Frankfurter, we knew, could not be persuaded. As Mayor William B. Hartsfield of Atlanta, who became the plaintiff in one county unit challenge, said of that distinguished jurist's policy: "The segregationists ought to erect a statue to Felix Frankfurter on the capitol lawn alongside that of Tom Watson and Eugene Talmadge."

But I was hopeful that a majority of the Supreme Court could see that it was absurd to contend, as Frankfurter did, that the injustice of malapportioned representation could be corrected through the political process. Couldn't any fool see that the Georgia legislature, which reflected the same distortions as the unit voting system, was not about to give up its hold on the body politic? The political channels for reform worked only when open, not blocked, as in Georgia, by the very device we were attacking.

In early Spring of 1950, I told Helen Mankin I was ready to file another attack on the county unit system. I had even secured a plaintiff who bore the disarming name of South—Bernard South, a local automobile parts supplier. The nominal defendant was James Peters, the irascible Democratic State Party Chairman.

To give us the most time and the best chance, we filed before the State Democratic Committee had even called for a primary. Just as in 1946, the county unit chief legal defender, Talmadge's lawyer, B. D. Buck Murphy, had argued that the Talmadge case was brought too late, he now snarled that it should be dismissed because it was premature.

Literally, Murphy was right. The county unit law only applied in primary elections, in which state political parties could nominate candidates; or if the governing committee chose, the nominations could be made by convention. Of course, the Democratic State Committee did hold primaries; it proudly proclaimed that Democratic candidates were popularly elected, whereas Republican nominees were "chosen by bosses in smoke-filled rooms."

Murphy knew that if he could bounce us out of the court for having brought the suit too early, he could attach a subsequently filed suit as "too late." We were, as I kept saying to the courts for fourteen years, always teetering between being premature or moot—too early or too late.

The day of the trial arrived. Judge Samuel Sibley, the most venerable judge in the United States Court of Appeals for the Fifth Circuit, presided over a three-judge panel. Sibley had sat on the 1946 county unit cases and his judicial views on the subject were as rigidly set as Frankfurter's. Sibley was also a very smart lawyer, and he would look for the way to make his judgment as irreversible as possible. This prematurity thing was almost made to order and almost foolproof.

Murphy knew Peters would not volunteer to help me, so he led him through his witness script: "Yep," the committee had not decided whether to hold a primary in 1950 or to nominate by convention. In fact, no date had been set yet for holding the committee meeting to decide.

Smirking, Murphy sat down. After Peters' testimony, Murphy would argue for dismissal.

"Mr. Peters," I cross-examined, "are you aware of the fact that the Democrats have traditionally held primaries?"

"Yep."

"Are you aware of the fact that no Republican has been elected to important statewide office in Georgia since Reconstruction?"

"Yep."

"Are you aware that whoever wins the Democratic primary is as good as elected?"

"Yep."

"Are you suggesting that the Democratic Party, of which you are Chairman, is now going to nominate its officials behind the closed doors of a convention?"

"There definitely will be a primary this year."

The courtroom burst into laughter, and though his lawyers tried to retrieve his position, explaining, "Mr. Peters cannot call a primary; he merely summons the Executive Committee into session," the prematurity ploy was over.

However, Judge Sibley again upheld the county unit system on the basis of the 1946 case and the Frankfurter principle of staying out of the "political thicket."

We then rushed to the Supreme Court, urging fast action before the results of the primary were certified. Although we beat the clock, the court denied jurisdiction and dismissed our appeal by a vote of 7 to 2. We had gained a foothold, however, for Justices Douglas and Black entered a vehement dissent in which they said the court should have taken the case and outlawed the unit system.

Governor Herman Talmadge had prevailed, though he clearly was shaken. His stakes in the unit system were so great that he now huddled with Murphy and others to devise more legal protection against future attacks.

In 1950 and again in 1952, Talmadge's controlled legislature submitted constitutional amendments to the voters in successive general elections "to protect and defend" the county unit system. Baxter Jones, Jr., a brilliant lawyer of about my age and a scion of a distinguished Georgia family, and I led a campaign to defeat the Talmadge ploy. Our crowd had almost no money; Talmadge raised and spent large sums. He attacked Jones and me by pamphlet, newspaper, radio, and television with such scurrilous claptrap as this:

Baxter Jones, Jr., Atlanta lawyer and professor of business law at Atlanta University, a negro college. Jones teaches under Dr. Rufus Clement, who has been cited by Cong. Committee for his "affiliations with communist-front and subversive groups."

Morris B. Abram, Atl. Att'y, bosom pal of Jones. Nat'l leader in World gov't movement. (Atl. J'nl., Mar. 28, '49), which, according to Cong. Record, "was created and is dominated by Reds and fellow-travelers."

If I hadn't been Jones' "bosom pal," I soon so became. His great joy was to take a radical idea and make it sound conservative, though I, who was much more conservative, always appeared to be more liberal—perhaps because of the language and emphasis of my presentations. Together we made a great pair. In 1952, Jones decided to run for Congress against James C. Davis. I raised the money.

I recall a political meeting at the fashionable Cactus Club, an establishment political organization of which Jones was a member by right of his wife's social position and I by grace of my education. Everyone there was denouncing Jones' candidacy. The chairman of the committee appointed to recommend a candidate to the Club had the poor taste to repeat some of the insinuations which Talmadge had been broadcasting. My wife Jane kept nudging me to stand up and defend my friend.

"For God's sake," I said, "his wife, his brother-in-law, and two of his partners are here and they're all sitting still on their dignity. Why should *I* stick my neck out?"

Before nudge came to shove, however, I was on my feet. If anyone there thought I could be a political trimmer, my vociferous attack on those who had slandered my friend Jones told them otherwise.

After the meeting, Bobby Troutman's uncle, Henry, counsel to the Georgia Power Company, asked me to accompany him to the club's bar. A tall, gaunt, delightful man, he was totally without cant. "Morris," he said, half amused. "You're an unusually bright lad, but if you want to be successful you've got some lessons to learn. You can be an important influence in this town if you learn the rules. Now, I'm not sure you'll like what I am telling you, but it is a fact. You should represent your clients or those whom you want to make your clients, and those should be the better-off people and companies."

"But, Henry, I believe what I said."

"I know you do and maybe I do, too, but I'm telling you straight, to be successful you must become a legal whore."

In Jones's race against Davis, the sitting congressman smeared my friend all over three counties. Davis supporters scrawled "Professor" in bloody, emblematic red on Jones's posters. Their campaign literature hammered on Jones's part-time position at the Negro college. Nevertheless, Jones won the popular vote, and I gained experience as a fund raiser.

It was this campaign, along with my experience from the legal battles waged for Helen Mankin, that made me feel I could take on

Davis myself in 1954. Davis, however, gave me a discouraging start. Six days after I announced my candidacy, he began to exploit the fears raised by the decision in *Brown* v. *Board of Education*. Even labor, against which the incumbent had openly fought, was not solidly behind me, for their racial fears outweighed their immense distaste for Davis. Davis, of course, had the money of Georgia to draw on, while I had to struggle to raise thirty thousand dollars. He looked unbeatable.

But I was determined and thought that I might succeed, where others had failed, in stirring voter indignation against the county unit system. In our first debate, I named Davis "the minority-vote Congressman" to call attention to the fact he had taken office first over Helen Mankin and then Baxter Jones, each of whom had won the popular vote. Davis struck back, naming me as the candidate of the CIO radicals and, above all, Negroes. Davis made his charges with a quiet contempt, while I was much too vehement for a young man facing a silver-haired former judge, dressed in gentlemanly summer linens.

I was particularly upset when the race issue became central to the campaign. I avoided a direct attack on segregation but pressed the fact that desegregation was now the law of the land which had to be obeyed. To drum up support and money, I went to the unions, the black voters' league, the League of Women Voters, who all wanted to know how I expected to win when Baxter Jones had lost the unit vote. I told them I thought I could carry rural Rockdale, since, unlike Jones, I came from a country town.

It was a strange sort of reply coming from a Jew, and that, of course, was another problem. Not only did that fact cost me votes, but I was also very visibly involved in local Jewish affairs. Much of this involvement derived from simple economic necessity. When I started practice I earned a whopping three hundred dollars a month. Teaching Sunday School at the Reform Temple provided a much needed thirty-dollar supplement. I was also counsel to the Anti-Defamation League, which paid a small stipend, and then I was asked to be the paid secretary of the Atlanta Chapter of the American Jewish Committee, bringing in another thirty dollars.

I was particularly vulnerable as coauthor with Alex Miller, the Anti-Defamation League Regional Director, of a widely distributed pamphlet suggesting five laws to curb the Ku Klux Klan, entitled

"How to Stop Violence in Your Community." Five states and fifty-five cities adopted two of the most important of these laws, which prohibited the wearing of masks in public and the burning of crosses as an act of intimidation, except with the written permission of the owner of the site where it was to be done.

It was this pamphlet that led to an association with Osgood Williams, then a state senator from Taliaferro County in Georgia, a tough, lanky man variously reminiscent of Abe Lincoln and Ichabod Crane. He walked into my cubbyhole of an office one day in 1950, stuck out a bony hand to introduce himself, and slumped into a chair. "I hear you've got yourself some laws against the Ku Klux Klan," he said, "and you can't get nobody to introduce them."

After examining my propositions, he said, "Hell, these don't prohibit anybody from joining the Klan. They just say that you can't be burning crosses in places where you got no business to be, and you can't hide your face when you're demonstrating."

"That's right," I answered.

"Well, I'll introduce them," said this highly principled scarecrow of a man.

He did, and they zipped through the legislature. Herman Talmadge was governor and made the painful choice to sign them, but he resolved to drive Williams out of the Senate. In the next election, the Talmadge machine spent thousands of dollars in Williams' district, defeated him, and deprived him of a political and financial base. Williams, at 42, migrated to Atlanta and set up a law office in the building where we had first met.

Davis was certain to use the KKK legislation to identify my campaign with integration. There was a heavy concentration of Klansmen around Stone Mountain, and they were doing everything they could to help him. My best weapon, I felt, was to point out that Davis, a Democrat, voted most of the time for Eisenhower policies. My campaign slogan, "Vote for a Democrat in a Democratic primary," made the point abundantly clear.

But I was concentrating too much on facts and figures to carry a county like Rockdale, and since Davis was likely to carry his native DeKalb, Rockdale would have to be won. In fact, I opened my campaign there. I drove out with Jane and our children—Ruth was eight; Ann, six; and Morris, four—in a horse and wagon. I spoke long—much too long—in the broiling sun. It might have been a good speech in Atlanta, but I don't think I moved those farmers.

I eventually lost the district-wide popular vote by 5,000, but I did carry Fulton County/Atlanta. That was really remarkable considering that besides being a Jew I was marked as a liberal.

I must give full credit for my respectable showing to my campaign chairman, a real estate lawyer named Stephens Mitchell. Mitchell, known throughout the area for being writer Margaret Mitchell's brother, had been one of my closest advisors since my earliest days in Atlanta. When I showed him the first county unit brief I had written for Helen Mankin and her friends, he said, "It's fine, but let's go through it and knock out every word that isn't Anglo-Saxon in origin."

Anglo-Saxon words, he explained, are usually short, direct, and effective. "You think that Churchill could have gotten away with blood, perspiration, and lachrimosity? Now, Morris," he went on, " 'spit' is a good word and 'expectorate' isn't, and 'made' will also do for 'manufactured.' Don't forget that."

I particularly appreciated his support because he was very much of the Georgia establishment, and there is little doubt that his association with the Abram campaign caused many of his peers considerable consternation. One day he called me urgently at my home and asked, "What's all this about you're being a member of the ACLU?"

I acknowledged I was a member, and more, one of the organization's legal correspondents.

"Oh, that's bad, that's terrible." Mitchell, an Irish Catholic, staunchly supported Joe McCarthy. "I'm coming out to see you at once. We've got to have a talk."

He arrived in ten minutes. "This ACLU thing—I don't like it one bit, not one bit," he said. Then he shook his head and, to my great astonishment, said, "Well, you've got a right to your views. At least you have never been associated with the Klan. Now, we've got to hammer Davis. Get some television time, and we'll roast him together."

Mitchell's tenacious loyalty to me tells something about the Jewish/Catholic connection in the Deep South. Both groups were minorities, and they shared a common enemy. Besides, Mitchell was an elitist. He felt I could give intellectual tone to the office that Davis held as a messenger delegate for greedy interests. Finally,

Mitchell had the analytic ability to sort out my views on race and democratic values from my positions on economic questions. He supported me because I stood for the preservation of the more important values that he cherished. I would need him more as the battle heated.

If I was initially discouraged to see the race issue becoming the center of the campaign, it would fall now to an even lower level. At a Junior Chamber of Commerce debate, Davis charged that in opposing the Smith Act and favoring civil rights legislation, the ACLU was giving clandestine aid to the Communist party. I responded, "The ACLU is not listed by the Attorney General as a subversive organization, but Mr. Davis once belonged to the Ku Klux Klan, and that organization incontrovertibly *is*."

Davis had indeed been a member of the Klan for five years. What I soon realized, though, was that no matter how a rural farmer or a member of the Atlanta Junior Chamber of Commerce despised the KKK, it was still a known quantity. They could understand it. The ACLU was alien. If they were deaf to indignation they could still be stung by sarcasm. Looking Davis solemnly in the face, I said, "Sir, it is a very serious matter for a grown man to put on a bedsheet and go around scaring people." Davis, as I've said, didn't carry Atlanta, though only a few Negroes were voters then.

From the outset of the campaign, Davis' staff had organized an anti-Semitic network. My staff overreacted and attempted to counter with a dirty trick of their own. They decided to put out a hate sheet attacking me that they would blame on the Ku Klux Klan. It was to be widely distributed among blacks and then brought to my attention as a "smear job." They counted on me to react emotionally and go on television to denounce the perpetrators. Since I myself would be in the dark, my outrage would be utterly convincing. Davis would have to spend the rest of the campaign on the defensive.

But one of my staff members thought better about such a strategy—it was doubly dishonest, and insubordinate as well—and confessed the plan to me. "Thank God, you've let me in on it!" I said, "I've got to live in this town when the campaign is over. I can't have a tin can tied to my ass; nothing is worth that. All I need is a potential blackmailer getting wind of this." That was the end of it. When Watergate was unlocked and rushed to its roaring climax, I remembered my own narrow escape from the dirty tricks department of political life.

Jane and I stood from 7:00 A.M. until dusk on the September primary day shaking hands at the location of the biggest box in DeKalb, Davis' home county. A few feet away, Davis' wife greeted the voters, many of whom she had known for years. The physical and emotional effort exhausted both of us. Before going to campaign headquarters, I called an osteopath to bring his massage table to our house to revive our bone-tired bodies. Without confessing to each other, we both knew defeat was certain. Too many people at the polling place had averted their eyes as they politely shook our extended hands.

The aftermath of defeat was very hard. First of all some of those who had cooked up the "dirty trick," were now openly deriding me for throwing away the race. They pointed out, correctly, that all they had proposed to do was to bring to light what the Davis camp was doing covertly. I felt deeply hurt. I knew I was better than Davis; could not the citizenry at large see the same obvious fact?

I had overcome my squeamishness about the unchallenged self-blandishment which is required of all who seek public office. To have endured it only to be rejected was doubly humiliating.

I especially felt the rebuke of my father's silence. His and mother's bi-monthly visits to Atlanta ceased from May until the primary was over, and neither ever spoke a word about the campaign. Not even the magnetic pull of the three grandchildren could overcome daddy's anxiety during the hard-edged political campaign between his Jewish son and a former Klansman. In exposing my name on billboards and on TV, in behaving as a politician must, I had forced him to doubt whatever little assimilation he had achieved, but more significantly, I had threatened his fantasies about his son's place in the world.

I took my family up to North Georgia where I might bind up my wounds. They were festering still when we returned home. I especially regretted that I had not directly confronted the anti-Semitism in the campaign.

Today I'd not hesitate, but in 1954 I was dependent on campaign contributions from the Jewish community I lived in and which remembered the Leo Frank lynching. On a sunny day I would see

Frank's widow outside the Howell House apartments on Peachtree Street. The Reform Jewish contingent with which I was affiliated still downplayed ethnic differences and tried to "quarantine" anti-Semitic manifestations. Confrontation was reserved for the crudest practitioners of hate, such as the Klan. A whole generation of Atlanta Jewish leaders had been reared in the temple of Rabbi David Marx, who had stood tall during the Frank case but who reveled in the role of Atlanta Jewry's apostle to the Gentiles. In his Temple he abolished many Jewish rites, obliterated Hebrew from the Sunday school and denounced Zionism from the pulpit, as did many of his generation. In 1948 he told me that anti-Semitism arrived in Atlanta with the influx of Eastern European Jews forty years before. By then, Rabbi Marx's tradition was waning, for beginning with the birth of Israel, members of Marx's congregation were joining those of Conservative Rabbi Harry Epstein and Orthodox leaders in fund-raising campaigns for that new and beleaguered state.

When the temple was bombed, just before the children arrived for Sunday school in 1958, Rabbi Jacob Rothschild, Marx's successor, helped lead the Jewish community out of its ridiculous divisions and disabling inhibitions. By the 1970s Atlanta had a Jewish mayor who had openly challenged the anti-Semitism which he felt had been used against him in his election campaign.

The most important lesson I learned from the 1954 campaign was that there would always be a limit to what I could achieve in Atlanta. That realization would worry me for the next nine years. Yet I knew I would never leave Georgia until I had licked the county unit system and one man, one vote was established.

I recall an incident which crystallized the frustrations of many southerners like myself. No one had a better-deserved reputation as a southern liberal than Ralph McGill, the famous editor of *The Atlanta Constitution*. Ralph was very fond of Baxter Jones and me, and his political views approximated my own. Yet the voice of the *Constitution* was never raised on behalf of either of us. Though McGill did not support Davis either, his neutrality was deadly.

One night in 1955, while the memory of my defeat was still fresh, Ralph McGill relaxed at the Inquiry Club, of which he, Jones, and I were members. So was Julian LaRose Harris, son of the author of *Uncle Remus,* whose newspaper in Columbus, Georgia, had won the Pulitzer Prize for his attack on the KKK many years before mine. McGill began to defend the acquisition of the *Constitution* by James Cox, former governor of Ohio, and said that the *Constitution* could now operate with greater daring because its budget was securely in the black. But when he waxed eloquent on the "freedoms" that the new ownership were providing him, Julian Harris's rubicund face grew beet red.

"Free!" he exclaimed. "Free! Ralph, if you're so free, why didn't you support Baxter or Morris?"

McGill was abashed. Without saying a word, he rose and left the room.

He never again seemed really comfortable with me. Perhaps, I think, because I was a mirror in which he had had to face the limits of his own freedom.

I, on the other hand, was forced to face the limits of opportunity set by my religion and my views as long as I remained in Atlanta. I grew more and more frustrated. In spite of ambivalence I had to acknowledge to myself that I was becoming an increasingly aggressive, ambitious man. I knew I had better qualified and trained myself than scores of others who held public responsibility. I was also, unlike many or most, honestly motivated by what I saw as the public good. Yet I was handicapped by my Jewishness and my irrepressible candor. I thrashed about for the opportunity to be what Cecil Rhodes had required his scholars to be, men engaged in the public service. Doors didn't open, but I pounded on them, close to despair.

Eventually I came more to terms with my situation and did as much good work as I could find. I lectured yearly at Agnes Scott College, the alma mater of my old teacher, Lucy Goodrich Henry. I tried to bring a breath of fresh air to those bright young women, struggling to free their minds from upper-middle-class southern conventionality. I remember particularly a gasp from my audience as I reminded them that outside the loveliest of genteel antebellum parlors one might hear the clangor of chains binding recalcitrant slaves in work gangs.

I spoke at many forums in the days of McCarthyism, emphasizing the importance of respecting minority opinion. At Shorter College I pointed out that majority, orthodox views do not require protection by law as they possess the force of numbers; that the dissenting voice is most often the key to historic progress and is too often in danger of being snuffed out.

In the fifties, an anti-intellectual current ran strong and damaged Adlai Stevenson's chances for the presidency. I wrote of the danger in ridiculing professors and educated leaders as "eggheads" and decried the decline of a "hard-core" curriculum in the American university. Perhaps describing what I felt was my own predicament, I wrote in the Georgia Review of 1957, "The intellectual must, of necessity, be lonely. He is not able to surrender his mind and to subject his opinions to the vagaries of a mass public opinion poll."

It was not, however, only the intellectual part of me that felt isolated. My social practices were unacceptable, not that I transgressed against conventional morality. I didn't drink too much, I didn't gamble at all, and I stayed close to my marital obligations. My sin was the one *non plus ultra* in the South of the fifties. I went out of my way to form relationships with blacks as social equals. It wasn't easy, though I felt the need to do it as a moral imperative. I was emboldened by the example of George Mitchell, a Rhodes scholar, a Virginian, and executive director of the Southern Regional Council. It is hard to believe now, but I can vividly recall the ridiculous sense of noblesse oblige when Mitchell and I and a very black man took a sleeper to New York on a hunt for northern money to keep his outfit going. Even in those days the interstate diners and pullmans were exempt from Georgia's Jim Crow laws. So the three of us dined together and slept in adjoining pullman berths. Incredible as it now seems, it was, at that time, a giant step forward. Sooner or later I would have flouted Jim Crow, but I was relieved to have a white Protestant southerner as my buffer on this memorable excursion. The news of this breach with southern traditions got around, and before long I found I was being followed by a camera-toting aide of Governor Talmadge, who hoped to catch me doing something outrageous. Shaking hands with a well-dressed black would do very nicely.

I continued my involvement in local politics, usually supporting losers, and became the chairman of the Atlanta Chapter of the American Jewish Committee. But I obtained nothing in the way of local office until Mayor Hartsfield appointed me chairman of the Atlanta Citizens Crime Committee. Hartsfield, like Osgood Williams, had a rugged decency. They were examples of that distinct and marvelous southern prototype, the rough-hewn, even comical character who knows the difference between right and wrong and has the guts to act accordingly and the wits to survive. Twenty years earlier I had known one such in Sheriff Elisha Dorminey.

The Crime Committee was a useful experience—for the first time in my life, I had a clear view of the utter irrationality permeating the criminal justice system. I would have much rather served on the Board of Regents of the University of Georgia. But there was no chance of any governor admitting a Jewish integrationist to that body.

Another Jew, Charles J. Block, a brilliant lawyer from Macon, was a permanent member of the Regents. Block could spin legally respectable arguments upholding segregation as easily as a carnival vendor spun cotton candy. He was the unofficial legal counsel to the Dean of the Southern Senators, Richard B. Russell of Georgia, in his long fight for "states rights," which became the euphemism for white supremacy. I was not in Atlanta two years before Block, though twenty years my senior, recognized me as a natural enemy and succeeded in sabotaging my appointment to a judicial commission for which the Chief Justice of the Georgia Supreme Court was considering me. During all my years in Georgia, Block would be on the other side of almost every politically significant case I argued. I think he really saw himself as the Judah P. Benjamin of the new Confederacy.

My law practice consumed an inordinate amount of time. I dealt with crime, torts, contracts, land disputes, domestic relations, taxation—whatever came through the door. Many of the cases went to jury trial, and I gained an immense respect for the Georgia jury. Compared to the Judge Sibleys of the world, the juries I met were like the twelve Apostles. I won some cases, lost others, but only once did I feel that a verdict was totally beyond the pale.

I was representing an Atlanta woman in a suit against a local resident of a Georgia mountain county, where I went to try the case. The defendant had rammed into my client's car, and I thought the case was open and shut. But I was in a wholly alien, almost primitive environment, and there is nothing more impenetrable than an Appalachian community protectively encircling one of its own.

The August trial term was held in a sweltering heat, and the court followers assembled early in the morning, some of the adults barefoot as they leaned against the antebellum structure, untouched since the day it was spared in Sherman's march. The Superior Court judge was perched on a stool. Directly in front of him was a water bucket with a common drinking dipper. I risked tuberculosis for my client as I took a murky sip, figuring to convince the locals that I was as good as kin. I was so naive, however, that I thought the defendant's credibility would be weakened by the fact that her father was recently released from the penitentiary after serving time for bootlegging. I should have realized that moonshine was the community's principal industry, and the returning convict was regarded a veritable Sergeant York. My client was trounced, and I was angry as hell. Yet I cherished the very opportunity to experience such a case. I would never have been content in a large firm whose principal clients were banks or insurance companies.

The firm I began with—Heyman, Howell and Heyman—was ideal, but I went there only because two other firms would not have a Jew. The first was that of Bobby Troutman's father, as I have said, and I never sought employment there. Incredible as it may seem, Bobby appeared unconscious of the restriction, but how could he have been unaware of the fact that not one Jewish lawyer had ever been employed since the founding of the firm in the 1890s?

I was certain I could rejoin Allen Post, now no longer a partner of Hugh Howell. Allen had written that he had teamed up with Warren Moise in a firm that represented the First National Bank and he looked forward to my return. Moise, also a Rhodes scholar, had sat on one of the boards that chose me for Oxford. The idea of one Atlanta firm with three Rhodes men should have been very attractive. When I said I had decided to return to Atlanta in April 1948 to practice law, Allen was all set to hire me. But suddenly there were delays, and I could not get a straight answer from Allen, who was cordial but evasive. Obviously something was amiss and I thought Allen, too, seemed perplexed. I grasped for an explanation. I knew that once upon a time the family name of the Moises of Sumter, South Carolina, had been Moses. In Atlanta, Warren Moise was a fixture of the legal establishment. He had come out of a firm in which no professing Jew had ever served to form this new firm. Did he fear that any break with the tradition would injure the future of the firm, or worse, that it would raise doubts as to where

95

he fitted into the social order? These, of course, were issues with which Allen Post did not have to grapple.

Moise & Post did eventually hire its first Jew, but after Moise was dead and buried—his anxieties finally laid to rest.

And so it was that I found my way to Herman Heyman. I went to work with him reluctantly, at first, but my connection with the firm permitted me to become an independent, free-wheeling, and accomplished lawyer.

In addition to Arthur Heyman, in his eighties, and his son, Herman, there was Hugh Howell. It was my affection for that man, really, that resulted in my association with the firm. I had dropped by to see him, with no intention of asking him for a job. He greeted me warmly and introduced me to Arthur Heyman and his fifty-two-year-old son, Herman, who reminded me that I had taught his boy in Sunday school in 1940. After asking me about my future plans, Herman invited me flat out to come to work for him. I called Robert Troutman, Sr. to check on the Heymans' reputation as lawyers. I already knew Hugh Howell, of course. Troutman said there weren't better lawyers in all of Atlanta than the Heymans, father and son. So I brought my family to Atlanta.

This time the association with Howell was uncomplicated by his political ventures. His "running days," he told me truthfully, were over. Not once did he attempt to interfere with my assaults against his way of life, which included the unit rule, to which he had repeatedly sworn public fealty.

Because of my contacts in the black community and Howell's knowledge of Title 608 federally insured housing, we joined as sponsors of the largest apartment project available to middle-class blacks ever built in the South up to that time.

Highpoint Apartments, set on 35 landscaped acres, opened its 452 units in 1951. For the first time in his life, Howell met educated blacks as a suitor for their help. One of his new acquaintances was an influential black woman, Grace Townes Hamilton, who later became the first black woman to serve in the Georgia Legislature. I was present when he crossed the Rubicon and prefixed her last name with the title "Mrs." For there was no escape. He could hardly address this splendid lady, the executive director of the Atlanta Urban League, as "Gracie."

When Herman and I went out on our own in 1953, we used our

modest capital to rent offices in Atlanta's Healey Building. Space was limited, but we managed to shove in half a university law school library. Herman believed in fanatic research. We had the whole West Reporter System, as well as standard texts. The fact is, it was Herman who spent hours in these musty alcoves. Of course, I had to do wills, corporate charters, and pleadings, but I never did preparatory work gladly. I aimed at practicing law like an English barrister, who takes over a case when it becomes a contest. Once Herman had thoroughly researched a case and it was ready for contestation, then I was glad to master its details.

When our firm began to expand, we tried to maintain a balance between research and presentation. There were two brothers we hired named Hicks; one of them, whom Osgood Williams named "Weak Hicks," eschewed court but could race Herman through any pedagogical labyrinth. His brother was exactly the opposite. Whenever Osgood called for one or the other, he would say, "Give me Weak Hicks," or "Give me Strong Hicks."

We also prospered because Atlanta was growing. Civic improvements were the rule, which meant that a lot of property, particularly when it stood in the way of an interstate highway, had to be evaluated, and a lot of new zoning regulations were concocted, interpreted, and contested.

My most frequent adversary was Johnny Westmoreland. I invariably ran into him in contested divorce cases. Once I was representing a man who was divorcing the daughter of the Woodruff family, which had control of Coca-Cola. Westmoreland represented the defendant. The judge was Durwood Pye, a stern, formal, and fanatical man, whose wont it was to sniff and twitch.

The Woodruff case was scheduled for trial the morning of the worst snowfall in modern Atlanta history. When I called Judge Pye to confirm what I was sure would be a postponement, he said stiffly, "Court will convene at nine thirty and all counsel are expected to be there." I immediately called Westmoreland to ask if he would appear, but he had had a hernia operation three weeks before and had no intention of straining himself.

I picked up Strong Hicks, and we stumbled through the storm into the court. My client was there; Pye was there, but nobody else—no reporter, no bailiff, no stenographer. Pye, in a stentorian voice, started calling out the cases anyway. Then he called our case and glanced around to see if Westmoreland would materialize. When he did not, his Honor proceeded to grant the injunction I was requesting on the papers before him. "Your Honor," I said, "we can't proceed in the absence of Westmoreland."

"Don't you want this order?" he asked.

"Yes, your Honor, but not under the circumstances."

He was furious, and I had difficulty persuading him to adjourn long enough to call Westmoreland. I volunteered Strong Hicks to bring my colleague into court. Poor Westmoreland, not only did he have to brave the storm after all, but he lost.

The only man who ever really knew how to handle Durwood Pye was Osgood Williams. He'd imitate Pye in court; he'd sniff, twitch, ape the modulations of Pye's speech, and Pye figured that Williams and he were cut from the same loaf and was invariably courteous to his mimic.

The long hours and anxious moments of Atlanta practice in the 1950s were punctuated by intervals of relaxed yarn-telling, thigh-slapping laughter, affectionate teasing. In many ways Atlanta lawyers in the smaller firms were merely the better qualified and more ambitious counterparts of rural practitioners. Osgood, "Weak," "Strong," and I were from country towns, and so was Herman's father.

Throughout the years, my relationship with Heyman continued to grow. He was not only a friend but also a surrogate father, which I never ceased to need and seek. He was tailor-made for the role. Nearly Sam Abram's age, he possessed my father's humanity, sense of humor, and deep love of family. Yet, unlike my father, he knew how to navigate in this world and to elicit respect from his peers. He also found the time to teach me and was willing to let me have a public role. Neither Post nor Troutman would have had the time to teach, and their firms would not have long tolerated my political leanings.

Herman gave me a big case to work on just a few months after I was employed in his firm. Western Union was the client; the legal aspects were complex, and the confidence of the client was at stake. The results could have set a national precedent and cost the company hundreds of thousands of dollars. It was the kind of case an apprentice lawyer would usually labor ten years to get a crack at. But Herman passed it directly to his newest and youngest associate.

He had advised Western Union to close its uneconomical branch offices in towns like Ludowici, Nahunta, and Willacoochee, even though the state's Public Service Commission said they had to remain open. He also had advised Western Union to contest the fines, one hundred dollars per day for each office "illegally" closed. The sums involved were astronomical and were mounting.

It was our opinion that the Federal Communications Commission Act superseded the directives of the Public Service Commission. The Georgia Attorney General contested the legal opinion on which Western Union had acted. Herman was not only giving his untried associate a case that was important to the client and the firm, but also an opportunity to thrash out primary legal problems of the day.

As he had already anticipated, he was defeated in the lower court; the appeal to the State Supreme Court was the next step, and I wrote the brief. He read it, liked it, and after revisions asked if I wanted to argue it. Of course I did. The morning the appeal was scheduled for argument, John Waters, general solicitor of Western Union from New York, unexpectedly appeared at the office to advise and observe. He politely began to tell Herman how he thought the case should be presented. But Herman intervened. "Don't talk to me, talk to Morris, he's arguing the case." Waters turned red and then pale, but there was too little time for him to do anything. He didn't even have time to warn Western Union that an untried youngster was defending the company's fate in this landmark litigation.

I figured the best way to argue the case was to arouse the Baptists and Presbyterians and Methodists who sat on the court—to rivet them, if possible. I began by explaining that there is a Judaic text used in the Passover service called the *Haggadah*. Part of this Haggadah is a song called *Dayyenu*, which translates, "it would have been enough." If God had only done X for His people, dayyenu. If God had only done Y for His people, dayyenu. And so it was with Western Union. And, I argued to the court, if statute X were our only defense, dayyenu; if case Y were our only defense, dayyenu.

When I finished I thought the Supreme Court of Georgia would pass an ordinance against drinking milk with meat. Within a month, the court ruled with Western Union.

From that first experience I learned the cardinal rule of the courtroom: To dominate the forum by presence, by striking example, by drama. As I say to young lawyers: "From the outset, establish, if possible, that there are only two forces in the room, yours and the court's. You must do so by tactful power and knowledge. But knowledge alone is not enough. A good trial lawyer is one who gets his own way most of the time."

7

ONE DAY in mid-1975 while Eli and I were recalling our recent trip to Georgia, he observed that none of my old schoolmates he had met would have dreamed of a moment's struggle, let alone a lifetime's, against the political mores of their community. We wondered together why I had dared. I suppose it was because I never felt a part of that community. Success never quelled my determination to advance good government and racial justice in Georgia and I saw the struggle to eliminate the county unit system as the least heroic and most effective way for me to proceed.

In 1952, Baxter Jones and I had fashioned a new attack on the unit rule. We would not seek an injunction ordering the end of the unit count. We'd simply make this practice too expensive to continue. This time we elected to bring the case in the State Court system and filed a damage suit against James S. Peters and others for failure to count equally and fairly the vote of our client, Mr. Cox, in the primary of 1950. Since 1702 the English Common Law cases, adopted as Georgia law in 1776, have recognized that a voter can sue for damages when deprived of his vote.

The Georgia Supreme Court ducked the issue, and contrary to all opinions since 1945, held that the Georgia Democratic primary election was not an election at all. Even more astonishing, the Supreme Court of the United States declined to review this deliberate affront to common sense and to its own recent white primary precedents, probably because of Justice Frankfurter's determination to avoid another county unit contest.

In 1958, I had brought a third county unit suit—again for injunction with Mayor William B. Hartsfield as the plaintiff—claiming that the 1957 Civil Rights Act overruled Frankfurter's objections. Federal District Court Judge Boyd Sloan scoffed at this renewed effort and refused even to send for a three-judge court to hear the case. My response was to sue the judge in the United States Supreme Court for an order of mandamus to force him to send for the three-judge court. This action posed the real issue which was again the constitutionality of the county unit system. The county unit politicians were frightened out of their confidence when the Supreme Court declined to mandamus the judge, but by a mere 5 to 4 vote.

There is an interesting sidelight to this 1958 effort. Shortly after that Supreme Court vote, I was in the office of Federal Circuit Court Judge Elbert Tuttle, a great jurist and possibly the most ethical man I have ever met. He said to me, "I just want to tell you something. I'm sure you think that if Judge Sloan had convened a three-judge court I would have been the circuit judge sitting on that case, but I would have disqualified myself." "Why?" I asked, deeply interested. I had indeed counted on his participation, which would have been perfectly normal, since he was the only circuit judge residing in Georgia.

"Because I've run all over the state denouncing the county unit system."

"Yes," I said, amazed, "but that was when you were the head of the Republican party. That was your political opinion, not necessarily your professionally judicial one."

"Nevertheless, I'm on record."

". . . as a politician. Now you're a judge."

"But I've said what I have said."

"Look, Judge Tuttle, Judge Sibley ruled against the plaintiffs in every county unit case, yet he had no qualms about sitting again.

The same is true of Judge Scarlet. You know that's the trouble with decent people bending over backwards, while less scrupulous men take over. You never ruled on the legality of this thing, did you?''

Tuttle shook his head; a shadow of doubt was perceptible. I thought: the day will come when he'll wrestle with himself and decide that he is indeed qualified to pass legal judgment on the county unit system. I would be proven right.

The 5 to 4 decision in *Hartsfield* v. *Sloan*, the mandamus suit, made me think that, Frankfurter notwithstanding, we were on the verge of getting a majority of the Supreme Court of the United States to admit that the federal courts had jurisdiction over a county unit suit. Up to now all of the county unit cases in federal court had been claims seeking an injunction against the application of the unit vote rule after the popular votes were counted. Courts have traditionally claimed a certain discretion as to whether to grant an injunction, but a plaintiff either is or is not entitled to damages. I reasoned that if we posed to the United States Supreme Court the constitutional question in a damage suit, even Frankfurter would be hard put to prevent his colleagues from deciding the merits of our claims since we would not be asking for any judicial interference with a pending election. A federal Reconstruction statute, as well as Anglo-American common law, recognized the right of a citizen to bring suit for damages against an official who deprived him of the right to vote or to have his vote counted. The officials who applied the county unit system were certainly diluting and thus improperly counting the citizen's ballot. Hence, such an aggrieved voter was entitled to at least nominal damages. If the Supreme Court so held, the ruling would necessarily mean that the county unit system was unconstitutional and that it could be employed only at the risk of multiple damage suits.

The plaintiff with the best possible test case walked into my office in 1959. He had voted for the loser in the Congressional race of 1958, but as the winner had carried his county, the force of his vote was cast for the man against whom he had voted. Unfortunately, the case had to be tried before Federal District Judge Frank Scarlet, one of the three who had upheld the unit system in 1946. I was certain that Scarlet would rule against me, a fact which he confirmed in the very first hearing when he flatly asserted from the bench—following the Frankfurter logic—that the county unit case was non-justicable, that is, beyond the power of the federal judiciary to decide. I asked Scarlet to promptly dismiss the case so that I could scurry to the Federal Court of Appeals on the blunt and precise legal question of whether or not the issues were justicable. By this time, some new faces in the Supreme Court, appointed by President Eisenhower, were giving the Georgia political establishment concern. The lawyers representing the Democratic party officials were determined, therefore, to keep the case bottled up in Savannah. We begged Scarlet to dismiss our claim so that we could appeal his decision. He would not budge. Those of us who had struggled for ten years to open the federal courts to these "political" controversies, were thus denied the right to win that decisive phase of the battle because we could not get out of Savannah. If we had, it is almost a certainty that the new Warren Court would have ignored Frankfurter and the unit system would have perished three years sooner than it did.

The next challenge was in *Sanders* v. *Gray*. It proved to be the historic case that finally destroyed the political dinosaur. The three-judge court consisted of Judges Frank Hooper, Griffin Bell, and Elbert Tuttle.

A Tennessee case, *Baker* v. *Carr*, set the stage. It was now generally acknowledged that the United States Supreme Court would overrule Frankfurter's objections to entering the "political thicket." I had told Hartsfield, who had good access to the Washington press corps, to let me know the moment the expected decision in *Baker* v. *Carr* came down and I would immediately refile the county unit case.

Shortly after noon on March 26, 1962, Mayor Hartsfield called me breathlessly. "Let's go. The Supreme Court has just ruled our way in *Baker* v. *Carr*. My reporter friend in Washington tells me the court referred to all previous county unit cases, including *Hartsfield* v. *Sloan*."

"Fine," I replied, "the complaint is typed. All the mathematical calculations are up to date, and your name is on as plaintiff."

"Morris"—I could detect a note of anguish—"don't file until I can talk with the 'cigar.' " It was the moniker for his friend and staunch supporter, Robert Woodruff, head of the Coca-Cola Company and Atlanta's great community leader and anonymous philanthropist.

The office of the court clerk had closed by the time Hartsfield called back and said with resignation, "You've got to find another plaintiff."

The next day a suit with an Atlanta businessman, James O'Hare Sanders, as plaintiff was filed. Hartsfield could not refrain from walking with me to the court house to meet the gaggle of press assembled.

We were now on the spoor in our sixteenth year of attack on the county unit system. Its defendants were in power. The governor, Ernest Vandiver, had vowed to fight, bleed, and die for it. Having married Richard B. Russell's niece, he probably had little choice in the matter. His strategy was to render inoperable whatever petition we filed by legislatively reorganizing the county unit system. He would gerrymander and regerrymander so that the moment we pointed to the inequities existing at the time the suit was filed, his lawyers could say, "But that's no longer true; this suit has nothing to do with the revised distribution of units." Tactically, he could go on like that for some time. I had to credit the Talmadges, Russells, Murphys, Lawrences, and Vandivers; they had always managed to put up a shield against whatever sword we drew.

Vandiver was now frantically forging his defenses. He dispatched telegrams to the state legislative leaders to meet with him "to discuss a proposal to meet the threat to the county unit system posed by the pending court litigation." On April 16, he convened an extraordinary session of the legislature, whose sole assignment was to shore up the system.

Even if everything had gone smoothly on Georgia's Capitol Hill, Vandiver and his cohorts were going to be frustrated. Unbeknownst to them, we had hired mathematicians to compute every single permutation and combination of counties and county units. No matter what "political reality" they could contrive, we had a written amendment to the complaint all ready to file.

I was not, however, heartened about the composition of the court: Tuttle was a just man; and Hooper a decent man, conscientious but cautious. Finally, there was Griffin Bell, a conservative, then more a politician than a judge. It was he who could provide the swing vote. He had been a Kennedy appointee, a friend of Troutman, Kennedy's southern strategist. Well, Bell was there now and I saw him as a younger, shrewder Judge Sibley, who had twice ruled the county unit system constitutional in carefully written opinions.

The court met at 10:00 A.M., April 27, 1962. The room was packed as I proceeded to present the case. Suddenly, at about 11:00 A.M., a courier rushed into court with the tumultuous news that the legislature had just passed a new county unit law and that the governor was prepared to sign it. I will never forget the look of undisguised self-satisfaction on Buck Murphy's face as he rose and said, "Now we've got a complaint before us which does not state the facts as they exist, and we therefore move for a dismissal." This was the moment we had anticipated. We now dramatically produced an amended complaint that fit the new law precisely and proceeded with our attack.

The defense was taken aback, for they could never have imagined that we were prepared to argue against the artfully contrived new statute. When they looked at our amendment and saw that it did indeed accurately designate the inequities of the statute, they were chagrined. Murphy's usually immobile face for once registered dismay, and I had the distinct psychological advantage for the rest of the trial.

One of the high points came when Murphy objected to the introduction of an affidavit from Atlanta Mayor Hartsfield on the grounds of his well-known bias against the system. I replied that surgeons were well-known enemies of cancer, but that didn't disqualify them from testifying as to its effects or operating to excise it. Murphy pursed his lips, sighed, and sat down.

Not only was I worried about Bell, but oddly enough, Tuttle began to concern me, because of scruples about his past statements against the county unit system. I feared he might unconsciously overcompensate in favor of the other side.

The final opinion was a seventeen-page document, which Bell took exquisite pleasure in reading. He was obviously savoring the high drama of it all. About halfway through the reading, it became clear that the issue was now considered within the court's power to decide and that the new county unit act was unconstitutional because the geographical disparities were too great. Then Bell said, "We do not strike the county unit system as such. We do strike it in its present form," and he went on to further define the boundaries within which a legal county unit system might be devised. Clearly, there was no way the legislature was going to come up with a system that could meet the court's specifications, but I had wanted a judicial proclamation that one man, one vote was the sole constitutional basis of the election. Practically speaking, I had won the case, but not quite the principle.

What ensued could only be described as a political liberation movement. I was jubilant. Celebrations went on for hours, climaxed by a joyous party at our home. The frustrations of a fourteen-year-old political and legal battle were worth the prize which had been bestowed by Griffin Bell's opinion. I said to Jane: "Now if I die tomorrow, my epitaph can read, 'He restored democracy to Georgia.' "

Promptly every wag in Georgia announced for governor. Atlanta poured out its suppressed energies with scores of people who, just a few years before, would never have dreamed of public office. And the Fifth Congressional District witnessed an event that was fifteen years overdue. James C. Davis was finally defeated by a decent moderate, Charles Weltner, who had been associated with me in several county unit cases.

In the midst of these upheavals, the state requested a stay, and applied to the Supreme Court, but Hugo Black was the judge who had primary jurisdiction over the area, and he wouldn't grant one.

As the state wrangled with the court, we decided to match their offensive with one of our own. We challenged Bell's opinion that some sort of county unit system was constitutionally permissible. If we could win, the system would be totally beheaded and a fundamental principle established. No sooner did we file with the Supreme Court than the Attorney General of the United States, Robert Kennedy, announced that he wished to intervene and personally argue as a friend of the court. I was delighted, for I had always relished courtroom drama, and Bobby's appearance would certainly provide that.

Archibald Cox was Solicitor General and had prepared the government's brief. He asked me to come to Washington and meet with him, Bobby, and Burke Marshall, the chief of the Civil Rights Division, in order to coordinate our arguments. Bobby set aside two weeks to prepare himself, for this would be the first case he would argue in any court. I really had no idea what Cox wanted to coordinate, at the beginning of the afternoon session in Bobby's cavernous office.

We sat around a circle. Photographs of the Attorney General's brood were displayed in every nook and cranny, as well as an assortment of his kids' primitive art. Bobby wore no jacket. His collar was unbuttoned, his tie loose, and his sleeves rolled up. His general appearance might be described as that of a tightly coiled, rumpled youth.

After the preliminaries, I said to the group: "Look, the government's brief supports the lower court's opinion. I will argue that no county unit system is permissible, that the court must overrule so much of Bell's decision as holds that there can be any dilution of a man's vote. We stand squarely on the principle of one man, one vote."

"Well, we don't agree with you," Cox responded. He was a conservative, able but headstrong, and moreover, he had absorbed some of Frankfurter's temperament. If he were prepared to enter the political thicket, he didn't want to thrust too far.

"You don't agree," I said, "but grant me this: it's one thing to disenfranchise a man because he is illiterate, or a felon, or even unpropertied, but once you give a man a vote how can you give someone else twice a vote? You can't grade the franchise and give qualified voters varying amounts of voting strength. A man either is a voter or he isn't."

Cox wouldn't budge. Kennedy, who had been sitting silently, finally said, "Archie, I think Morris is right." Exasperated, Cox turned to Kennedy and said, "Well, that's beside the point. Tomorrow morning you're arguing the government's position, and you must argue the government's brief." When the Court convened the next day, almost every Kennedy in the clan was on hand—Bobby's wife, Ethel, his three sisters, and Jackie. Three cabinet wives showed up and the wives of two justices as well.

I will never know whether the show Bobby proceeded to put on before the Supreme Court was deliberate. He launched into what sounded like a Kiwanis Club toast, a bland moral pitch about democracy which never once alluded to the government position that some sort of county unit system was constitutional. Chief Justice Warren, who was a shrewd man, detected an unspoken reservation in Kennedy's argument and said: "I was just going to ask, General, do you believe there is any place in a state system of voting for weighting the votes in a general election for Senator, Governor, or state offices?''

Kennedy replied: ''Mr. Chief Justice, I don't think it is necessary for us to reach that point. I do say that, although I have given it a great deal of thought, I have difficulty coming up with any system that makes any sense which is a unit voting in connection with a statewide election.''

I was seated next to Archibald Cox, whose distress showed upon his face. Bobby Kennedy had just undermined the government's reservation and placed the United States flatly on our side.

On March 18, 1963, the Supreme Court, Justice Harlan dissenting, ruled that ''within a given constituency there can be room for but one constitutional rule—one voter, one vote.'' One man, one vote had advanced from a political slogan into a constitutional principle.

It is historically significant that even during the period between Griffin Bell's opinion and the Supreme Court's ruling, Georgia political powers had made no real effort to barrel a new county unit system through the legislature. The powers knew the jig was up, and they would not try to retain control in different ways: Intimidation of blacks, literacy tests, and various other ploys to exploit the blacks' reluctance to assert themselves against tradition. My work was done, but Vernon Jordan's—the mammoth job of getting black voters registered—was just beginning.

Several years later, while practicing law in New York City, I received an anonymous telegram. It read: ''Abram, you have gone all over this state saying in years past that if we got rid of the county unit system it would make it possible for an Atlanta man to finally be governor. Congratulations, one did. All hail Lester Maddox.''

Indeed, my anonymous friend: progress is a matter of pebbles.

I could not have faulted the county unit system for fourteen years from the base of an establishment law firm. Nor from such an office could I have taken on another controversial litigation, one which created many enemies and several social reprisals.

The case was the first successful major malpractice suit to be brought against a distinguished doctor in our section of the country.

I tried it before a jury three times before obtaining a verdict, and over this long and tortuous journey I discovered that doctors are even more sensitive than lawyers or politicians. They possess, besides, enormous influence in their communities. In fact, our family pediatrician, in the course of the litigation, offered a warning, thinly veiled in jest. "If you should ever need a doctor for yourself, you may well have to go to a veterinarian."

The case began one day when a woman named Agnes Railey was brought in a wheelchair to my office. She presented the situation that would preoccupy me intermittently for the next three years. She was twenty-nine, married to an architectural draftsman, and had two children. Since childhood she had had epileptic spells in which her head drooped and she became virtually comatose for a few moments. It was hardly a crippling condition; aside from her competence as wife and mother, she was a superb swimmer (though she did not swim unaccompanied) and had been secretary to John O. Chiles, the most prestigious real estate broker in Atlanta. Her most serious fear had been that she might fall unconscious at a PTA meeting and embarrass her family.

She had come upon a newspaper story a year before, that told of a new operation that cured epilepsy. Investigating further, she was referred to Dr. Exum Walker, a surgeon who had studied with Wilder Penfield, one of the world's leading neurosurgeons, at the Montreal Neurological Institute. It was Penfield who had developed the operation. I knew his name well, for we were at the same ceremony at Oxford in 1953, when he received an honorary degree and I picked up my M.A.

When Agnes experienced a seizure in Walker's office, he observed it closely and told her that she was lucky, that she was one of the small percentage of epileptics who could indeed be cured by the type of surgical intervention Penfield had developed.

There followed two operations: the first was neutral in effect. Under local anesthesia, Walker opened Agnes' scalp at the point of the right temporal lobe, and stimulated the cerebral cortex at the place where he identified the problem. He noticed, much to his surprise, that Agnes' speech was affected by the slightest stimulation. As she was a right-handed person (and thus her speech center was assumed to be on the left side of her brain), he concluded that the wiring of her brain was somehow transposed, and he prudently withdrew. Six weeks later, after consulting other neurosurgeons, he recommended that Agnes undergo the full operation under general anesthesia.

In the days immediately following the excision of a very small segment of her right temporal cortex, she was unable to coordinate her arms or legs and her speech was slurred. She now no longer could fulfill any meaningful domestic role.

I took her case despite the odds and the silent complicity that existed between establishment physicians and lawyers. I read the medical literature voraciously and primed myself with more details than most lawyers would have deemed necessary. It was in the family tradition. Had Morris Cohen and Lewis Abram not fought malpractice in their own ways? Was I not a doctor manqué myself? In any event, Agnes Railey had picked the most temperamentally suited attorney in town to take on the medical establishment. Furthermore, Agnes' husband, Walter, would be able to continue fighting indefinitely because our firm advanced the expenses for travel and depositions.

For two years I flew all over North America—California, New York, Wisconsin, Canada—gathering evidence. The Georgia Medical Association and Walker's private and insurance company lawyers who were defending the suit were determined to wear us out either with overwhelming support from the most distinguished neurosurgeons in North America or with our mounting expense bills.

Despite the fact that Walker's neurosurgical colleagues rallied around him, I knew that his treatment had been flawed and that the operation had not been medically justified. Before the first operation, he had performed the standard tests: first an angiogram, which charts the blood vessels in the brain and which revealed no irregularities in the area from which he thought the epilepsy derived. Then he did a pneumoencephalogram on the brain cavities, and found nothing amiss. Finally, he sent the patient for an electroencephalogram to locate the point of the improper firing of electrical impulses. That test failed to pinpoint the problem. Nevertheless, lacking all laboratory confirmation and in the face of the surprising evidence that Agnes' speech centers seemed to be located on the right rather than the left side of her brain, he recommended and performed the operation on the right temporal lobe. Walker claimed that Agnes Railey had become a half-articulate cripple because of multiple sclerosis, which happened to afflict her the very week she was recovering from the operation.

Every comment in the available major medical texts made clear to me that Walker had performed an operation against the accepted standards of those qualified to engage in this procedure. He made his judgment and persuaded Agnes Railey to submit to the second operation on the basis of his clinical intuition, from having observed her in seizure—but without confirmatory objective findings.

Walker's defense was that he had done what the established experts advised. His insurance companies and the Georgia Medical Association were prepared to back him all the way. The resistance of a united medical establishment was intense. Most memorable was my encounter with Dr. Penfield himself in a deposition taken at his clinic at the Montreal Neurological Institute.

Waiting for him in his office while the insurance lawyers interviewed him in his consulting room, I just happened to notice among his many books a monograph containing an article by him on Indications for Operation for Focal Cortical Epilepsy. I read it.

Later, in answer to questions by Walker's lawyers, Penfield gave his expert opinion that Agnes Railey's condition "could not have been caused by the removal of the sliver of brain from the right temporal lobe."

Finally, Walker's counsel asked for his opinion of Walker's qualifications to perform the operation on Agnes Railey.

"He was my assistant and chief resident for a period of twelve months. During a period of two years we were in daily contact at the Montreal Neurological Institute."

"During that time did you, assisted by Dr. Walker, perform operations on the brain for focal epilepsy?"

"Yes, a good many."

The ball was now in my court. Since Dr. Penfield had said that Agnes' condition could not have been caused by the removal of the part taken by Dr. Walker, I asked:

"Now, doctor, is it not true that the boundaries of the temporal lobe and the functions of the temporal lobe are not yet completely mapped?"

"The functions are certainly not completely mapped."

"All you know about this woman's brain is contained in these various letters and the report that Dr. Walker has given you?"

"That's right."

"From time to time you find anomalies in the brains or differences from person to person?"

"Yes."

But when I tried to obtain Penfield's admission that Agnes' condition might have resulted from the operation on her right temporal lobe, he hardened:

"I think that it is perfectly absurd."

I reminded him of the differences in human brains, and he admitted, "Those differences make us tremble always for every operation."

Referring to his publication which I had read in his office a few minutes before, I asked, "Have you made the statement in one of your works of recent publication that 'Fools, alas, and charlatans, too, have traded on the credulity of the epileptic in his great need'?"

Penfield was visibly startled, demanding to see the source from which I appeared to be reading:

"It is true."

Off the record, Dr. Penfield demanded, "How did you get that?"

I told him. He was livid as I continued the questioning, referring to the Hunterian Lecture delivered by him in 1954: "In that lecture you set out the generally accepted practice and indications with respect to the surgical treatment of temporal lobe epilepsy, did you not?"

"I tried to."

"Doctor, do you agree that the decision for or against excision and the extent of cutting depends on the discovery of the part of the cortex which is grossly abnormal as shown by electrographic spike discharges on electrography?"

"Yes."

Penfield then chided me for attempting as a layman to comprehend the intricacies of his delicate subject.

"I am not a doctor, sir," I said, "and I therefore have to read the medical journals if I am to be of any use to my client."

"You've done a good job," he told me grimly.

Though Dr. Penfield was unshakeable in his praise of Dr. Walker, he agreed that "in good practice one needs to use every tool that is available to localize and to differentiate the actual point of firing," a concession damning to his disciple.

Though I could not expect to get a neurosurgeon to testify directly against Dr. Walker, I now had extracted by cross-examination the necessary expert judgment to get the case past the judge to a jury. Penfield, the master of the subject, had stated flat out that in failing to use the necessary tool to localize and to differentiate the actual point of firing, Dr. Walker had not followed the accepted procedures of his peers.

Twice I tried the case before Judge George Whitman and a jury, and twice the juries were divided and a mistrial was declared. By the end of the second trial all the principals, myself included, were worn out. Every retrial is a chore and takes longer than its predecessor because no witness retells the story in precisely the same words, causing lengthy legal fencing over small contradictions in testimony. Too much was at stake for me, for my firm, and for the Raileys. I would not give up. I became more resolute after having lunch with one of the jurors in the second trial.

"You'd have won that case except for me," he said after a couple of drinks. "I hung that jury."

"Why?" I asked, somewhat hurt.

"I would never give a verdict against a neurosurgeon for ordinary negligence, of which I thought Dr. Walker was guilty. You see, I think a neurosurgeon ought only to be held liable if guilty of gross negligence, and I don't think that that was the case."

"But the judge told you that the law required a verdict against the doctor if he were guilty of ordinary, not gross, negligence."

"I know," he said, "and if you had asked me when you were examining the jury whether I would pass judgment against a doctor on the showing of ordinary negligence, I would have told you I would not. So, Mr. Abram, if you try this case another time, you'd better question the jury panel more carefully."

The circumstances of the third trial were hellish. There was Agnes Railey pitiably flailing her uncoordinated arms in a wheel chair. My firm had sunk more money in the case than it could afford. A further aggravation was Walker's attorney, Hop Dunaway, a political ally of James C. Davis and himself a passionate, reactionary man whose very presence was an irritation. Then there was the judge.

George Whitman was the wisest fool on the Superior Court bench, an honest, impractical lawyer who enjoyed what I can only describe as legal embroidery in the smallest detail. His son, also named

George, was chairman of the Democratic party under Herman Talmadge. It was George, Jr. who procured his seventy-year-old father's judicial seat.

His Honor had another son, a doctor in Albany, Georgia, a fact which I believe eventually turned the tide in *Railey* v. *Walker*. Through the first two trials, Whitman could not conceal his distaste that a distinguished surgeon was being attacked and in his own courtroom. Knowing that Whitman was a man of integrity, I employed a tactic which is advisable only when things have come to a deadly impasse.

"Judge," I said, before the opening of the third trial, "I want you to disqualify yourself. If you want Dunaway here while I argue this, fine, but I don't want to cause you any embarrassment."

"What's the reason for disqualification?" he barked. "I know of no legal disqualification."

"I don't know of one either," I replied, "nevertheless, you are, I grant quite unconsciously, prejudiced in favor of the defendant."

"Well, that's a new one," said the judge. "Tell me why you say that."

"Well, Judge, you've got a son who is a doctor who pays fees to the Georgia Medical Association which is defending the case, and who presumably carries malpractice insurance himself. Every time I examine one of these doctors appearing for the defendant, I can tell you're extremely upset. Somehow you identify the doctors with your son. It isn't wilful and it certainly isn't malicious."

He demanded an instance on which I based my reading of his psyche. I replied, "One day I had one of Dr. Walker's witnesses under cross examination and I asked a question to which there was an objection on the grounds that the question was leading, as indeed it was. You then said, 'Mr. Abram, the question is leading, rephrase it.' I replied, 'Your Honor, I am entitled to ask a leading question on the cross examination of a witness for the opposite party.' You replied, and these were your words, 'The doctor isn't a witness for anybody. He is an expert.' "

The judge said, "Morris, I reversed myself instantly and let you ask the question as you wished."

I replied, "Of course, you did, your Honor. You know the law and when I pointed out your error you corrected it on the spot. My point is that you would never have made an error on so obvious a point except for the fact that you elevate doctors to a godlike position.''

Whitman was furious; he was so furious he grabbed the arms of his chair as if to rise. But he refused to disqualify himself, and in that third trial he went out of his way to prove to me and to himself that he could lay his feelings aside.

During the selection of the jury, I took great care in selecting the twelve men and women. Not only did I ask them if they were willing to deliver a judgment against a doctor guilty of ordinary negligence, but I probed their entire attitude toward doctors. There was one man, for example, who seemed perfectly suitable until I got him to burst out: ''When a neurosurgeon is operating, the hand of God is moving.'' He may well have been right, but even George Whitman knew that as a matter of law he had to be disqualified.

The trial lasted three weeks and Agnes Railey obtained the largest verdict ever obtained up to that time in Georgia against a doctor of the first class.

Today I am one who owes his life, certainly in large part, to daring and aggressive doctors who are my friends and colleagues, as I serve as the chairman of the President's Commission for the Study of Ethical Problems in Medicine and Biomedical and Behavioral Research. There has been much progress in the doctor/patient relationship since the days of the Railey case. Recently, I wrote out what I espouse as the standard governing informed consent between doctor and patient, and the philosophy that lies behind it. In fact, I believe that the skillful doctor, metaphorically speaking, throws out a rope to the patient drowning in illness and by encouraging the patient to hold on furthers the healing process. Dr. Walker and others like him are too absorbed in empirical scientific procedure to be total healers.

My professional accomplishments during the 1950s did nothing to ameliorate the growing social isolation I felt on behalf of myself and my family. Even if I had succeeded in abolishing the county unit system in 1958, the garlands, I think, would have long since withered. Although I had a beautiful home and some interesting friends, I was distinctly still an outsider, respected by many, admired by some, but not considered ''safe.''

The most painful hurt of all was separation, not of my own choosing, from the University of Georgia friends, even former roommates. This pain I nursed alone. I don't even know if Jane was aware of my feelings, for it was one of the many things I felt too deeply to discuss. Some of these classmates were now lawyers; they all shared an understandable desire to move up in Atlanta's pecking order. Too intimate an association with me would have been an impediment. Few men are as brave as Stephens Mitchell or as secure. I'd see these men in private circumstances but seldom at big parties or clubs. They casually joined groups which excluded Jews, and if any of them supported my congressional candidacy— Troutman or Cleveland, for example—I did not know it. Some were brilliant, fascinating people, and not only did the rejection sting but I sorely missed their company. The reasons which underlay this schism hurt the more, for I knew there was nothing I could do about it. I could never transcend the barrier, not as long as I lived in Georgia.

It is perhaps because of these rejections that I remember friends like Mayor Hartsfield with such affection. His expansive humanity bridged most social chasms. He was simply too much of a maverick himself to be constrained by the pettiness of status-seeking. Wednesday dinner with us could easily be followed on Thursday by a quiet evening with Robert Woodruff.

The Jewish community in which we moved included some of the most interesting people in Atlanta. There was, for example the well-to-do set which had founded the Standard Club at the turn of the century. We belonged and attended its elegant, tasteful parties, but the conversation was generally banal or repetitive, for though many of these men and women possessed startling knowledge of the world in which they lived, they were loathe to display it and seemed ruled, instead, by a code of refined but strictly superficial social intercourse. The men worked hard; and the women supervised their homes, did voluntary work, regularly went to their beauty parlors. To do something new of a Saturday evening required imagination and planning; Atlanta was essentially provincial.

In the 1950s I defended two movies banned by the local censor: *Tunes of Glory,* because Alec Guinness had spoken the word *bastard,* and *Never on Sunday,* on account of its suggestive theme. Atlanta then did not possess a towering skyline, and it certainly had no adult bookstores.

In addition to my boredom with the city's social and intellectual life, I was rediscovering the whole painful experience of anti-Semitism through my children. They brought home the phrase "Christ-killer" before they were in their teens, and I had to explain it, unfortunately, to children I had thoughtlessly failed to root firmly in their own ground, to provide the identity they needed as a shield, precisely as my parents had failed to provide one for me. All the hurts of my childhood were resurrected; my children were myself all over again.

This is how my daughter Ruth learned her lesson:

All of our children had attended a private school, Lovett, which ended after the seventh grade. Ruthie, and her friends, Laura, Sally, Jennifer, Lucy, Margaret, and Beverly felt lucky they were going on to the same high school, Westminster, a Presbyterian prep school.

It was 1957 and Ruthie was twelve. She reported to school with a new haircut with bangs, and wearing a hoop skirt with petticoats, saddle shoes, bobby socks, a Peter Pan collar, and a circle pin. At the first recess at Westminster, she dashed over to meet her friends who were gathered outside.

"We're really sorry, Ruthie," Laura began. "We really like you a lot. This is nothing against you. Please understand, it is not us—it's our parents."

"What do you mean?"

"You can't play with us any more; you can't come to our parties. We're all going to the cotillion, but you can't. You're Jewish, you see. . . ."

Ruthie didn't see, but she was about to see. Being Jewish in Atlanta was to mean the end of cherished friendships, being left out, loneliness, becoming a stranger in her own land, having more in common with the black women who worked in her home than with the girls in her school.

A few years later my wife Jane responded uniquely to these pressures. As our youngest child was about to be born, she declared she wanted to convert to Judaism. I had certainly never encouraged her to do this; indeed, I was amazed when she proposed it. Our other children had been attending a Jewish Sunday school, but Jane wanted to guarantee that they could lay undisputed claim, not only to what they professed, but to what the world would, in any case, consider them. It is my belief that Jane's conversion was most deeply motivated by a desire to protect our children from scarring confusions of personal identity. There is nothing about Jane that I admired more than this capacity to assess such needs in our children and act accordingly. She has always had an intelligent respect for the Jewish tradition; I can recall how she staunchly rebuffed her mother, who, in Oxford, suggested, "How nice it would be for Ruthie to be baptized in the lovely Pembroke Chapel by that nice young chaplain. He's such a good friend."

We were in that awful no-man's-land between the ghetto and total assimilation. Scarsdale, Woodmere—they're ghettos, too, and the children there never experience the yahoo until they're older. But in Atlanta, it was different. The Jews were few and too dispersed, too open to the random insults. And with their father a liberal to boot, Ruthie, Ann, Morris, Jr., and Adam were easy targets.

In 1957, my preoccupation with the subject of identity was intensified by the news that my father was in the Fitzgerald Hospital. An aneurysm had burst. I rushed home, but he was already dead. My brother and sisters were there. The funeral was to be the last time we'd all be assembled together in Fitzgerald for close to twenty years. My older partner had been a surrogate father for years, but now Sam Abram himself was gone, my blood cried to his blood.

We were growing financially more secure. My father was able to will me no legacy, but in the thirty-nine years I had known him he transferred to me every one of his own well-founded anxieties about earning a living. Jane laughed off my fears and offered to make and abide by budgets. I preferred not to know our precise financial condition—a hangover from my father's practice of eschewing all business controls—because in his case, he knew that the news would always be bad and exacerbate his tensions.

In 1959 we decided to upgrade our residence. Both Jane and I liked early American antiques and domestic architecture. We found the perfect replica of an eighteenth-century Tidewater Virginia mansion, which we eventually bought. It wasn't easy. It was everything we had been looking for, but since it was I who first discovered the house, Jane balked about buying it immediately. We both had strong competitive streaks. I, as a man, had infinitely more opportunities to exercise mine. Jane had only her home. Decisions on decor, landscaping, table manners, and even menus were turned into contests of style and taste. Earlier in the marriage, I would have deferred happily to her decisions. The trouble came with an increasing self-confidence in my own social grace.

8

In the late 1950s, although the fight to destroy the unit system would keep me in Atlanta, forces were working to propel me beyond Georgia. One was an invitation I received in 1959 to join the Twentieth Century Fund in New York City. Here was the kind of intellectual stimulation and contact with opinion molders that I was starved for. It had happened quite unexpectedly. Jane and I were invited to a dinner party in Athens by Mildred Thompson, a retired dean of Vassar. Mildred had returned to her native state to accept a teaching post at the University of Georgia. The guest of honor was her former student and protégé, Beatrice Berle. Adolph Berle, also present, had been one of FDR's original braintrusters. An admirer of Berle, I was happy to have been invited.

It was Adolf Berle, a few months later, who secured the invitation for me to join the Board of Trustees of the Twentieth Century Fund. A well-endowed research organization which produced scholarly books, it attempted to disentangle political, social, and economic conundrums.

I sat quietly through the first meeting. There they were, the kingpins of the New Deal, almost legends, and deservedly so—for they had brought to Washington its first essentially political, rather than corporate, culture since Andrew Jackson. Berle and Benjamin Cohen discussed government regulation. David Lilienthal, first head of the TVA and AEC, elaborated on issues of energy development. James Rowe, who had served Democratic presidents from Roosevelt on, lectured, as did Robert Lynd, author of *Middletown*. Francis Biddle, former Attorney General, was there, and so was Charles Taft, William Howard's son.

The most electric presence, however, was a man only peripherally connected with the New Deal, although he was responsible for an event ten thousand times weightier than the Depression or the future of American liberalism. J. Robert Oppenheimer was a thin, ascetic man who always arrived late, his hair ruffled, a pipe hanging from his mouth. He looked like a poet, and an academic one at that.

What a relief from the parochialism of Atlanta! I had struggled to escape it by running for Congress, by immersing myself in the affairs of the American Jewish Committee, and by striving to enlarge the windows through which Georgia viewed the world—but here, around this table, was a collective experience and expertise that surpassed the sum total of everything and everyone that I had yet known. Why was I elected to this group of notables? I had not published, held high office, or lectured from a distinguished university chair. Had these men picked me as a southern liberal, to bring to their round table an informed viewpoint of the changing South? As an educated Georgian with a national perspective on questions of race and constitutional law, I belonged in this society for precisely the reasons that I did not fit in the power centers of my own region.

About the same time and for similar reasons I was invited with Mayor Hartsfield to have dinner with Ruth (Mrs. Marshall) Field in New York to talk to the Board of The Field Foundation, of which Adlai Stevenson was then president.

Beforehand, Hartsfield came to my home in Atlanta with Harold Fleming, the executive director of the Southern Regional Council, the prime biracial organization in the South at that time. We talked and drank until midnight. Hartsfield became very relaxed, stretched out on the sofa in the study, and delivered himself of opinions on race far exceeding the limits that southern conservatism permitted its politicians. He had never spoken so frankly even to me before. I was amazed and gratified. It seemed that a civil rights activist was lurking within my cagey friend.

Suddenly, he himself seemed startled by what he was saying, and as if to interrupt his own stream of consciousness, stammered, "You know, this is damn heady stuff we've been talking here to-night. I wonder where I got all these ideas. Well, I don't suppose I'd have gotten them if the niggers hadn't got the right to vote."

The thought of Hartsfield saying this to Adlai Stevenson, Ruth Field, and Lloyd Garrison sent shivers down my spine.

"Well, it doesn't matter now," he continued, "wherever I got them I now believe them and I'm stuck with them."

At the risk of hyperbole, I would say that a large, solid minority of the white South was speaking at that moment. The new ideas were coming, and the Hartsfields would have to adjust and so would lesser men than he.

In New York, in the presence of Ruth Field and her guests—Adlai Stevenson, Lloyd Garrison, Ralph Bunche, Clarence Pickett, Judge Justine Wise Polier—I spoke of Georgia as the great fulcrum of southern opinion.

"What happens in North Carolina, Tennessee, or Florida doesn't matter much. North Carolina has a heavy mountain population; it isn't South Carolina, and its actions can be dismissed as the aberration resulting from the indoctrination at the University at Chapel Hill. Tennessee is a border state. The largest Union Army and hospital was located in Johnson City, and its population was bitterly divided even in the Civil War. Everybody knows that South Florida is an extension of New York. On the other hand," I said, "there is no possibility that Alabama will take the lead in desegregation, but it would eventually accept the accommodations made in a state such as Georgia. So, Georgia is the pinwheel. If Georgia integrates its schools in obedience to the Supreme Court, the real resistance is over."

I discussed Georgia's bondage to the county unit system and, in a rather uncommon argument for those days, I pinpointed class not race as the heaviest burden weighing down the South.

"Most whites are in the middle class; most blacks are underprivileged. When, therefore, whites are asked to have close association with blacks, it requires surrendering not only traditional race prejudice but class distinctions. The whites of the South and of the North, too, will not find this easy."

"What, then, shall be done?" asked a board member whom my words had apparently depressed.

"The class gap has got to be closed," I replied. "When the color of people's skin is the only thing we have to worry about, society will be in much better shape."

As commonplace as this may seem today, one must remember the temper of a time when Eastern liberals thought that racial prejudice involved little more than a primitive fear of people who looked different.

I was pleased by my own performance and had the distinct impression that the lords of the liberal world were interested in what I had to say and would show it by word or deed. Indeed, I was invited to join the board, and when Adlai Stevenson died five years later, I succeeded him as president of The Field Foundation.

By the time of the presidential election of 1960, I had several footholds in the North. My association with the campaign of John F. Kennedy planted my feet more firmly in northern soil. Circumstances conspired to have me play a major role in procuring the release of Martin Luther King, Jr. from an Atlanta jail during the middle of the Kennedy-Nixon campaign, an event for which Jack Kennedy received full credit. That credit earned him untold black votes, and I needn't emphasize that it was a close election.

Ever since 1956, when Jack Kennedy came close to the vice-presidential nomination on the Stevenson ticket, Bobby Troutman had figured in Kennedy's plan to head the ticket in 1960. Troutman had known Joe Kennedy, Jr. at Harvard, and after the death of that scion he attached himself to the hierarchal successor to the Kennedy political mantle. As a southern Catholic with luxuriant political roots, Troutman was a natural man to carry Jack Kennedy's banner in Dixie.

Troutman relished the role as the bridge over ideological chasms—holding the Dixiecrats in line, keeping the South solid—and he began to work hard to tie Herman Talmadge, now a United States Senator, and me to some cause of mutual interest. I didn't foresee any political motive behind his suggestion in 1957 that Talmadge and I should stump the state fund raising for the University of Georgia Foundation, and I was shocked at the audacity of the proposal.

"But, Bobby," I said, "in my 1954 campaign for Congress Herman was asked, 'Do you think Abram is a subversive?' And what do you think he said?"

"I don't know, and these so-called political issues are all a bunch of crap anyway," replied Bobby, whose only ideological commitment was to his Catholic faith.

"Well," I said, "Herman told the listening radio audience he couldn't say Abram was a subversive, but it was rumored that he had studied abroad."

"Poppycock," Troutman said impatiently. "Can you imagine what an impact it will have on fund raising for the university and on healing political divisions among the alumni if Morris Abram and Herman Talmadge campaign together for their university?"

Indeed, the image Bobby invoked was as intriguing as it was astonishing. He didn't have to win me; and he bowled me over when he revealed that he already had Herman's approval.

It was not until three years later that I first suspected Bobby's proposal had another motive behind it. He must have reasoned that if Jack Kennedy had to have the support of the whole South to get the nomination and win the election, the Talmadges were the key. Yet, there was a New South arising, with ties to the Democrats and Independents in the other regions. It would be dangerous, maybe fatal, for Kennedy to ignore the moral and political claims of these liberals in the pursuit of Talmadge-type delegates and the support of entrenched southern office-holders of which he was an archetype.

During the 1960 campaign my wife and I found ourselves, through Troutman's skillful arrangements, spending the weekend at the Talmadges' in Washington and dining with Senator and Mrs. Kennedy on Sunday evening in their elegant Georgetown house.

Then came the convention and the debates. At first I was, as I had expected to be, a marginal figure, kept mainly in the closet. But in October, just days before the election, I was hurled into the vortex. Harris Wofford, a staff aide to Sargent Shriver in the civil rights division of the Kennedy effort, caught me on the phone one

Saturday morning as I was leaving home with my nine-year-old daughter Ann, for her "promised day with Daddy." "Morris," Harris said, "Martin Luther King, Jr. is in jail in Atlanta."

"Surely, you don't have to call me long distance to tell me," I replied. "Everybody knows that."

"But I want you to get him out and claim the credit for Senator Kennedy."

"How in the hell do you think I'm going to spring him?" I asked.

"Go see Mayor Hartsfield, since he was arrested by the Atlanta police, and explain that the two of you, after his release, will say that you did it because of Senator Kennedy's interest and concern."

I pointed out that I was one foot out the door with Ann. Harris would have none of that: "Take her with you," he said, and he refused to believe that, even with Hartsfield's total cooperation, it might be an impossible chore. There were nineteen civil rights demonstrators keeping Martin company in the Fulton County jail. Were they to be released as well? King, moreover, had said he wouldn't come out on bail; the charges filed by Rich's Department Store, where the sit-in in the Magnolia dining room had occurred, were unjust. His cry was "jail, not bail." And at the climax the police had also arrested a contingent of Klansmen for anti-black demonstrations. It was a tangled mess. Yet, as Harris saw it, all that was required was merely to persuade Hartsfield to brandish his seal of office. I agreed to call the Mayor, if only to get Harris off the phone.

Hartsfield was extremely excited: "Yeah, come down at once," he said. "We're negotiating right now with every important Negro in town. They're all sixty of them in the council chamber." He asked me to bring Harold Fleming, too. When I arrived at City Hall with Ann and Harold, it was a mob scene. We shut outselves up in the Mayor's office, and he gave us some unsettling news. "I've just told the Negro leadership in the council chamber that representatives of Senator Kennedy called and asked me to release Martin Luther King, Jr. There was an AP reporter in the room and the story by now is on the wires."

I was barely able to digest this potentially catastrophic development when I noticed that J. H. Calhoun, the leading black Republican in Atlanta, was talking excitedly over the telephone in an adjacent room. We couldn't help but overhear the hapless Calhoun trying to arouse Nixon headquarters to the danger that King was on the verge of obtaining every black vote in the country. "A report!" Calhoun shouted incredulously into the mouthpiece. "We don't have time to write a report; you've got to get through to the vice-president at once." He listened for another moment and then dropped the phone slowly in its cradle. Calhoun and I were friends, and since he knew I had heard him, I said with concern, "What did they tell you?" "They told me to send in a report air mail, special delivery," he replied, shaking his head.

Well, Vice President Nixon had his problems and we had ours. I had to work something out with Hartsfield, and though he was totally willing, the procedure would be intricate.

We had to obtain the consent of the police, because Hartsfield didn't want to break their morale; the consent of the prosecuting officer, because it was necessary; the approval of the black leadership, because of the local political implications for Hartsfield; and the consent of Rich's, which had made the charge against King and his nineteen followers; and finally, the consent of Martin Luther King, Jr. himself, which proved as difficult as all the above put together.

We began at ten o'clock in the morning and we negotiated until eight that evening without stopping for food. My hungry little daughter received a political immersion she will never forget. By the end of the day we had worked out the simpler parts of the deal. Hartsfield recommended the release of everybody, the blacks and the Klansmen, without bail; but our troubles were just beginning. Martin refused to leave jail. He announced that he had not been legally vindicated, that the charge, under an unjust and unconstitional law, would still be hanging over his head. And he was right. He had another, more pragmatic reason as well, which I learned a few days later. At the time, he flatly refused to walk out of that prison until all charges were dropped, but getting them dropped would be no mean feat. Richard H. Rich, a friend of Hartsfield and mine and a Hartsfield supporter, was the very practical president of Rich's Department Store. He was in terror that his company would be charged with caving in to black pressure, a public relations gaffe that could cost him millions of dollars. Moreover, what would happen if black crusaders should then target in en masse on Rich's to really integrate its segregated dining and rest room facilities, while his competitors had a free ride? Hartsfield and I would be asking Rich to become a frontline combatant in a cause for which he cared little. He just wanted to sell shoes, furniture, and perfume.

Even before we began to wrestle with these complications, Bobby Troutman burst into the mayor's office. He had heard the AP story on the car radio and was envisioning the whole of his southern political strategy going right down the tube. "Who," he demanded to know, staring straight at me and Hartsfield, "is this representative of Senator Kennedy who is trying to get this King fellow out of jail?"

"Well, I don't know," answered Hartsfield, an experienced dissembler.

"I do know," said Troutman, livid. "You two have just blown the election. Do you understand that? You have just blown the election. We had it sewed up, but now you're going to lose the South. These southern politicians are going to turn against us. They'll never accept Kennedyism with Martin Luther King tied to its tail."

I have never seen Troutman so out of control.

"I have already heard from Fritz Hollins," he continued. "He called me from the governor's mansion in South Carolina. What do you think he said? He said that if Kennedy is trying to help that rabble-rouser, he's off the team. Who've you been talking to, how do I get in touch with him?"

"You're asking *me* how *you* should get in touch with Kennedy?"

"Ah, forget it," he said as he started for the phone, but then he suddenly realized he'd require privacy. He stormed out of the City Hall and I knew at once what he planned to tell Kennedy. I called Harris at Shriver's office.

"Now, Harris, goddam it," I said. "Troutman was just here and he's madder than a hornet. He's trying to call Kennedy now and tell him that Hartsfield and I have lost the South. He's going to advise Kennedy to repudiate our efforts." In case Wofford couldn't visualize what was at stake, I said, "Wait for the headlines in Sunday's paper, 'KENNEDY RENOUNCES EFFORTS TO HELP KING.' "

"Oh my God," he said, "we'll lose the north."

"Call him, Harris."

128

"No, Morris, you call him. You know the facts." And he told me that in a few moments Kennedy was expected to land for a campaign appearance in Joplin, Missouri. He gave me the contact number.

Then it dawned on me. Wofford and Shriver were winging it. They hooked up this whole scheme with no prior clearance with anyone else in the Kennedy campaign. I should have known that from the first; I should have known that Jack Kennedy would not have rocked so delicate a balance as the 1960 election in October by permitting direct intervention on behalf of Martin Luther King, Jr., not when he had conferred upon Bobby Troutman the obligation to court every Dixiecrat whose ancestor had survived Pickett's Charge.

I called Joplin and got an advance man on the phone. Kennedy's plane was arriving. You could hear the whir of the engines. In fact, it was hard to hear anything else. I shouted, "If Senator Kennedy is asked anything about Martin Luther King, Jr., let him say *nothing*. Do not let him say that he has encouraged what has been going on in Atlanta, but for God's sake, do not let him say he *didn't* encourage it. Instead, have him and his principal staff members call Shriver at once." The catastrophe that Troutman's impetuous reaction threatened was thus averted.

We now turned our attention back to King. He still wouldn't leave the jail. Nothing could persuade him, not even a visit from the black president of Atlanta University, whom he knew and respected. He continued to say that charges against him and his young ones would all have to be dismissed. Of course, an agreement with Rich would have to precede our efforts with the prosecutor. So, very late Saturday evening the mayor and I barged in on Rich at home in dressing gown and slippers.

"Atlanta is getting a horrible image, a horrible image!" Hartsfield exclaimed. Rich shrugged sympathetically, but as if the words did not implicate him. "Look," Hartsfield went on, "I've agreed to release the Klansmen. Their supporters are delighted. If you drop the charges against King, those happy rednecks will barely notice."

Finally, Rich agreed if the prosecutor, John Kelley, would sanction it. That would give the department store the benediction of the legal establishment.

Sunday morning, we drove out to see Kelley, a pleasant, rotund little man who was more impressed by a visit from Hartsfield and the significance that Richard H. Rich attached to his endorsement than he was by our arguments. So he, too, agreed. The charges were lifted.

Blacks nationwide were jubilant. A national voice had been raised, they thought, in defense of their leader. Soon, however, we discovered that King's reluctance to leave jail may have been based on a very realistic fear—for after the charges in Fulton County were released, he was promptly picked up on a warrant for a parole violation of a court in the neighboring county of DeKalb. It was a problem of which Hartsfield and I had no prior knowledge.

It was not simply a second arrest that King was dreading. He had felt the hand of the law too many times already, but this warrant had been issued by Judge Oscar Mitchell, a close friend of James C. Davis, and a man after the white knight's own heart. The problem had arisen because of an earlier charge against King for driving with an out-of-state license. He had simply failed to get a Georgia registration when he moved his operations from Montgomery. No one had paid it much attention, not even Judge Mitchell when he had sentenced King to a term in the state prison at Reidsville, an isolated, benighted part of the state, for Mitchell had immediately suspended the sentence provided King did not violate any Georgia law during the period of probation.

Mitchell was a shrewd, bitter-end segregationist who would relish holding a tether around the neck of the nation's foremost practitioner of civil disobedience. King would either toe the line during the probation period or, if he persisted in challenging the laws on the books, he could be summarily sent to prison some three hundred miles away where the inmates were particularly vicious. King's incarceration there, far from the media, could even spell death. So, Mitchell had read the headlines and had King taken into custody as he left the Atlanta prison. After a cut-and-dried hearing on a simple question of parole violation, Mitchell sentenced King to six months' hard labor in Reidsville where he was promptly taken in handcuffs. At that point, Bobby Kennedy phoned Mitchell to protest, outraging every tradition in the South. In a sense, Bobby Troutman's earlier fears were coming true.

In the meantime, Shriver had cornered Jack Kennedy and persuaded him to call Coretta King to express support and sympathy.

Shriver had waited for the moment when he and Kennedy were alone, for he knew that the rest of the entourage would try to prevent the candidate from going so far out on a limb. Impulsively—and let us hope intuitively—Kennedy consented and called Mrs. King as she and Martin Luther King, Sr. were on their way to my Atlanta office.

For whatever reason, Judge Mitchell released King on bail. Now the whole campaign was enmeshed in the Georgia situation. The political damage of King's release from Atlanta charges had been fairly well contained, but Bobby Kennedy's call to Mitchell had cost dearly. Kennedy strategists now plotted to milk the exposed position for every possible benefit. To this end, Harris Wofford called me again and asked if I could get King to announce his support for Kennedy in view of "all we had done for him." I told Wofford that I knew King would not endorse any political candidate, but it dawned on me that Martin Luther King, Sr. might not be bound by such self-imposed restrictions.

"That's great," said Wofford jubilantly, "a Martin Luther King is a Martin Luther King; the public will never know the difference."

But would Dr. King, Sr., or Daddy King as his friends called him, endorse John Kennedy? I had long admired him. In fact, years later I teased his famous son by saying that "the really great King is your father. You couldn't have failed with a daddy like that." And Martin had smiled broadly and agreed. My present chore was facilitated by some other legal matters I was handling for King, Sr. He was going to stop by at my office. As I waited for him, I remembered a speech I had given some years before at the Hungry Club, a kind of black Rotary which met at the Butler Street black YMCA. There I had criticized the poor black voter registration and especially the shameful totals in Fulton County, where blacks were freer to participate than elsewhere. There were some in that audience who sharply attacked my views for what they characterized as casting the blame on the victim. Nobody rose to defend me except Daddy King. "Look here," he said, "nobody here can accuse me of being an Uncle Tom. In fact, I am going to go tonight to help my son in Alabama." He benignly stared his audience down. "Now there's no use putting the blame on others. Do what Mr. Abram says, register and vote."

This was the man for whom I was waiting. Daddy King arrived with another son, Reverend A. D. King. As we concluded our business, I said, "Dr. King, Senator Kennedy would like Martin to announce for him."

"He can't do that in his position."

"What about you?"

"Well, Mr. Abram, as a Baptist I have been opposed to Senator Kennedy on religious grounds."

That startled me. It seemed to belie the whole morality of the civil rights movement. I had simply forgotten that black Baptists were Baptists who were black. They are not exempt from the same prejudices that distinguish their white counterparts.

"Nevertheless," Daddy King continued, "in view of what Kennedy has done for my son, I'm going to vote for him."

"Will you say so publicly?" I asked, realizing that Daddy King was drawing out his reply as much as possible. His flair for the dramatic was not limited to the pulpit.

"Mr. Abram," he said, "have your reporters at the Ebenezer Baptist Church on Sunday." This was a few days before the election. "I will say that, uhmm, I will say that because of what Senator Kennedy has done for my son, I want to get for him a whole bushel basket full of votes." Daddy King was as good as his word.

John F. Kennedy was elected president of the United States a few days later by a margin of about one hundred thousand votes.

Following the election, I was at a crossroads professionally. Kennedy would probably lift me out of Georgia with some federal job, I thought, but Talmadge and Russell, though personal friends, would not think of supporting me for a federal judgeship in the South. That would have been too dangerous politically. Indeed, because of Kennedy's deference to Democratic committee chairmen such as Senator James Eastland of Mississippi, his appointments to the federal judiciary in the South were deeply compromised. Eisenhower, who had no southern Republican senators to placate, had been free to appoint Elbert Tuttle, John Minor Wisdom, Skelly Wright, and others of their intellectual and moral caliber. The election of John Kennedy put the traditional southern congressional chairman back in control of southern judgeships.

Shriver offered me a position as general counsel to the Peace Corps, which I accepted on a temporary basis. Later, the president offered me the first American ambassadorship to the emerging nation of Tanganyika. It was a pivotal state and its leader, Nyere, was one of the more interesting men in Africa. I was flown out on Air Force I for a visit there as a delegate to Nyere's Independence Day inauguration.

After much thought, however, I decided to decline the job and stay put in Atlanta. There was, after all, the county unit system and my family to worry about, and I didn't quite believe Kennedy when he proclaimed Mennen "Soapy" Williams' appointment as Assistant Secretary of State for African Affairs "a job second in importance to none."

The lure of New York intensified. Adlai Stevenson was at the United Nations. He asked me to serve part-time on a subcommission for the Prevention of Discrimination and Protection of Minorities. I saw no reason to decline. In alternate years I would be visiting Geneva.

In the meantime, Stevenson's former law partner, Lloyd Garrison, heard that I had turned down the Tanganyika post and offered me a partnership in Paul, Weiss, Rifkind, Wharton & Garrison. The firm was a band of independent souls, each with his own outside interests, who could have formed the faculty of a distinguished liberal arts college. The offer was enticing. I would already be spending a lot of time in New York at the Twentieth Century Fund, The Field Foundation, and now at the UN, and it was suggested that I might be in line to become the national president of the American Jewish Committee. Yet I hesitated finally to pull up my Georgia roots.

I was forty-four years old, and I could earn a splendid living in Atlanta with my left hand. *Sanders* v. *Gray,* the final assault against the county unit system, was looming, and I knew that changing political conditions would change my own. The prospect of being a big fish in a little pond was attractive. New York had enormous drawbacks. I would not be able to afford to live in the center of all the glitter and delight that had first attracted me to the city, yet suburbia entailed a frightful commute. The city would mean private schools for four children, and a fifth child was coming. It would also mean the trauma of change from grass to asphalt. And, finally, there was the fear of failure. My accomplishments in Atlanta entailed fifteen years of professional connection with men and women who trusted me. I could count on them. How much could I count on Adlai Stevenson or Lloyd Garrison to ensure that my children would be properly housed and fed? I would have to learn a totally different practice, serving a totally different clientele. Could I do it? In Atlanta I was the virtual head of my own firm; now I would be one man among twenty-nine partners. I might get lost.

Two incidents, small in themselves, tipped the balance. I lunched one afternoon with George Goodwin, an old friend, a political liberal and devout Presbyterian—a man sufficiently ensconced on the side of the angels to have won a Pulitzer Prize for exposing Talmadge vote frauds in his home county, Telfair. Symbolically enough, we were sitting in the restaurant on the top floor of the Bank of Georgia Building, the highest spot in Atlanta. I asked him what he thought about my future.

George, who was a cautious, solemn man, pondered my question. I could almost hear the gears turning. On the one hand he wished to be truthful; and on the other he did not wish to hurt me; and above all, he would have preferred that I stay in Atlanta. He finally laid it on the line:

"Morris, you can live a comfortable life here and be an important figure, but you will never be accepted on merit. You will not go as far as your talents would justify."

George was the first person to say what I suppose I had known for years, that my views were too broad, my tongue too sharp, my determination too unrestrained, and my legacy too Jewish for me ever to be admitted as a member of the power structure of Atlanta. That coterie would have to deal with me and even bend when I pushed, but I would forever be consigned to do my work outside the fence rather than within.

If I needed further encouragement to move to New York, Leonard Reinsch, the manager of Cox Broadcasting, provided it.

"Do you want to play ball with the New York Yankees or the Atlanta Crackers?" he asked tersely, and smiled as he saw me grope for a response. "Morris," he said, "the New York Yankees play in New York City."

That did it. For years after, lawyers and politicians in Atlanta said the same two things about my departure. They said I left because I wanted to make it to the Supreme Court and that as long as I maintained my Georgia ties that could never happen. And they also said I was leaving Atlanta at the one time in all its history that was propitious for someone like me to attain high public office there.

In fifteen years I and my colleagues had filed half a dozen suits in an effort to destroy the county unit system. We had finally won the battle, and I, its principal general, was now in October 1962 leaving the fruits of victory to anyone else with money enough to subsidize a candidacy. And many who never before had a chance gained important elective office, including Charles Weltner and Andy Young, in the very congressional district in which Helen Mankin, Baxter Jones, and I had been defeated. Elliot Levitas, a Jew, was soon elected to Congress in a newly created adjacent district. Within a few years a veritable sea change occurred in the political climate, sending Jimmy Carter and George Busbee to the governor's chair. Race baiting disappeared from Georgia political campaigns.

Of course, I've pondered what I might have become had I stayed in Georgia. I probably could have been elected to Congress. But I'd have been a one-termer. I would have voted my convictions, not necessarily the same as those of my constituency. After the initial thrill was worn, I would have loathed the endless courtship of the electorate and the banalities of public events. And if I'd gone to the court, like Osgood and other liberal friends, I'd have chaffed from the restrictions of that cloistered life. Still, I could have remained a private citizen with more influence than George Goodwin and I forecast that day we dined atop the Bank of Georgia in 1962. Sometimes I daydream of that scenario. Yet, I have never been so unsure of my decision as to forfeit what was to come: that exhilarating feeling of being at the center of the center of the world.

9

ON A GRAY WINTER DAY in 1976 as Eli and I were taping, Ruth Field called from Chelsea, her plantation home near Beaufort, South Carolina, to extend an invitation for a visit in early spring when the azaleas and camillias would be in full flower. As I returned to my conversation with Eli, I was thinking of the role Ruth had played in my transition from Atlanta to New York.

I was already a middle-aged man when I went North to begin my new career. There was one connection that proved especially helpful: The Field Foundation. That meeting at Ruth Field's apartment turned out a rich harvest. It was there, as I have said, that I met Adlai Stevenson and Lloyd Garrison, who were senior partners at Paul, Weiss. In addition, the firm represented the Field family.

The fact is, my grounding in the ''liberal'' establishment, however elitist and northeastern the phrase may sound, began because of my work in Atlanta. My northern counterparts saw me as a virtual fifth column in the southern flatlands and whistle stops. Because I was a man of law and business and not merely of causes, I was an unusual southern liberal. When I pulled up stakes and came

136

to New York, my reception was decidedly warm. In 1965, two years after my arrival, I became the president of The Field Foundation, then the bellwether of American liberal philanthropy.

In the first few weeks of my commute from Larchmont, New York, where we bought a home, I was depressed, particularly during the slow shuffle up the ramp of the underground cavern at Grand Central Station where the trains discharge their thousands of passengers. I caught myself recalling the words of a poem, "Thanatopsis," memorized in my youth: ". . . a quarry slave . . . scourged to his dungeon. . . ." But I had made the choice and had to live with it. New York was not as exhilarating as I remembered it on my first trip in 1936 as a member of the University of Georgia debating team. "Thousands of people choking the streets after the theaters are empty," I wrote my family. "Boys screaming paper editions, beggars selling papers. Lights flashing news and advertisements all stun one into submission to the fact that you just ain't used to such things in the country."

I had even rhapsodized the YMCA Sloan House; today, no one who could afford something better would go near the place, but in 1936 I thought it an exquisite monument. Now thirty years later I was back in New York laden with the responsibility of a family of five children. For the next eighteen years I would work in diverse and challenging fields. As I view this period, I understand that two essential facts of my life would continue to dominate. I was a Jew and a rural-born southerner.

The fact that I was a Georgian, as well as a Jew, would extinguish one of the vague hopes that had brought me to New York. I had left Atlanta not only because its ceiling was too low, but also because part of me was so tired of being a marginal figure. In Atlanta I would always be the maverick. I left hoping for a new sense of belonging. In many ways I found it. Here, for every taste there is a satisfaction; for every interest, there is a person or institution through which to pursue it. But in all my New York years I have not found the counterparts to the few southern friends who accepted me for what I was, who criticized my foibles mercilessly and with whom I felt totally relaxed.

I used to spend two or three hours a day talking things out with my law partners in Atlanta. You don't do that in a New York law firm where partners number more than sixty. When I was near death, the men to whom I felt the need to speak were Osgood Williams and a former law partner named Joe Lefkoff. These southerners, and others, are part of my being. Among the scores of friends and colleagues in New York, the contacts are too infrequent or too fleeting and too recent to forge the bonds of shared experience which make for human family. In the days that I lay in Mount Sinai, my bone marrow ravaged, my gums bleeding and fever raging, I pondered a conundrum: A man is supposed to be buried at home, but where was home? Not Fitzgerald, where my father lies in an unshaded plain in the Jewish section of Evergreen Cemetery, for I left there at sixteen vowing never to return; not in Atlanta, where I suffered the wounds of rejection and ostracism and was part of a netherworld of marginality; and certainly not New York, which yields no ground in which a man may finally be laid to rest.

On the other hand, my marginality was perhaps one of my main assets—a southerner with a national point of view who made his living not in philanthropic or religiously supported movements but in the world of law and commerce. In New York my qualities, I believed, would be appreciated, at least I would not always swim upstream. But perhaps, in the end, I have always been an outsider—in New York not less than I was, though for totally different reasons, in Atlanta.

I soon learned to play up my regionalism. If I couldn't escape it I would exploit it. Once I stood in a New York federal court and requested that my opponent get down to the "lick log."

"What is that, Mr. Abram?" asked the judge.

"Your Honor, in every cow pasture there's a log of salt which the cow must lick lest she perish. Getting to the 'lick-log' is getting to the vital point."

"I guess if it's southern it's got to be a good expression," said another judge.

I readily agreed.

If dayyenu could help me in a Georgia court, how could log-licking hurt in New York? My career would thus be underwritten by my race, my religion, and the unlimited possibilities of the city—yet each of my experiences would perist in reminding me that I was essentially a stranger in strange lands.

If there was a single instant which best represented the transition from Georgia to New York, from the sun-broiled courtrooms of

Fulton County to the plush apartments of Ruth Field, it was the case of *Aelony* v. *Pace*. That case unfurled in the depths of the South, but my own role in it was determined by my new colleagues of the northern Establishment.

On June 21, 1963, President Kennedy asked about one hundred leaders of the American Bar to the East Room of the White House where he, Vice President Johnson, and Attorney General Robert Kennedy charged the Bar with having failed miserably to uphold the rule of law in the civil rights battle raging in the South. The president was cool and factual; the vice president was electric, as he said, "It's a hell of a condition where a black soldier can get killed in a foreign foxhole but can't be served a hamburger in his home town."

The group formed itself into the Lawyers' Committee for Civil Rights Under Law and asked me, as a member of the Executive Committee, to undertake its first case:

Five youths, black and white, had been arrested in a voter registration campaign in Americus, Sumter County, Georgia, and were being held without bail under a discredited state sedition statute which carried a capital penalty.

No white member of the Georgia bar accepted my invitation to join in the attack on the sedition statute or the continued incarceration of these young people. The notables of Sumter County who expressed any position on this case supported the sheriff and the other authorities.

The county's state senator at that time was Jimmy Carter. He could have said something to the newspapers; at the very least, he could have told a few of his prominent friends that a sedition trial was an absurdity, and ought to be viewed as such. But the state senator totally ignored the travesty in his own county, and concentrated instead on quietly plotting his own future.

The case was, after all, a national issue and all Sumter County was in an uproar. I asked the local Superior Court judge at least to grant bail. He refused. The sheriff was worked up to the point of physically threatening any and all intruders, myself included. One of the demonstrators arrested was a fourteen-year-old girl, who came up before a Juvenile Court judge and was subsequently locked up in solitary confinement. Her circumstance was not known to me when the trial commenced, but it was later brought to my attention.

I requested the three-judge federal court to include her claim.

The court was convened with, fortunately, Elbert Tuttle as its presiding magistrate. The panel included, however, Judge Robert Elliot, who ten years earlier had declared his support of the county unit system, asserting: "I don't want these pinks, radicals, and black voters to outvote those who are trying to preserve our segregation laws and traditions."

Presiding Judge Tuttle subpoenaed the judge who had imprisoned the child. I undertook to serve the subpoena, accompanied by an enormous Irishman from my office named Tom Farrell, who wisely stood behind me. I knocked on his Honor's door. It was 10:00 P.M., and I could hear his footsteps clop threateningly in the night.

"Who's that?" he bellowed.

"I've got a subpoena to serve on you," I said.

"I don't want no damn subpoena," he said and slammed the door in my face. The next day Tuttle had the marshall bring the judge to court. While he was sitting on a bench outside waiting to be called, I asked him why he wouldn't accept the subpoena.

"Morris, was that you last night? It's a good thing the screen door was latched for if you had pulled it open I'd have shot you. I had a gun."

"You wouldn't shoot me, would you, judge?" I said in my best South Georgia drawl.

"Hell, I thought you were one of those federal whippersnappers."

We won the case, though Judge Elliott dissented. Tuttle had the demonstrators, including the hapless fourteen-year-old, released and the "sedition" law on which they were charged was ruled unconstitutional. Our victory robbed Georgia of a potent legal weapon, and represented a further inroad against the segregationist order. In a sense I *was* a "federal whippersnapper." After all, I had been retained by a Washington committee and, as in the past, I was relying on a federal court to guarantee that justice would be done.

It felt good to return to Georgia on a civil rights case, backed now by the pillars of the national legal establishment and no longer dependent on a livelihood in Georgia.

It is a paradox that in 1981 I would be a lonely dissenting voice in the Lawyers' Committee as it turned from the color-blind defense of individual rights and liberties to the promotion of racial

140

preferences of one group of Americans over another. This was the very evil I had traveled to Americus to oppose.

As a struggling lawyer in the year 1950 I had taken a part-time job as executive secretary of the Atlanta Chapter of the American Jewish Committee for the needed thirty dollars a month. I was attracted by the people I met and impressed by the scholarly cast of the Committee's national staff. Most of all, I was drawn to the character and intelligence of John Slawson, AJC's executive vice president and its prime galvanic force in the 1950s. Slawson was an extraordinarily cagey man, in the best sense of the word. He could circle around you for hours, managing somehow to draw out what he wanted—and what he wanted he conscientiously believed to be in the best, long-term interests of the Jewish people.

The American Jewish Committee, founded in 1906 by elitist German Jews, out of concerns generated by the Kishnev pogroms of 1903, was a small but influential institution in which the word *American* was emphasized. Under Slawson, the word Jewish in the name received equal emphasis. Indeed, the Committee became a redemptive movement in Jewish life for many such as myself. Its programs made identification possible for the Jew who was integrated into America but not necessarily drawn to a religious observance. Before my intimate associations with John Slawson, I suppose it can be said that I was a Jew not so much by my own choice as by the certain knowledge that the choice had been made by others. I realized that honorary white Protestant citizenship had always been open to me in Georgia, especially in Fitzgerald, but that the acceptance of the invitation would make me only a specimen, the Jewish convert, the baptized Jew.

As my ties with and associations within the Committee developed, I found the essence of what it meant to me to be Jewish. That essence lies in the collective unconscious of the people from whom I spring; the linkage of ourselves one to another; the ties that we all feel, to a greater or lesser extent, to Zion; and the determination to survive as Jews, free men and women wherever we may live.

I am not a religious man but I can cite an example of the collective unconscious from the pages of the Passover liturgy, the Hagaddah: "In every generation they arise to destroy us." The linkage of faith is referred to in the passage "All Israel is responsible for one another'' (Isaiah 2:3); the ties to Zion, in the phrase "for out of Zion shall go forth the law and the word of the Lord from Jerusalem'' (Micah 4:2); and the determination to survive, in a command from Deuteronomy, "Choose life.''

These principles perceived in the secular setting of the Committee compensated for my inadequate religious education and became the ties that bound me to my people and their service.

By 1963, Slawson was pushing my name for the AJC presidency. Slawson wished to broaden the Committee's constituency and particularly its leadership to include people from outside the Northeast and from other than German–Jewish backgrounds. He had once observed that what the Committee needed was "fewer bluebloods and more redbloods.''

As a liberal southerner with a Roumanian father, I was the perfect candidate. Moreover, at 45, I would be by far the youngest president in the Committee's history. The recent election of Kennedy had placed an emphasis on young leadership.

The job, which I accepted soon after arriving in New York, was no sinecure. During my four and a half years as president, the Committee continued to become more representative of the broader spectrum of Jewish life in America, while retaining its preeminence as a scholarly think-tank. It was officially known as a "non-Zionist'' organization, but since the mid-1940s had been fully committed to the importance and necessity of the Jewish state. My attitude toward Zion was now typical of that of the AJC membership. It was not likely that I would ever wish to settle in Israel, nor would my children—short of the unspeakable. I would like to have said "unthinkable'' but what Jew since the Holocaust can safely assume that culture is a shield?

When I was first associated with the Committee, I deliberately eschewed the phrase "the Jewish people.'' I was a Jew and an American—period. By the time I handed over the office to Arthur Goldberg, I felt there was no incompatibility between membership in the Jewish peoplehood and the American nation.

The Committee, even when it was no more than a small group of German Jews in New York with a number of correspondents around the country, was composed of what Edmund Burke might have called "the weightiest people.'' Once David Ben-Gurion asked me how many members we had, to which I responded, "We don't count AJC members, Mr. Prime Minister, we weigh them."

The "weight" of its members and the scholarship of its staff thrust me almost immediately after I became president into a struggle to remit the Roman Catholic church's charges of deicide against the Jews. Vatican II had taken steps toward that momentous end upon receiving elaborate studies by the American Jewish Committee, including citations of anti-Jewish references in Catholic literature. But with the death of John XXIII efforts to eliminate the derogatory references were languishing. John Slawson decided that direct intervention with the new pope was necessary.

We were fortunate to have on our side a Dutch cardinal, Augustine Bea, who had been appointed by John XXIII to oversee Catholic-Jewish relations. Not quite as warm and expansive as John himself, Bea was more intellectual and perhaps a bit shrewder; his role as intermediary would prove indispensable to our efforts. The Committee's staff had learned through Cardinal Bea's secretariat that there was powerful resistance in the Curia to the changes outlined in Vatican II before John's death on June 3, 1963. The reasons for this antipathy to a clear absolution of the Jews were theological, political, and economic. To absolve the Jews would require a whole rethinking and reinterpretation of scripture. In addition, the Vatican was irked because Israel had not internationalized Jerusalem; and finally, the church had economic interests and missionary outposts in key Arab countries.

An audience with the pope himself would be essential if we were to penetrate the intricate Vatican bureaucracy. We were granted that audience, but there was a catch. Our hearing could, if we wished, be public, in which case the pope and I, as president of AJC, would read our respective statements, and that would be the end of it. Or we could meet in private, but then the occasion would be unreported. We opted for the latter, as it was our only chance for a meaningful dialogue.

We wanted to take as much ammunition to Rome as we could. In particular, we wanted a powerful ally within the Catholic church. Ideally, he would be a conservative and not, like Cardinal Bea, tied too closely to Vatican II, to Pope John XXIII and the ecumenical effort. Slawson suggested that most redoubtable of all American

Catholic leaders, Francis Cardinal Spellman; we scheduled him to address the AJC on April 30, 1964. It was our hope to get him to condemn the deicide charge in his speech.

John Slawson and I met him in his Chancery two weeks before his appearance, and what a strange meeting it was. We were met at the door of his residence at Fiftieth Street and Madison Avenue by an Irish maid, clad in black with a lace collar. Ushered into the parlor to the left while we awaited the cardinal, I mused on the old-world Irish decor—plush, but certainly not stylish. The windows were framed in curtains that were adapted from what I imagined would have been seen in a Dublin town house in 1900.

Soon, Spellman padded into the room wearing his red yarmulka-type cap, his beady eyes glistening behind his glasses, which reflected the morning light from the windows facing Madison.

He was convivial until I stated our business. Then he visibly bristled. I tried to both flatter and needle him; I told him that he was the second most important Catholic in the world and that his voice would be heard in every antechamber in Rome. He didn't appear impressed. He grumbled that he did not yet know what he planned to say in his speech and I would have a copy the afternoon of April 30. I was therefore astounded when he finally stood in front of the AJC and pronounced the deicide charge "absurd." His theological arguments may not have equalled Cardinal Bea's, but his statement was unequivocal and the whole world would know of it. As it was, the speech was heard by Secretary of State Dean Rusk, who was a Committee guest on the dais that same evening.

Before departing for Rome, I went to see Rusk, reminded him of what Spellman said, told him the purpose of our trip, and asked if he would help us.

"The Embassy in Rome will do everything it can," he said, "but you know, we don't have diplomatic relations with the Vatican, and it's really a religious matter. I have to act very circumspectly."

"Can I tell him that you heard Spellman, and that you hope he'll issue a similar declaration?"

"Oh sure, you can tell him that."

This, then was the ammunition I took to Rome, accompanied by five other members of the Committee. I have never seen such dazzling opulence. All the princes of the church, it seemed, emerged from the pope's apartment as we approached. Their morning conferences were ending, and now it was our turn.

When Pope Paul VI appeared, I was struck by the way the glittering white garb flowing from head to toe utterly dwarfed his diminutive figure. Here was no jovial John XXIII, exuding warmth. Paul was an austere figure, pinch-faced, unsmiling, resembling very much an intellectual bureaucrat. He shook hands with all six of us. Then he astounded me by withdrawing, from the ample opening in the sleeve, a typed paper rolled as a scroll. He unfurled it and read. The paper was positive, defining the Jew in three general ways. The Jew was, first of all, a religious being, and the church acknowledged the patriarchs as spiritual antecedents. The Jew was also an ethnic creature, and, in this context, the church unequivocally asserted the equality of all men before God, a principle of the natural law. Finally, he said, the Jew was a political being, and on this—the State of Israel—he took no stand. The pope "strongly deplore[d] the horrible ordeals of which the Jews have been victims in recent years." He finished, and waited for us to voice our pleasure.

But I had come to Rome for something other than polite dissertations upon the obvious. I felt we were at the crossroads. I would not, as president of the American Jewish Committee, return to America with a pocket full of platitudes. At this juncture of Vatican Council II, I was determined that the occasion would produce a reaffirmation by Paul VI of the grace of John XXIII. But would pressing the issue of deicide be interpreted as disrespectful? If I wrangled with the pope, might it not create a sorrowful breach? On the other hand, had I not prepared for this moment? Didn't I have something also up my sleeve? Weren't Spellman and Rusk in our corner? I decided to advance: "Your Holiness, you know we're here to talk about the deicide charge."

Stiffly, he replied, "The matter is *sub judice*," By which he meant under judicial consideration.

"Millions of people are sorely distressed," I said.

"What do you mean?" he asked.

"There are millions of people hoping the Council will condemn the charge of deicide, and one of them is our own secretary of state, Mr. Dean Rusk."

The pope's face tensed. I then spoke of Cardinal Spellman's

speech, mentioning that he had stated flatly in public and in the presence of Mr. Rusk that the deicide charge was "absurd."

"Cardinal Spellman has spoken my sentiments," he blurted out.

I was taken aback. Had a significant victory been won? But the meeting was private. We could not release the pope's comment to the press. For two thousand years the Catholic church had helped propagate the belief that the Jews were to be held responsible for the crucifixion of Jesus, and now, in 1964, the pope himself told me it wasn't true. And I had to sit on it!

No more was said about deicide. One of our delegates had rosaries for her Catholic friends. When she asked the pope to bless them, he waved his hand and said, "I bless everything in the bag," and walked away.

He seemed somewhat upset.

Apparently no one had told him explicitly that we had come for a candid discussion of such a substantial matter. He had been prepared with pleasantries to which there could be no exception. Hearing Spellman's name, the pope, I believe, instinctively adopted his ally's position. Yet, it didn't have to be a public commitment. It could have died right there.

After we returned to our hotel, a messenger arrived to tell us that His Holiness had decided to publish the text of his statement defining the Jew in the *Osservatore Romano*. It was a happy surprise. I replied that our dialogue was supposed to be private, and that I would interpret publication of the pope's remarks as permission to make public the *whole* of our conversation. The messenger rushed back. He returned some time later with the news that the pope *still* intended to publish the material, and that I could release the text of the dialogue in New York. That is exactly what I did.

The pope had made a remarkable decision. Confronted with a situation perhaps more complex than anticipated, he chose to agree with the position of the American church as expressed by Cardinal Spellman. But he also demonstrated considerable good faith. He had not wanted to talk about deicide; that reluctance was what *sub judice* really signified. But when pushed, the Vatican chose to take a stand, the right stand.

Now the American Jewish Committee could spread the news throughout the Catholic world. The words of the pope were undeniable—there they were in the press. A mission I headed carried that news to the primates of Argentina, Chile, Peru, and Brazil.

My visit to Argentina raised issues in that country's large Jewish community which resonate today in the case of Jacobo Timerman, the tortured and exiled Argentinian Jewish publisher, and with respect to American international human rights policies as applied to Argentina.

When the American Jewish Committee accepted the invitation of its sister organization, the Argentine Instituto, to visit Argentina, the central Jewish body of Argentina known as the DAIA objected, arguing that the Jewish community should speak through its voice. The Instituto, as well as the Committee, rejected this view, contending that Jews were no more unified on religious, social, and political issues than others, and that no umbrella group could represent their diverse views.

Argentina was then undergoing one of its frequent outbreaks of terrorism. Over our protest, our delegation was escorted by police to guarantee our safety. While we were in Buenos Aires an attempt was made on the life of the former President Frondizi.

There is a pervasive anti-Semitic strain in Argentina. Of the half-million Jews in the country, not one was an officer in the army or air force, and the constitution required that the president be Catholic.

We visited the primate, who circumspectly told us that he agreed with the pope's view on the deicide question, "first because the pope is the pope" and second because of his own convictions. The Instituto arranged a dinner for our delegation. Despite a high admission charge, the main ballroom was sold out, and adjacent rooms were used. The glittering audience, Jewish and non-Jewish, was composed of government officials, diplomats, clergy, intellectuals, and professionals. The Instituto later reported that never before had such a cross section of Argentinian life turned out for a meeting under Jewish auspices.

The leaders of the DAIA had urged me not to confront the audience with the overt anti-Semitism in the country. As I rose to speak, I scanned the tense faces of the leaders of the "official" Jewish community.

"You and I," I began, "live in nations of immigrants. In this diversity there is strength when all elements are bound in national unity based on common respect and freedom."

I attacked extremists, drawing on the American experience with the Ku Klux Klan, and explaining how this organization was contained by "the outspoken opposition of a broad spectrum of decent citizens of every creed and color."

The audience broke into applause. The editor of *Criterio*, the Catholic intellectual journal, was standing, soon to be joined by waves of others. At a glance, I saw that the DAIA leaders were stunned, and, at first cautiously, then enthusiastically, they joined in this demonstration for the support of a principle. If anyone expected special pleading of the Jewish cause, they were to be disappointed. I was determined to go to the heart of the Jewish problem in Argentina without referring to anti-Semitism. But I was understood to be speaking for Jews, as I universalized the claims of all citizens in a pluralistic society. Argentinian Jews wanted no special treatment but only to be embraced in full and equal citizenship, a claim that I underlined, saying: "When a nation fails to protect any minority, in the long run the majority is at risk. Forces unleashed against one group cannot and will not be restricted. Persecution weakens the very fibre of the nation." I learned that night in Buenos Aires that the human heart yearns for social harmony and that human rights have a universal appeal although they enjoy a limited practice.

It was after this meeting that we went to the presidential palace for a conference with President Illia, a democratic centrist, and by profession a country doctor. On his desk was a picture of his hero, Franklin D. Roosevelt. Illia, regarded by many as too weak, was soon turned out of office by the armed forces. Terrorism escalated and even Jacobo Timerman's newspaper, *La Opinion,* supported the return of Juan Peron from exile. It was Timerman himself who arranged for our delegation to meet with a high military commander, who warned of the anti-Semitic forces in Argentina, then well supported by Arab money.

As I traveled through the Catholic world reminding it of the pope's words, Cardinal Bea became the standard-bearer in Rome itself. We still needed an official decree from the Vatican. It was Bea who drafted the document, and, after numerous amendments and emendations, the guilt of the Jews for the murder of Jesus Christ was officially remitted: ". . . What happened to Christ in His Passion cannot be attributed to the Jews of today." With that decree in hand, the American Jewish Committee was then able to instigate its campaign to expunge from Catholic textbooks all offensive depictions of the Jewish character.

What had we accomplished, really? I would not delude myself that even a single anti-Semite was transformed by the decree. Myths entrenched for ages are not erased simply because a pope in Rome is persuaded to say that he agrees with a cardinal in New York. But that is beside the point. We had done no more, and no less, than destroy an institutionalized justification for bigotry. Neither *Sanders* v. *Gray* nor *Aelony* v. *Pace* had eliminated racism, but they significantly eroded the legalistic tools of racist hatred. And so it was in Rome. No anti-Semite can now rationalize insidious prejudice by claiming to draw sanction from the Vatican.

Within two years, with the outbreak of the Six-Day War between Israel and seven Arab nations, I was forced to revise my view that the orthodox forms of religion were the chief obstacles to the development of warm ecumenism between Jews and Christians. I have never forgotten the uncomplicated acceptance and love for my Jewish family of some born-again fundamentalists such as Sheriff Dorminey in Fitzgerald. But by and large, conservative, mainstream, institutionalized religion did not, from my experience, practice the teachings of Jesus Christ. Jews felt far more comfortable with liberal churches and churchmen, who emphasized the social gospel of Jesus Christ rather than religious obscurantisms. It was in these circles, particularly with Quakers, Unitarians, and social activists within the larger denominations, that Jews could and did cooperate in programs for progress, on race, poverty, disarmament—the prophetic themes of Judeo-Christian culture.

The National and World Council of Churches and the segment of the Catholic church represented by John XXIII were the Christian elements with whom modern Jews felt the greatest commonality of spirit and purpose, more so perhaps than with the ultra orthodox of the Jewish faith.

When the Six-Day War erupted, on June 5, 1967, I, as president of the American Jewish Committee, called on liberal Christian church allies to join together in support of Israel at a giant rally in Lafayette Park across from the White House. I expected an outpouring from these churches with whom we had been linked on so many fronts. After all, Nasser had challenged not only Israel, but also the United Nations and internationally recognized maritime laws.

By the time the rally was mounted in Washington, Israel had destroyed the Egyptian Air Force; David of the Middle East had half-slaughtered the Arab Goliath. The underdog had triumphed, and many of our Christian allies vanished. Yet, Israel's cause was not less valid on the fourth day of the war than on the first. I could not believe it, but the "advanced" religious leaders of the Protestant establishment began turning their backs on Israel and Jewish-Americans, whose history and fates were intertwined with the survivors of Hitler's gas ovens.

In the thirteen years since, with notable exceptions, so-called liberal church organizations have made common cause with Arab, African, and other Third World nations which conduct campaigns of vilification of Israel, even siding against fellow Christians in Lebanon who are defended by Israeli arms.

The portents of this shift have reverberated within American political and social life with enormous consequences still not fully grasped and certainly not resolved.

But June 1967, the date Nasser ordered the UN observers out of the Sinai and marched on Israel, marks the beginning of the revival of a fearful collective unconscious in world Jewry. On the day after the attack there appeared in the halls of the American Jewish Committee Americans of Jewish ancestry so totally assimilated as to have changed the actual pronunciation of their names, haunted now by the specter of history and the common fate of Jews. I recall, for example, how Admiral Lewis Strauss (pronounced by him Straws) appeared at the Committee's headquarters and offered his services. My former wife Jane was strikingly perceptive, when she observed: "Jews are a people who hold hands around the world."

Since 1963, I had been serving in the human rights organizations of the United Nations. I was first sent there by President Kennedy in 1963 as representative to the Subcommission for the Prevention of Discrimination and the Protection of Minorities and later as our representative to the Human Rights Commission. I did not see this position as a platform from which to battle anti-Semites, though Soviet conduct would soon create the cause. My overriding preoccupation, of course, was the involvement of the American government in the whole spectrum of human rights around the world. I was keenly aware that I was representing the only great power that stands for human rights, though the United States in the 1960s took great abuse from quarters in which freedom and liberty were unknown or unpracticed. Doubtless we have shortcomings, as well as our share of historical shame. A society with its windows open to the world would be hard put to deny them. But this openness gives us, as well, the opportunity to flaunt the glorious difference between our society and that of a country such as the Soviet Union, whose vast engine of repression operates in the name of government.

I was no more "diplomatic" than our UN Ambassador Daniel Patrick Moynihan ten years later in my blunt comparisons of the United States human rights record with that of the Soviet bloc. One fact to which I was fond of alluding was undeniable: After American occupation, former totalitarian states such as Germany, Italy, and Japan became functioning democracies. Soviet occupation never birthed a democratic regime and, in the case of Czechoslovakia, strangled one that was full-grown.

In the mid-1960s the United Nations Human Rights Commission was engaged in drafting two international treaties, one outlawing all forms of racial discrimination, the other against religious intolerance. I was deeply involved in both, and worked to keep out of these draft treaties prohibitions on free speech and press. The Soviets, and most of the so-called Third World, were anxious to make criminal any expression which could be interpreted as "racism." When representatives pointed out that this would make a mockery of constitutional liberties in the West, most other delegates were totally unconcerned.

The racial covenant was completed, and though not ratified by the United States is in effect among 107 states. The 1975 General Assembly resolution that declared "Zionism is racism" attempts to employ this treaty as a Soviet instrument against Jewish nationalism rather than for its original laudable purpose.

I was soon directly embroiled in a struggle against institutionalized anti-Semitism in the USSR. I had gotten hold of a book entitled *Judaism Without Embellishment*, written by Tromfim Kichko and published by a Ukrainian press, whose lurid paperback cover resembled a reprint of Streicher's *Der Sturmer*; the crudest imaginable caricatures of Jews polluted its pages. I had sat patiently through a meeting while a Russian representative expostulated on the vitality of civil rights in the Soviet Union as guaranteed in their "Codex and Constitution." When he finished, I brandished the book and asked him to comment. He stormed, fumed, ranted—I was "provocative," my conduct was impermissible, and so on.

The basis of Russian opposition to all comments on their human rights practices was that the critic was intruding on the "internal affairs" of the USSR. Of course, one of the contradictions in trying to deal with human rights on an international level is that a violation always occurs within some country. After all, genocide today is seldom committed by pirates on the open seas. And if a country wants to participate in the open forum of the United Nations, it must be prepared to confront the indignation of others. This exchange is, after all, one of the reasons the UN exists. No one has ever suggested an invasion of Russian soil to liberate its captive Jewish population or for that matter its Lithuanians, Georgians, and Muslims; but if the Russians expect to participate in the international community, they, no less than the United States, have to hear the views of others. As I put the matter: Since the adoption of the Universal Declaration of Human Rights by the General Assembly in 1948, no nation has the sovereign right to violate the human rights of its own citizens.

In any case, on this occasion the Russians were very sensitive about Kichko's book. The Soviets actually promised to stop its publication, probably because of the uproar the exposure generated in the French and Italian Communist parties—a significant concession, because the book was published by the prestigious Ukrainian Academy of Science, and no one in Moscow wanted to offend the historically irritable citizens of Kiev.

It turned out to be an impermanent victory, for the Russians since have embarked on anti-Semitic programs, directly and by proxy, on a scale instituted by no great power since World War II. Kichko's books are again being circulated in the Ukrainian language, and in Russian as well.

As I got to know my Russian colleagues, I began to confront them not only with their anti-Semitism but with the wide-scale violation of human rights in the Gulag Archipelago and throughout their vast dominions. I also chastised them for their enormous miscomprehension of American society. I felt very frustrated because I knew that in any fair debate our society, for all of its flaws, could stand inspection, but Soviet society could not. On the other hand, I was being constantly taunted by the Russians about the glaring inequities in my own country, particularly before the passage of the Civil Rights Act of 1965, which ended segregation in places of public accommodation in some of the southern states. My answer was to invite twelve delegates of the UN Commission, including two Russians, to be my guests on a visit to Atlanta, Georgia. When we arrived, Atlanta was pure tumult. Lester Maddox was not yet governor but already an influential political force, and every pocket of the city was seething.

Mayor Ivan Allen, a pillar of the business community, as well as Martin Luther King, Sr., would help guide my guests through the byways of the city, which was then emerging from its past with much accomplished and much more to do. The Russians were particularly flabbergasted by our openness. We showed them angry black Muslims, Ku Kluxers, and our urban slums, but finally we drove into affluent black suburbs, stopped off for tea and morning coffee at one of the gracious, sprawling homes that make up the neighborhood. A few even had private swimming pools.

"Are all these homes lived in by black people?" asked one Boris Ivanov.

"I'm sorry if the facts don't fit your views, Mr. Ivanov," I said. "Mayor Allen is an important capitalist who has been working like hell to achieve racial justice. But if you want to listen to the beating of proletarian hearts, we can always go back and see another Klan demonstration."

I did not view the black problem then in terms of the diminishing significance of race and the persistent growth of a black underclass. But even in 1964, if Ivanov and I had engaged in an informed and honest discussion, he would have been obliged to admit that a black middle class was emerging rapidly in a capitalist society. I would have been obliged to confess that generations of prejudice and neglect left the United States with a group of blacks who were not making it. The fault, however, as Ivanov would have argued, did not lie with the capitalists, a few of whom had even been in the forefront of the civil rights struggle.

Such a person was Mayor Allen, at the top of the pyramid of Atlanta's power structure. He published an account of how he came to support the Civil Rights Act in the mid-1960s, relating that I visited him at the request of President Johnson to obtain his testimony, as a southern mayor before the Senate Committee on Commerce. As Allen remembers, he was seated in a rocker in his office while I spoke about the point of my mission.

"You're familiar with the public-accommodations bill," I said.

"That's all we hear down here lately."

"The South's pretty upset, I understand."

"Upset?" he said. "I don't know of a single important official in the South who's come out for it."

"That's what I came to see you about. The president wants you to support the bill. He wants you to go to Washington and testify."

This stunned him, but he ended up as the only deep South mayor publicly in favor of the bill.

It hadn't taken me long to realize that the decision to come to New York was correct. Within two years I was president of both The Field Foundation and the American Jewish Committee. At the United Nations my voice, however frustrated by circumstances, was being heard. I was actively engaged in drafting two significant UN conventions, outlawing all forms of racial discrimination and upholding religious freedom. On a side trip to Bonn from the Human Rights Commission meeting in Geneva in 1965, I presented to the German Minister of Justice Ewald Bucher a legal framework within which West Germany, without violating its constitution, could extend the statute of limitations for Nazi crimes still unpunished. Bonn did subsequently extend the period for these prosecutions.

I was ascending, indeed, and my next step was Washington. In 1965, Lyndon Johnson, acknowledging my roots in the civil rights movement and my service in cases like *Aelony* v. *Pace*, asked me to cochair with William T. Coleman a preliminary White House Conference on Civil Rights. The venerable A. Philip Randolph would be the honorary chairman. The auguries were encouraging, but the task would turn out to be an unhappy experience, one that would permanently influence my attitudes toward radicalism and unbridled social expectations.

The conference had been promised by Johnson, always aware of the moving finger of history, in a burst of exuberance following his landslide victory over Goldwater in 1964. He expected the blacks, as they now wished to be called, and maybe whites to acknowledge the administration's vast accomplishments and to celebrate the leader who had dared to say to Congress in a speech following Kennedy's assassination, "We shall overcome."

But the Watts riots intervened between the decision and the conference, and Vietnam sapped resources for Johnson's war on social neglect.

I had enormous respect for Johnson's commitment to racial justice. He was ten times bigger than the prejudices of his background, and his political passion was infectious. Never a Kennedy lover, he was delighted to have legislated what Kennedy could only rhapsodize about. Even after certain newly discovered black leaders were becoming publicly disaffected, he believed that the conference could be an LBJ showcase.

Anyone who expects praise and is criticized instead feels rebuffed, hurt. When I met with Johnson in 1965, a few months before the conference was scheduled, he was seething with wounded vanity. I remember him bending over his constantly chattering ticker tape news machine and reading that Joe Rauh, Jr. had complained about a black in South Carolina being persecuted by the local authorities. "Goddamit!" Johnson roared at an aide. "Tell your friend Joe Rauh that the president of the United States hasn't got the time to take care of some stoplight violation in Abbeville, South Carolina."

Then he calmed down, proud and patriarchal. He was appointing Thurgood Marshall Solicitor General. "I'm getting that man ready for the Supreme Court."

The conference had been promised by Johnson at Howard University that June, in a triumphant commencement speech, written by Daniel Patrick Moynihan, then an official of the Labor Department. Paraphrasing Michael Harrington, Johnson called the blacks "another country within our country."

The executive committee of the conference included the mainstays of the civil rights movement: Roy Wilkins of the NAACP, Whitney Young of the Urban League, Martin Luther King, Jr. of the Southern Christian Leadership Conference, James Farmer of CORE, Dorothy Height of the National Council of Negro Women, John Lewis of the Student Nonviolent Coordinating Committee, and Jack Greenberg of the NAACP Legal Education and Defense Fund. They were joined by black academicians including Kenneth Clark and Vivian Henderson. There was also a generous representation

155

of sympathetic whites. Only the black firebrands were missing.

I opened the planning session—the plenary conference was to be held the following spring—with a speech in which I tried to emphasize that the purpose was to address solutions rather than to assign blame; that the problems facing blacks were not theirs alone, but should be understood as the collective agony of the American people. I stand by that speech, although to some it may appear outdated by the great tides of black separatism and anger.

Three storm signals were immediately evident. The first came from Martin Luther King, Jr. He was profoundly at odds with Lyndon Johnson over Vietnam. Martin's early opposition to the war was, at first, very disturbing to black leadership. The war itself, however, was not enough to keep him away. What seemed to trouble him was that he equated the government's Vietnam policy with American racism. He was convinced that such a wanton expedition could never have been sustained against whites. Therefore he could hardly view a White House conference of the Johnson administration as a legitimate expression of the black struggle. Bayard Rustin, his old mentor, was importunate, but Martin stood his ground. Only reluctantly did he agree to attend one meeting to reaffirm, no doubt, his continuing respect for Rustin, Wilkins, and the others.

In addition, there was a vociferous reaction against the conference by radical blacks. Bill Coleman, a brilliant, successful black lawyer, had met with some of the radicals in Philadelphia to explain our purpose and to elicit a degree of understanding if not support. But they remained hostile and told Coleman that they would use the conference as a forum for attacking the government. They proved as good as their word. Their leaders appeared on television and in the newspapers to lambast Wilkins, Randolph, and everyone else. The old tigers of the civil rights movement were being set upon by their would-be successors. Perhaps it is the sad way of all revolutions. For me, the most telling sign that the old common crusade had splintered was the undisguised reluctance to invite Pat Moynihan. Moynihan was the author of a recently published Labor Department report on the black family. It was a deeply disturbing tract that identified the pathologies in the lives of many black families as main stumbling blocks to social and economic progress. The "Moynihan Report" thus committed the cardinal sin of focusing on conditions which could not now be solely attributed to racial persecution, though the report admitted that the problem had its roots in past mistreatment. Moynihan's clear implication was that court victories and legislation would not suffice to elevate the state of growing numbers of black families with absent fathers. It was doubtless a national problem and had to be addressed.

Though deploring the situation, Moynihan had never suggested moral or intellectual inferiority. The object of his attack was American society. I was dismayed that some conference leaders did not wish to hear his views. This was ironic because it was Pat who had planted the idea of the conference in the president's speech in the first place. The obvious role for him in the conference would have been participation in a panel discussion on the black family. The executive committee wavered until the last moment. Then the White House finally stepped in guaranteeing that Moynihan could participate if he chose. I was asked to invite him, apparently because no one else volunteered.

"Do you realize what a hornet's nest you've stirred up?" I asked him. "Do you know how hard it's been to get you invited? I assume you've read the dissection of your report by Benjamin Peyton, research director of the New York Council of Churches."

"No, what did he say?"

"It's a very serious attack."

"What kind of academic writes an attack on another academic without sending him a copy?" he asked, not disguising his scorn.

When Pat did appear at the panel he was assaulted mercilessly. Speaker after speaker rose at the conference to condemn either Johnson or Attorney General Nicholas Katzenbach for failing to enforce civil rights statutes. Political or social strategies that smacked of self-help or applied work ethic were condemned. One dominant demand was for federal spending, lots of it. But Johnson thought that he, through his war on poverty, was already doing enough for a now palpably ungrateful constituency.

The conference had not achieved LBJ's purpose. Neither Coleman nor I was asked to chair the plenary spring conference called "To Fulfill These Rights." We had failed to make the people stand up and cheer, and our punishment was assignment to the executive committee. When the plenary conference commenced the White House held its breath.

The sole purpose now was to contain outbursts, ward off demonstrations, and avoid physical confrontations. Invitations were carefully screened, and security precautions were given high priority. The ill-starred conference passed over without violence, but it accomplished little.

This was my first experience with raw black militance, my wound from black colleagues in the struggle for racial equality in which I had been engaged for twenty years. But my hurt was obscured by my anger at LBJ because of his insatiable desire for praise. At the same time, I had witnessed the first black outburst that I could honestly describe as black racism. In 1965 I was still unwilling to do the black man the honor of examining his conduct as critically as that of whites.

Beginning in 1969, when I became president of Brandeis University, I no longer gave automatic support to prevailing black opinion and came to recognize such response as patronizing at best and a reverse form of racism at worst, hurtful to whites as well as to blacks. Some black friends have been offended by my attempt (not always successful) at the neutral treatment of color. But this principle was at the core of my earliest objection to segregation and support of equality for blacks.

After the White House Conference, my active life in New York temporarily erased bad memories of the breach opening between white liberals and black leadership. I returned to the United Nations confident that the American record in civil rights, fortified by recent advances in legislation and court decisions, could, like our American productivity, be valuable foreign policy assets.

Arthur Goldberg was now the UN Ambassador, and while still holding my position on the Human Rights Commission, I was made his senior advisor. Unlike his predecessor, Adlai Stevenson, Goldberg was not a skillful public performer. But even more than Stevenson, he was a man who would fight personally for you if he believed in your cause and respected your intentions. Amid the rhetoric and frequent treacheries of the United Nations, his comradeship would prove valuable.

His support was particularly welcome because the Soviets had not forgotten the Kichko affair, and I was singled out as a particularly troublesome American. The matter came to a crisis during a human rights controversy over an American statement summoning all nations to cease persecuting Jews, to extend cultural freedoms, and to liberalize emigration statutes.

The Russian response was that the Americans were in no position to raise these issues as long as we were engaged in aggressive actions in Vietnam. Then they zeroed in on me. Jacub Ostrovsky, the Russian delegate to the Human Rights Commission and my most persistent antagonist at the UN, saw fit to remind me on the commission floor that I "was not at a meeting of the American Jewish Committee"; that I was trying to serve two masters; and "obeying the orders of the Zionists and the Jews of America." He added further derogatory comments about the AJC.

Ostrovsky was really attempting to show that no Jew is qualified to speak on human rights in the United Nations forum because no Jew can approach the subject disinterestedly, and his statement resounded with distinct overtones of a charge against me of dual loyalties as an American Jew. Repetition of such remarks on three occasions demonstrated that he represented an official position of his government. The same mentality that had produced the Kichko book was now present in the rooms and corridors of the Human Rights Commission.

I accused Ostrovsky and his government of bigotry. Goldberg's support was immediate and strong, but I needed a voice from Washington as well. The Soviets had to know that this sort of behavior would not be tolerated by the organs of government that determine American policy vis-à-vis the Soviet Union.

To a plea that the State Department reject Ostrovsky's ploy, Dean Rusk responded: "I should like to inform you that . . . the United States Mission to the United Nations, under instructions from the Department of State, made formal representations to the Soviet mission in New York, at a high level, to make it absolutely clear that Mr. Ostrovsky's conduct was considered to be a regrettable departure from the standards that should prevail. . . ."

This, in the language and practice of international politics, was the appropriate move. After some hemming and hawing, the Russians desisted. It was for me one of those small but telling victories, drawing the line between what is and what is not permissible in civilized discourse. And for the second time in two years I had watched Dean Rusk throw in his weight in defense of a principle of human dignity.

The following year the Human Rights Commission was embroiled in yet another collision with the Russians. We had received reports of widespread oppression of intellectuals in the Soviet Union, and Goldberg was very upset. He asked if he might sit in my chair at the Human Rights Commission and deliver a speech. It seemed that the Soviet's brutality toward the ornaments of Russian civilization had touched the man's deepest moral nerve.

As soon as he began, Ostrovsky left his chair and was replaced by Malik, the Russian ambassador. He and Goldberg dueled. A new and more significant battle began when the time came to draft a report. I was amazed and impressed with how much the Russians cared. The fear the great Bear lives with! He fears the most subtle statement in the most obscure journal, and he fears it because he fears having the outside world learn truths in official documents that are distributed worldwide.

Goldberg's statements were successfully published in the final report of the Human Rights Commission—another victory. Whenever I hear it said that the actions of the United Nations make little real difference, I recall the Russian frenzy over that report. If they care enough to be embarrassed, perhaps they may care enough to exercise at least some restraint the next time a Sakharov or a Solzhenitzyn chooses to speak the truth. But the UN, in which the Maldive Islands and Granada have the same vote as the great powers, is a Tower of Babel, especially when the United States tries to win favor rather than lead by consistent adherence to principle, standing alone when necessary and using our veto in the Security Council in extreme cases.

It was in the midst of the 1960s that the condition of Jews behind the Iron Curtain took on a dimension far more personal for me than the cloistered debates at the United Nations. Under the auspices of the American Jewish Committee, I traveled to Roumania and visited the surviving fragments of my father's family. On this journey I would see firsthand the conditions under which Roumanian Jews lived.

My trip was not, however, spawned by an interest in sociology or politics. I wanted to find my dead father in the community that shaped him, and through him find more of myself. I wanted to learn all the facts that daddy would never discuss, no matter how I prodded.

And I hoped I would find and bring to my mother proof that Sam Abram was correct when, in moments in which he felt diminished, he would say to her, "I didn't come from *drek.*" Sometimes he would add that his mother bought him a handsome overcoat for the trip to America, and he would mention the pocket money that permitted visits in Central Europe before the steerage passage to the New World.

I wanted to be able to say to mother, "It all was true," and so it was, except that my father's name had not been Sam but Elijah, for "Samuel" in Yiddish is *Schmul*, and Schmul was the name of my father's brother, whom I met in Vaslui, Roumania. And this fact unraveled for me the mystery of why Sam Abram never, never called himself Samuel. But why he used the name Sam in America I do not know.

In 1964 I drove out of Bucharest with my wife and daughter Annie and Abe Karlikow, an AJC man who would act as our interpreter. That afternoon we reached Vaslui, where Schmul and his family were waiting. He was so much like the old man—that full face, the twinkling eyes, the squarish body, and familiar smile. He even dressed the same, in a button-down sweater and a broadbrim hat. The similarity in gestures was uncanny—the hand reaching into the pocket to extract a round, ponderous watch could have been my father's hand.

Schmul and Sam were two of nine children, the only Jewish family in the nearby village of Buchesti. Sam, aged nine, was apprenticed to a harness maker in Vaslui, ten miles away. Five thousand Jews had lived in Vaslui, but now there were only 250 families. Many of them, like my father, had left long ago to avoid army service. The government prohibited emigration, however, and just one out of five made it to America. You had to walk to the coast to a town named Costanza and there wait your chance. Two of Sam's brothers were killed in World War I; only Schmul returned from the trenches. A nephew died in the Fascist pogrom of 1941. Two nieces made it to Israel, and a third landed in Los Angeles. Sam had long since wound up in Georgia.

When I walked into Schmul's humble house, I saw framed on his wall a faded photograph of myself and my sister Ruthanne, aged four and two, respectively. For all these years Schmul had been expecting us. He opened his heart with hospitality, pressed us

161

continuously with brandy, cherry cake, wine mixed with soda, and Turkish coffee. He would not let us take them to a restaurant, for they were obviously cautious about being seen outside with foreigners, and we did not do much talking with them in cars rented from the Roumanian tourist service.

Vaslui was a railroad town. The locomotives were steam engines, some larger than those daddy and I had stoked forty years earlier in Fitzgerald. I gazed bemusedly at these hissing, chugging behemoths, remembering the long Sundays Sam Abram and I had spent in the round house.

I visited my father's synagogue and the old harness shop. The synagogue was run-down, but it was probably beautiful in Sam's day. It was painted like a Moldavian church and still had a flavor of an almost medieval Judaism.

Schmul was surprised that I did not speak Yiddish. "Didn't your father teach you Yiddish?"

"No," I replied, concealing from him the fact that Sam, in my mother's presence, did not acknowledge that he knew the language at all.

I learned what I had come to find out. I didn't need to reinvent these people; their dignity loomed before me. It was, to be sure, something that Jane had recognized in my father, years before.

So impressed was I with these gentle and intelligent relatives— Schmul, his wife Gizella, my aunts Sarah and Rifka, the nieces and nephews—that I took my mother there four years later. On that visit, after much importuning, I persuaded Schmul to ride in our rented car to Buchesti to see where dad lived until his apprenticeship and, incidentally, to see the grain mill, the largest village industry, confiscated from Schmul when the Communists took over at the end of World War II. Schmul, dressed in a brown prewar suit of excellent quality, rode uneasily. He had not seen his mill since it was seized and was concerned that he would be remembered as an exploiter of people or that some apparatcheck would report his sudden interest in his old capitalist enterprise.

We arrived in Buchesti. I alighted from the car to take color Polaroid snapshots. A crowd assembled to watch the magic in amazement. The postman recognized Schmul, who was afraid to get out of the car. A shout went up, "Schmul is back!" A crowd of friendly people jostled to see him in the car. Now reassured,

162

Schmul alighted, shaking hands, hugging old people, pointing to me and my camera and displaying both proudly.

For a moment my father was restored to me, the frightened man who could nevertheless make such warm human contact as would wipe his fears away.

Had I succeeded in showing mother that daddy came from a solid family? I don't really know. By then mother was seventy-seven and her personal thoughts more private than before. However, she was visibly moved when Schmul initially embraced her.

10

I CONFESS that if there was ever an experience in my life that toughened me for the crucial battle with illness, it was my tenure as president of Brandeis University.

Brandeis, founded as I was leaving Oxford, had long loomed to me as the new promised land, the nonsectarian university founded under Jewish auspices where the Jeffersons, Hamiltons, and their Jewish equivalents could meet and espouse their differences. Athens had, in its small way, encouraged my ideal; the University of Georgia, for all of its shortcomings, provided my first broader visions; the atmosphere of Chicago and Oxford were further reinforcement. And Brandeis, the Jewish contribution to academic society in the new world, was synonymous in my mind with cosmopolitanism at its finest. And there was room for everybody— Jew, Gentile, white, and black. I was deluded enough to dream that America's ferment in 1968 could somehow be shaped and put to good ends on a distinguished university campus. Now, my only regret is that I did not find a way somehow to fight harder for that dream. My disenchantment was with people, not with the idea of a university, and certainly not with Brandeis.

If Brandeis fulfilled a long-standing dream, from a personal and practical viewpoint it was also a godsend. I was at an impasse; the war in Vietnam was darkening my spirit and gutting my political ambitions. Senator Jacob Javits was up for reelection in 1968, and friends urged on me the idea that he was vulnerable. The Democratic nomination was mine for the asking, first, because not too many other people wanted to take on the formidable senior senator, and second, because Bobby Kennedy had been a friend since his brother's election in 1960. When I tested the waters, Kennedy, then the junior senator, and several state party leaders gave me their blessings. I was on my way. Even if Javits, as expected, beat me, I hoped to do well enough to guarantee that I would be a force to reckon with in the future.

Yet I, like most Democrats, could no longer ignore the hard facts about the Vietnam war.

In the fall of 1967, I expressed my agonizing concerns about the war to Kennedy, who said he shared them. I told him that while I was quite willing to oppose Javits with his and the president's support, I was no masochist and would not run if he and the president were divided on my candidacy. When I suggested that I might separate from the president's war policy, Kennedy, the practical politician, replied that I could not do so and run as the Democratic senatorial candidate on the ticket Johnson headed in 1968. As of that date Kennedy had not felt morally obliged to speak out firmly against the war, nor, I am sorry to say, had I.

In January 1968, President Johnson sent me, as head of a prominent Jewish contingent, to Vietnam to examine the swelling refugee problem. By the time I left Saigon just a few days before the Tet offensive, three events had convinced me that American policy in Vietnam was wholly disastrous.

The first eye-opener was a helicopter flight I took out of Da Nang to see an area supposedly cleared of Viet Cong by American bombardment and search and destroy missions. I was accompanied by a colonel and sergeant pilot. The sergeant refused to land in the cleared area; he said it was too dangerous. The colonel, conscious of my reaction, insisted. The pilot picked a spot where there was little foliage or underbrush and even then, he only touched down lightly and took off again, shooting straight up, making sure to avoid fire from the nearby bushes. The sergeant knew, if the colonel would not admit it, that bombardment and patrols had not made this area secure.

Another event was even more convincing. I was breakfasting at a military outpost when there arrived the most disheveled job-lot of United States soldiers that I had ever seen. The night before, they had survived a murderous firefight in support of a South Vietnamese unit to which they were attached. My colleagues and I were present when the American officer briefed his superiors. The South Vietnamese troops had apparently vanished. There was no choice but to retreat, sustaining serious losses in the process. "Why is it," I asked, no doubt embarrassing everyone present, "that a bunch of pajama-clad guerrillas are able to take on a well-trained, well-equipped unit, backed by the full force of American weaponry and manpower?"

"Because the enemy has a cause," he answered me, without blinking an eye, without hesitating, without attempting any excuse or even pretending that an excuse was possible. That officer knew what was coming; he was no coward, but he was ready to go home that day.

The clincher for me was a conversation I had with our ambassador to South Vietnam, Ellsworth Bunker, a former schoolmate of my law partner, Lloyd Garrison. "Do you think the Americans and the South Vietnamese can prevail?" I asked, and he replied that there could be no doubt of it, given sufficient persistence and more men.

"How many more?" I asked.

"We will need at least a half million more Americans for at least another five years."

"Would the American people stand for that?"

"That's a political question," said Bunker.

I was despondent when I returned home. If I supported Johnson, I'd be supporting a policy that would suck the life out of the American people. If I criticized the policy, or stayed quiet, he'd pull tight the purse strings of his supporters from which I needed to draw my campaign funds. I had no doubts that Johnson would do this; his man in New York, Edwin Weisl, National Committeeman and the president's personal lawyer, read me the riot act when

I told him that I could not defend the president's Vietnam policy as it then stood. I simply could not give my full support to the administration's policy in Southeast Asia. Perhaps naively, I thought that I could devise a compromise policy that Johnson and his surrogate in New York would tacitly agree not to oppose. With great care I drew up a memorandum showing how we might negotiate ourselves out of Vietnam while protecting the lives and liberties of our Southeast Asian allies. I did not denounce the war as immoral but acknowledged it to be unwinnable at any price America was willing to pay.

I went over the statement with Kennedy, whose disagreements with Johnson had widened by February 1968. Kennedy asked that I develop my ideas further with his close friend Burke Marshall, the former head of the Civil Rights Division of the Department of Justice, a man whom I also knew and respected deeply. When the policy statement was fleshed out, the proposal was again referred to Kennedy. He said that he felt it would enable him to campaign for me "without embarrassment." So far, so good. I then sent the statement to Weisl, who soon called to say that not only would the White House find the proposal totally unacceptable, but that his law partner, Cyrus Vance, also disagreed with it. I thought that I could change the White House opinion by discussing the matter with Vice President Humphrey, to whom I took the paper. Humphrey said that while he could not endorse the proposal, I should simply publish it and "run," for though the president would stew and fume, he would soon realize that he had no choice but to accept me if I won the nomination.

Meanwhile, Congressman Joseph Y. Resnick, a very rich man, announced his candidacy on a platform of complete support for Johnson's war policy. Now it was clear that the Democratic party would be split between the Kennedy and Johnson wings, providing a very poor base from which to take on Jack Javits.

As my public aspiration and private conscience wrangled, the other dream that had really been lurking in my mind for years became a reality. I wanted to succeed Abram L. Sachar, the first president and founding father of Brandeis University. Part of me, it seemed, had done nothing for years except compile the right sort of résumé for the job. I was old enough, I had served the Jewish community in any number of public capacities, and I was known

167

to be a good fund raiser. So many Rhodes scholars had fulfilled Cecil Rhodes' plan for public service through university presidencies. In 1948, the year I began my career in Georgia, Sachar was busy laying the groundwork for his new university in Waltham, Massachusetts. Sixteen years later I was resting on a beach in Miami when a friend said to me, "You're in your forties and you've done a lot. But do you have any final goals?"

"I'd like to be president of Brandeis if Abe Sachar ever quits," I said. I had not been dwelling on the prospect, but I was conscious that Sachar was approaching retirement age.

If I had a premonition in 1964, by 1968 I saw Brandeis as the best way to realize my dream of public service. I wanted Sachar's job more than I wanted Javits's and now the opportunity materialized. As if on cue, without the slightest initiative on my part, I received a call from Larry Wien, a lawyer, real estate tycoon, and philanthropist, who also happened to be Chairman of the Board of Brandeis University. He made an appointment without stating any purpose, but I knew—I just knew. When he came, I listened as he told me how much better it would be than the United States Senate. "I want to tell you," he said, "I know Abe Ribicoff, and that man would rather be president of Brandeis than senator from Connecticut. I can guarantee you that. But Abe just hasn't got the qualifications, and you have. Think it over."

I said I would.

As soon as I discussed the matter with Jane, I was ready to accept—despite the fact that we had just moved into the city from Larchmont and were still busy decorating our new apartment. I was a bit surprised when I encountered a strongly negative reaction from my two senior partners, Judge Simon Rifkind and Lloyd Garrison. The latter had been the dean of the University of Wisconsin Law School in the 1940s and said bluntly, "The university, like public life, is intensely political, except that professors are exceptionally petty." Indeed, both Rifkind and Garrison had been supportive of my senatorial ambitions, and their response to this new opportunity was disturbing. But my mind was made up.

I wonder how much more strongly Garrison would have worded his advice had he known that Abe Sachar would insist on retaining, with the newly minted title of chancellor, an office on campus, plus

168

his old presidential residence, and full secretarial assistance. He was thus in a position to try to hold the reins of power, with me as front man. Both former Senator William Benton, one of the trustees, and Arthur Goldberg warned that these concessions to Sachar would prove a mistake. "Insist that he be off the campus," said Goldberg.

I was confident enough to think that I could field almost any challenge, but Benton's words kept ringing in my ear. He said that any former chief executive, not to mention a powerhouse like Sachar, would create problems if he retained an office with a prestigious title and residential privileges. Benton openly urged the trustees to grant Sachar nothing more than a generous pension. I took these warnings to Wien, and to Wien's vice-chairman, Robert S. Benjamin, whom I knew better. Both Benjamin and his wife, Jean, were, in fact, colleagues from the United Nations, and I trusted them. It was their honest view that Sachar understood his new position and would stay within its boundaries.

I was persuaded. In addition to Wien's reassurances, and Benjamin's, there was my contract, which made me the sole executive officer. I had insisted on that clause, and my legally oriented mind assumed it would cover any misunderstanding. That was only the first serious difference between my experience as a lawyer and the realities of academia.

During the transition period before my inauguration, I commuted weekly to Boston, meeting faculty, administrative staff, trustees, patrons, and whatever student representatives were available during the summer. These months also included numerous meetings with Sachar and myself. By September, our relationship had begun to sour, although I doubt that he and I have any disagreement whatsoever about the nature of his or any other university. That's why I view his later enmity as so pointless.

Who could deny or forget that, when it mattered most, Sachar was Brandeis? Nothing I could do, however startling or innovative, could obscure his legacy. It was Sachar who had the vision, Sachar who got the money, Sachar who made Brandeis University respected, Sachar who brought such teachers as Abraham Maslow and had the good sense to appoint to tenure a leading critic, Philip Rahv, despite the fact he had no college degree.

Sachar had called his school "a school of the spirit . . . a dwelling place of permanent values." Like me, he believed in Brandeis as an elitist institution, a commonwealth of scholars, which would transmit the profound learning of the centuries from one generation to another and explore the frontiers of knowledge. It had been Sachar's vision of excellence that attracted me to Brandeis in the first place.

What I wanted to contribute was my own emphasis on a core curriculum, inspired teaching, and the importance of a university as a learning and research center. I would tie this conviction to the idea that the university must be free of outside political influences, and never itself become politicized. It was a very natural apprehension in a man like myself, who had grown up on politics, but who knew that only a university without ideology could be a place of learning.

I was also convinced that the private universities served as influential models for public institutions.

The nature of a young university will be largely determined by the way its chief officers conceive its purpose. I, like Sachar, was committed to keeping Brandeis' Jewish identity as a sponsored school that held open its doors to anyone who could qualify. Sachar had, after all, named the school after a Jew who reached every segment of the American population with his humane legal intellect.

At no point in our relationship did Sachar and I ever debate a matter of principle; if he saw in me some sort of threat to what he stood for, I never heard of it. But I did see in Sachar from the beginning an extraordinary and openly expressed rancor against many of the faculty, students, and community leaders. Through the summer he sought and received large sums of money from donors, and then announced each success as if he were in a competition with me.

The watershed event in our relationship occurred without warning just before I assumed the presidency. Late one afternoon, we were sitting together in his office when he turned and fixed me with a piercing stare, magnified by his thick glasses. "As I leave the presidency," he said, "I want you to know that I intend to abide by my agreement and leave the running of this university to you so long as you do not change its character or mission—because, if you

170

do, I want you to know that I will take the matter to the board and fight you until the bitter end.''

I was startled and angered. ''Abe,'' I said, ''there is no reason for you to think that I would try to change the fundamentals of this institution. We are as much in accord as a past and future president can be, and I resent your statement, particularly at this time and under these circumstances. I intend to be the president of this university, and you can do what you wish when you wish.''

After this conversation Sachar and I would never again be on particularly good terms. About a week later, I learned that the faculty, the students, and many trustees were upset, and rightfully so, that tight university funds were being used to build a Sachar Auditorium to memorialize the founder.

Another event would prove of far greater consequence. I was asked to meet with representatives of a faculty-student committee, which included delegates from the black student body. They wanted to take up a number of issues: Black Studies, black professors, black scholarships, black assembly spaces, Vietnam, the sins of Abe Sachar; everything except the standards of Brandeis University.

A few days before, Abe Sachar had implied I might be unwilling to fight for the standards that I believed in with my very soul. And now here was a collection of students and teachers who assumed I was responsible for what they thought Sachar had done to them, for what John Calhoun had done to the blacks, and for what Lyndon Johnson was doing to Southeast Asia. The irony of the last was particularly cruel because I came to Brandeis partially because I could not support the war effort. Vietnam had helped bring me there, and Vietnam would cloud my stay.

A few months before I took charge as president, in the wake of Martin Luther King's assassination, Sachar had agreed to a number of proposals in order to pacify blacks. I saw his agreement as a sell-out of the very principles to which he was committed. He knew that someone else would have to cover his promissory notes.

The first demand, and the one which eventually proved to be the most troublesome, was for a black studies program. In addition, the committee had wanted a number of scholarships, available only to blacks, to be named after Martin Luther King. Third, they had asked the president's committee to bring in a large number of disadvantaged black students; and, finally, they demanded the appointment of a number of black teachers and black student advisers. Sachar had promised it all.

I remembered how these same radical blacks had viewed King before his death as an Uncle Tom. Now, he was their martyr.

I had little choice but to implement the majority of their demands, since they had been promised by Sachar. I made that very clear to them, but I also felt impelled to express my opinion. Their reaction to my views showed how little they valued my reputation as a civil rights worker, my service as trustee of Morehouse College, which was probably the best black school in the country, and the fact that Coretta King had already accepted an invitation to speak at my inauguration.

I told them that, in my judgment, the entire humanities curriculum at Brandeis should be examined so that each discipline would reflect the role and contribution of all races in the society. That, I said, would serve both blacks and whites. A black studies program would merely isolate their culture, kick it upstairs, as it were.

As the blacks glowered at me—as if what I was saying was, after all, patently racist—the whites shriveled. Some white professors were delighted by the turn of events, for it meant that they would never have to modify their own syllabi to encompass the black presence as a major fact in American life.

Months later, the day came for the promised, though ill-advised, black studies program to be created. I considered research in black studies to be a very valid and constructive graduate enterprise at the few institutions equipped for the task. Maybe one or two undergraduate courses in black experience might be added as electives, courses open to all and taught by qualified scholars of any race. But I thought undergraduate concentration in black studies a fraud and a cop-out by whites through resegregation of blacks in a two-tier educational system. I kept waiting for someone to raise questions. No one would, so I did.

"What is the difference in these various 'black' courses which bear different titles but exhibit the same content?" I asked the startled proponents on the Educational Policy Committee.

When I received no solid answer, I said: "I do not wish to preside over a university of superficialities."

No one was anxious to come to grips with the real issues: How

172

do we get American history, political science, and economics taught with truthful relation to the critical role of the black/white confrontation on this continent? This task would require work, revision, reflection, time away from other specialized, esoteric research. Better that blacks be assigned to the backwaters of new black courses, where they seemed to want to go anyhow. But sloth and rhetoric were joining hands, and the ideals that brought me to Brandeis were caught in between. The story was the same at Harvard, Brown, and at all the really good universities, where some faculties treated students like customers—and "the customer is always right."

Not only did I inherit Sachar's mistakes, but my entire administrative staff was Sachar-appointed. This did not mean that the group was particularly loyal to Abe Sachar. Rather, the trouble lay in the conniving nature of their behavior. I found it impossible to trust anyone wholeheartedly or discover the motivations underlying the least word or act. Lloyd Garrison was right. Within a few months part of me was longing for the bombastic candor of Lyndon B. Johnson.

Now, with the Vietnam War worsening and the rhetoric of the left turning to violence, with universities in trouble all over the world, I needed men and women capable of acting beyond their own self-interest. The sources of money, so necessary to meet the growing needs, could dry up at the least show of campus unrest. My love of the academic ideal and my hatred for the barbarism that threatened it were passionate; could such passion engender wisdom in the heat of the moment? Perhaps I believed too strongly in Brandeis; perhaps Brandeis needed a compromiser like James Hester, whom I had known at Oxford, and who was now at New York University. Or a Kingman Brewster of Yale, who could bend with student protest, joining them in the line that a black radical could never receive a fair trial in America. Would I be able to dissemble in a position I regarded as a trust?

What bothered me more than any other aspect of the student revolt was that in Brandeis they had picked a decent institution as a vulnerable target. Brandeis was still fragile, capable of being damaged by student seizures and burnings. The protests could never harm their named antagonist, the vast and amorphous military-industrial complex.

When I accepted the presidency of Brandeis, the riots at Colum-

173

bia had not yet occurred. When they came, in the spring of 1968, I felt their leader, Mark Rudd, was the kind of demagogic politician familiar to me from the backwoods of southern Georgia. I observed the way the tactics of fascism lead to the dogma of fascism. Speaking with a professor there, I lamented the students' disruption and heckling of campus speakers. She replied: "There are some ideas so immoral and reprehensible that they should not be permitted on a university campus." She meant ideas in defense of American foreign policy. I remembered when Governor Eugene Talmadge of Georgia would not permit desegregation to be advocated at the university; and I imagined how that teacher from Columbia would have raged at Talmadge's attempt to fire the dean of the School of Education for one or two mildly progressive statements. As she spoke, her angry face was suddenly reminiscent of one I had seen in a lynch mob. The extremes of the right and left wear the same masks, though they think ill of each other's.

Was I the man to be president of Brandeis in 1968? The Columbia riots were on my mind as I wrote my inaugural speech. It thus foreshadowed the events that would, a few months later, also rock Brandeis to its foundations, for the issues that were obvious in 1968 were no less important a year later. "A university politicized," I would say, "is a university doomed, as the lessons of the German universities under the Nazis proved. I also give you the tragic example of many South American universities, which were politicized around 1918, and made cockpits for the invading forces of contending political parties who sought to manipulate the university as a tool. Such institutions . . . will not long be a residence of scholars.

". . . I am not prepared to reject the liberal methodology of fair play, civil liberty, and due process as the only way in which a civilized society can pursue truth, prevent the encrustation of error, and insure the fulfillment of man's creative talents and inclinations.

"The university has frequently been threatened from the outside. . . . Today, however, the danger comes also from a new direction. It comes from within." I thus inadvertently had drawn the battlelines for the forthcoming seige of Brandeis.

When I surveyed our ranks, the first face I saw was Dean Clarence Q. Berger. Sachar had introduced him to me as his only indispensable man, and Wien concurred. Berger, about fifty, was of less than average height, neither handsome nor ugly. He was ever accommodating to one's face, helpful especially in small things. He was a Byzantine infighter, unburdened by a philosophy. I found him fascinating, for in conversation he could unwind the skeins of Brandeis history like a novel; he also exploited my disenchantment with Sachar by delivering long diatribes against him.

I should have known, as Jane sagely warned, that a man who is disloyal to one superior is not likely to long support a successor. I should not have listened to him. I didn't realize that Berger wanted to protect certain friends of his, that he aspired to the executive vice-presidency, a post Sachar had always wisely refused to confer on him. Sachar preferred to keep Berger in a state of unrealized expectancy. Despite this, I would later appoint Berger executive vice-president.

Another formidable administrator was Berger's natural foe and sometime ally, Peter Diamondopolis, dean of the faculty, skilled in sadomasochistic encounter sessions that he called administrative conferences. They all needed each other, I suppose; Berger would attack Diamondopolis and Diamondopolis would sneer at Sachar who, in turn, would rage at both of them. Diamondopolis was also, I might add, hard working and a superb teacher, who charmed all sorts of people in all sorts of ways.

As long as Sachar remained in Waltham, there would always be the irresistible temptation to play the double agent. Abe Sachar was a ready listener to each new proof that I was not his replica; he relished my every fault as further evidence of his own indispensability. It would be months before I realized I should have insisted that Berger and Diamondopolis be replaced. By then it would be too late.

One administrator I had the opportunity to choose was David Squire, who had worked with me at the United Nations. He was a businessman who vowed to be a millionaire by the time he was thirty-five and thereafter to retire to do good works. He kept that promise and began his good works as a top official of the Job Corps under Sargent Shriver. Like Shriver, Squire did whatever he did well. He also possessed clarity and truthfulness, and would add an invaluable warmth to the Brandeis community. I offered him the job of vice-president of student affairs; he accepted, and arrived during the black student riot of January 1969.

175

A cabal immediately developed in the senior administration; its purpose was to expel him as a foreign object. Though no one could actually specify a single fault in his performance, he was made a fall guy for every trivial complaint. Things went so far that, at the commencement exercise in 1969, he was condemned by the valedictorian, who stood up on that sunny day in front of the whole assemblage and pronounced: "There will be no peace in this university until David Squire is fired." I was humiliated and Brandeis was shamed. Well, David Squire remained at Brandeis for a decade. Through sheer persistence and self-respect, he won the esteem of the campus. But in 1969, his case exemplified the mischievous forces dividing the institution when unity was never more necessary.

But at the time I was still optimistic. Naively enough, I thought that my relationship with my own children—three of whom were then in college—was emblematic of my relationships with the children of others, some of my close friends in Chicago, New York, and New Jersey. My college children and I always communicated; our disagreements, and there were many, never led to hostile estrangement.

Ruth, then twenty-five, a graduate student at the Heller School of Social Welfare at Brandeis, was very interested in campus issues and skilled in Socratic discourse. Her views on public issues were relatively close to mine, and she would never condone violence on any campus. One day when some student protestors tried to impede my passage, Ruth, heavy with her first child, placed her intimidating presence between the activists and me.

Ann, twenty-two, a student at Boston University, became upset by Judge Julius Hoffman's conduct in the trial of the Chicago Seven, charged with rioting at the 1968 Democratic convention. So I flew her out to observe a day of the proceedings in which Abbie Hoffman and crew were vying with the judge for bad conduct medals. Her fairness and good sense brought the wise comment at the end of the day that "the legal system is working to expose the flaws of judge and defendants."

Morris, Jr., twenty, was at Harvard, where he was the founder of a student newspaper, the *Independent,* to counter what he felt was a one-sided view from the *Crimson.*

176

But though he opposed the student disruptions as counterproductive and severely abusive of the rights of others, he strongly deplored President Pusey's use of the city police in Harvard Yard.

As for my own policies at Brandeis, Ruth, Ann, and Morris generally supported them.

It therefore was particularly painful when Brandeis students averted their eyes as we passed on campus, especially if they were in groups. I could not believe these young people were very different from my own children and I really did not expect either violence or its condonation.

Still the Columbia and Harvard examples made me wary, and the whole temper of the times put me on guard. I took small comfort in the fact that the student body was 75 percent Jewish, and that their parents most likely possessed a depth of commitment to the university that could not be matched by any other college in the country. I did not take into account that college-age children are often acting out rebellion against those very parents and that an identification with a black minority would have a strong appeal to a young, idealistic Jewish adolescent in 1969.

My elitist standards were obvious from the first day of my administration when the students found out how sympathetic I was to their plea for "relevance."

To make my point, I told students what Sir Otto Niemeyer had said to me in Sussex just after the war. My wife and I were visiting him as part of the Rhodes program, but I didn't know who he was though it was clear he was exceptionally well-informed about economics. That is why I asked him, "Why did England return to the gold standard in 1926?"

"Because," he replied, "I thought it was the best thing to do."

I was taken aback, and later I spoke with Niemeyer's male secretary. "Sir Otto," I was told, "is a director of the Bank of England. In 1926, he was undersecretary of the treasury. Winston Churchill was his political boss. Who do you think made the decision?"

The next time I saw Sir Otto, I asked him where he had gone to school—it was at Balliol, Oxford—and what he had studied there. "Why," he said, "the only fit subject for a man, 'Greats,'" by which he meant the Latin and Greek classics.

"Where did you learn economics?"

"Young man," he said, "when one has mastered Greats, one picks up the trade subjects for oneself."

When I told this story at Brandeis, I hoped that the students would understand that Sir Otto had had two advantages. First, he had read Thucydides, and learned to appreciate the noble constructions of Virgil. Prices would inflate and deflate, jobs would be gained and lost, and Sir Otto Niemeyer would have to answer for it; how much better for him that he had once glimpsed human perfection. Second, Sir Otto's classical education had taught him how to learn. The rigors of Adam Smith and John Maynard Keynes were nothing compared to the discipline of reading Plato in ancient Greek. I tried to make the students at Brandeis realize that such standards of academic excellence entailed both moral and intellectual benefits.

I was not opposed to students who felt keenly about social and economic problems, learning about them through personal experience in the slums and ghettos, but I did not regard such experiences as a substitute for learning from books. As I said to one student: "If you were studying chemistry you wouldn't think of going into the lab to perform experiments before you learned the periodic tables. So what makes you feel that you can get an education in the ghetto, which is at best a laboratory in which you might investigate and seek data *after* you have read Weber and Durkheim?" Experience without theory is as meaningless in the social sciences as it would be in the natural sciences. Such arguments often fell on deaf ears and even hostile, unresponsive minds.

So did my opposition to the lowering of admission or grading standards: "Sure," I'd admit, "some American universities have always had 'open admission.' I went to one—the University of Georgia, in the 1930s. But," I'd point out, "this and other Georgia state universities culled out the unqualified by the droves, a practice you'd feel was harsh and unjust."

One of the first problems I wanted to tackle at Brandeis was the proliferation of courses. I was already acutely aware of the issue before I came there. I had, for example, discovered that there were over a hundred social science courses at an Ivy League college at which there were but thirty several decades ago. Every Ph.D. thesis, however trivial, had to be a pretext for a course; the faculty committee members were better at scratching each other's backs than any Talmadge I ever knew. The net result was higher tuitions—somebody had to pay for Italian Revolutionary Theory between 1836 and 1837. My inclination to examine the situation earned me instant enemies. So did my proposal to establish several "university" professorships for charismatic scholars whose work cut across disciplinary lines. This idea, which raised fears that outsiders would get choice chairs, had to be abandoned. In later years it was implemented with the initial selections being made from within the Brandeis ranks.

Another goal was expressed in my inaugural remarks. Could the traditional slogan of "publish or perish" be rephrased as "publish and prosper; teach and prosper; teach and publish and prosper doubly"? One day the senior members of a social science department called on me proposing additional slots for an arcane branch in their discipline. I took the opportunity to ask if they intended to recommend tenure for their junior colleague, who had received rave reviews as a teacher in the student survey. His prowess was described glowingly as "making a dull subject sing." The department head spoke for the group:

"He'll not be up for tenure."

"Why not?"

"He's not published anything since his Ph.D. thesis four years ago."

"Was his thesis important and well done?"

"Well, yes."

"Does he participate significantly in learned discussions with his peers?"

"Well, yes."

"Does he have fine analytic powers?"

"Yes."

"Is it true what students say of him as a teacher?"

"He's the most effective teacher we have."

Something in me, certainly not caution, took control. I rose quietly from my rocker where I was seated, walked over to my bookcase, took out Alfred N. Whitehead's book, *The Aims of Education,* turned to and read aloud this passage:

"In every faculty you will find that some of the more brilliant teachers are not among those who publish. Their originality requires for its expression direct intercourse with their pupils in the form of lectures, or of personal discussion. Such men exercise an immense influence; and yet, after the generation of their pupils has passed away, they sleep among the innumerable unthanked benefactors of humanity. Fortunately, one of them is immortal—Socrates.''

My advocacy did not change a vote in the department. I was powerless in a just cause.

When I first met with the faculty senate, I hoped to hear some fresh ideas on curriculum and goals; I wanted to know what their priorities were, and how I could help them. Instead, the president of the senate offered an agenda featuring the faculty's, and particularly the senate's, role in running the university. The agenda was verbally supplemented by complaints about Sachar's suppression of the senate's demands for a university provost. As I had just taken on the presidency, I said, ''Gentlemen, I would be glad to discuss these questions, but it does seem to be very premature. I am disappointed that our first meeting should have brought forth from you demands that have so little to do with the scholarly mission of the university.''

I could sense the chill race down their spines. When the faculty wasn't asking for a provost, students were demanding, ''What are you doing to make the university more of a moral force?'' I felt, of course, that the university, by its very nature, and only by its very nature, was a moral force. Some students were more specific. ''What is the university doing about housing for the poor? Does Nixon know where you stand on Vietnam? What about the Chicago Seven?''

I attempted again and again to restate the principle of my inaugural address, that the university as an institution should stay out of politics. I reminded them that I myself had been a politician, and that I was convinced that the university should never attempt to be and could never be effective as a partisan supporter of this person or that cause. I told them that the university should only hold the soapbox for others to stand on. In short, I said exactly what they did not want to hear.

One incident, in particular, exemplified the polarities involved. In my first days as president, I was approached by a delegation of students who wanted to see the Brandeis investment portfolio. I asked them why. "To be sure that none of the investments are tainted," they said.

I laughed and replied, "Well, I can tell you for a fact that the whole portfolio is tainted. And it 'taint enough!"

They were not amused. "Look," I said, "the whole thing is twenty million dollars, and I'm very concerned about making do. Would you tell me now, so I'll know for the future, what sort of an investment you'd regard as tainted?"

"Dow Chemical!" they cried, as if by rote. I asked them what I should do if a donor offered me Dow stock yielding about a half million per year with the sole condition that Brandeis not switch to another investment. Refuse it, they said, refuse it!

"What investment would not be tainted?" I asked.

"Something like Bell Telephone," one of them volunteered.

"Are you opposed to the Vietnam War?" I asked her.

"Of course I am," she replied.

"I would suggest that the best way to end the war would be to get rid of Ma Bell. Have you ever tried to call a commanding officer without benefit of a telephone? Of course your social life would be impaired, but there could be no war."

"Then transfer it to something neutral."

"What's neutral?"

"United States Government Bonds."

I must have looked as disgusted as I felt. "Who do you think Dow Chemical makes the napalm for?"

"Then invest it in banks," said the girl, losing patience with me.

"Banks," I said, "there is no military-industrial complex without banks to finance it." Finally, I said, "On your premises there is no untainted investment in which the university could keep its money."

"That's your problem," she snapped.

I knew already that my impassioned faith in orthodox academic standards might get me in trouble, but it was only later that I realized what a disadvantage my rational approach to political questions would prove. In the politics of confrontation, both sides claim victory until somebody gets his head smashed in; that is the final tribunal.

Despite my exasperation, I walked the campus frequently, attempting whatever dialogue might be possible. From the very

181

first I noticed that the students did not reply to my greetings, and many went out of their way to avoid me. I suppose that they didn't actually want to be rude; the peer group pressure, which had been renamed "solidarity," must have been considerable. However, when they needed my help, they weren't shy.

One incident is particularly memorable. A young woman came to my office, very upset. "Mr. President," she said, "a terrible thing happened in our dormitory last night, and I wish you would take steps to protect us."

"What happened?"

"Well, around two in the morning a male student broke into the dorm shouting obscenities and threats."

We talked a moment and I realized that the young woman knew the man's name. She admitted that she did, but refused to disclose it.

"How in the world am I going to help you?" I asked.

"Can you post a twenty-four-hour guard at the dorm?"

I told her that that was not possible, that our security budget could not afford an additional burden. It suddenly dawned on me what the real difficulty was. "The student that you're complaining about, is he black?"

She hung her head and nodded. Dimly, but only dimly, I began to realize that I had quite a problem on my hands.

In later years I looked back on this experience as the beginning of a trend among good people, to stifle honest discussion where race is involved, for fear of being tagged "racist."

On the night of January 8, 1969, I was due to speak in Boston. The text of my address contained the following passage:

"I must caution you that the best university administration in the world is no assurance at all against physical confrontation. Administrators and faculty may be receptive and well-motivated, but this will not save the university from disruptions. In fact, our best universities seem to be the main targets."

That morning I had returned to Boston from a fund-raising engagement. My driver greeted me at the airport with the news that 65 blacks had seized Ford Hall, located in front of the administration building. I was shocked. Despite their earlier demands, I was not aware that their discontent had escalated, for Brandeis had increased the black student admissions from 58 in the spring of April

182

1968 to 120, the heavier concentration being from Boston. In addition, financial aid to blacks had jumped from $125,000 to $349,000. I had also recruited some competent black professors, and there were still no threats, no urgent appeals. No one could tell me why the takeover had occurred. But the fact remained Ford Hall was under siege.

The only warning that I had came from FBI sources. During the late 1960s they were in touch with university presidents. Bill Sullivan, eventually a deputy to J. Edgar Hoover, had called me several weeks before to say that during the takeover of a college in Canada, it was announced that Brandeis would be the next target. Brandeis was seen as a sitting duck, Sullivan related, because of its Jewish connections; Jews were very committed to black causes and might be expected to be tender in dealing with a black takeover. I thought Sullivan was an alarmist, and I had not taken his warning seriously. It would have made no difference anyhow, for I soon discovered one of the direct stimulants for the takeover.

On January 7, one day before the event, two members of the faculty of San Francisco State had spoken at Brandeis. They were a white sociologist named Arlene Daniels and a black instructor in international relations named William Middleton. Only black students had been allowed to the meeting; there, they were told that if they had any manhood at all, they would express their sympathy with the protestors at San Francisco State by disrupting Brandeis. Of course, while the blacks were proving their manhood at Ford Hall, provocators Daniels and Middleton had moved on somewhere else.

Other factors exacerbated the situation. The Admissions Committee under Sachar had accepted a number of unqualified and badly prepared blacks in the fall of 1968. Mid-year examinations were two weeks off, and their moment of truth was at hand.

Other motives behind the takeover were clarified later. A reporter from the student radio station appeared with the tape of a press conference that had been held that afternoon at Ford Hall in the office of the advisor to black students. The tape stated ten "non-negotiable" demands, many of which, to my surprise, were already policy, while others were being implemented.

The real sore point seemed the Afro-American Studies Department about which I had first been told the previous summer. The students wanted to have power over hiring and firing; and they also wanted various degrees of control over the selection of chairman, faculty, and curriculum. Every good university assigns this power to faculty, not students, and as I had already reluctantly agreed to implement the outstanding promise of a black studies program, any agitation for it was *per se* fatuous. No, they were making noise for the sake of noise.

As soon as I had listened to the tape, I convened a special faculty meeting. "I do not minimize this crisis," I reported. "I do not want to preside over any institution that can be held up for ransom by force. I have no desire to act hastily or vindictively. We must do what is right for Brandeis. The community is looking to the faculty for leadership, and so am I. The time has come for responsible action."

Professor Maurice Auslander announced that the Faculty Senate had met earlier to express its support for the administration; the full faculty now joined with that expression and adopted a resolution that "utterly" condemned the takeover and demanded that the blacks vacate the building and enter negotiations. I was very pleased.

The blacks then requested that I come over to Ford Hall to negotiate—alone. Everybody advised me not to go, that I'd be endangering my life. But I could not allow fear to rule me. When I arrived, an enormous chain was unwound from the latch on the front door and promptly put back once I entered. I spoke briefly, directly addressing the leader, Roy Du Berry. He was, as I shall explain, of particular interest to me.

"I came here to honor your request," I said. "I am always willing to listen to Brandeis students with grievances. I now urge that you leave the building at once so that we can proceed to discuss your legitimate requests."

"We have nothing further to say," answered Du Berry, "and we will not leave until all demands are met."

"That," I said quietly, "will not happen." I turned my back and faced the door. My heart was in my mouth but I held my ground. There was an ominous moment, then one of them stepped forward and lifted the latch.

I returned to my office to weigh the options. I felt it would be a grave mistake to bring in the police. The Waltham troopers were not like those of New York, not even as well-trained as those of

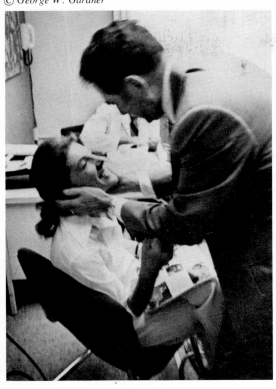

With Carlyn
in Dr. Cuttner's office,
following treatment, 1975

With Irene Abram in Fitzgerald, Georgia,
1976, wearing a hat to conceal a wig

With Carlyn, on the occasion of receiving the Learned Hand Award
from the American Jewish Committee, December 1977

The author in 1978

Cambridge. They were hardly more sophisticated than the college's flimsy security force, and were not likely "into" civil rights. But I wanted to explore the alternatives. I asked them if, should arrests be necessary, I could go in first, ahead of any troopers. The answer was no; the police would not tolerate interference of any sort. I asked if the troopers could take the building unarmed. No, they would not consider it, for there was no way of knowing what weapons the students might have. It was rumored, for example, that quantities of sulfuric acid were missing from the chemistry lab and were now stored within Ford Hall. No chances should be taken. That evening on television I watched with envy as the London police calmly dispersed a rowdy peace protest in Grosvenor Square. But Waltham wasn't London; my cops had axes to grind. I dismissed the option. America's preeminent Jewish university would not inflict official violence on blacks less than a year after the death of Martin King.

There was no sleep for me or my aides; we dozed at our desks, waiting for news. At 4:00 A.M., Eric Yoffie, the president of the student body, informed me that the Student Council had voted to condemn the Ford Hall seizure. I was exhilarated at the news, for now faculty and students were in accord; the unanimity I was seeking was achieved. Whatever might happen, Brandeis would not be another Columbia, and no one could accuse me of pitting myself against the rank and file.

In the meantime, the blacks remained intransigent and I was concerned that time might yet ignite a powder keg. I arranged a secret meeting with Roy Du Berry and told him that many of his demands were dishonest and illogical, and that even those that were fair did not justify the student revolt, for the processes of civilized intercourse had not yet failed. We agreed, almost amiably, that no immediate solution was possible.

. Du Berry had come to Brandeis from Mississippi via Boston's prestigious Commonwealth School. There was between us a common experience—the South. I had more roots in common with him than with any New York Jew; and he himself was closer to me than he could ever have been to some of the northern blacks fighting by his side, and perhaps egging him on.

The Mississippi draft board was breathing down Roy's back. It refused to acknowledge the student status of their black boy in a white school. Long before the Ford Hall takeover, I had said to him, "Roy, I won't let them take you from Brandeis." I had called the draft board and told them, "Don't you dare touch him! His grades are good enough for exemption, so don't you dare touch him!" It had seemed settled, but that was not the last we'd hear from Mississippi. When the Ford Hall confrontation was over, the state resubmitted its claim.

Roy was desolate. Who'd help him now that he had led an insurrection? I asked the university lawyer to intervene on his behalf, and Roy Du Berry stayed out of the army. He didn't thank me and left my office by the back door so that none of his friends would see him consorting with the enemy.

The black students negotiating with me during the eleven days of the Ford Hall occupation comprised a revolving cast. As soon as progress was made with one set, their powers were removed and new black spokesmen emerged. We were continually starting from scratch. Then ten black men and women, self-appointed leaders of the Roxbury community, joined them. Bags of food donated by the Freedom Food Market, also in Roxbury, were brought to Ford Hall. The takeover began to look more and more like a siege. Mattresses, desks, and steel lockers were pushed against the doors. An enormous sheet billowed from one of the second floor windows, proclaiming the building "Malcolm X University," and featuring a large photograph of the dead radical.

It was the Roxbury presence that disturbed me the most. These ghetto community figures would make the university a focal point for black grievances against whites, and Jews in particular. My sense of responsibility and burden was thus increased tenfold, and all my advisors were exhausted with anxiety and emptied of ideas. I was aware that twenty years of other men's labors could slip through my fingers.

Finally, however, after forty-eight sleepless hours, I realized that I didn't have to do anything more. That became the core of my strategy. Why should I care if the blacks held Ford Hall? Brandeis could operate indefinitely without it. The only threat, I thought, was a schoolwide strike and total faculty disunity. If I could prevent that, I'd win.

I immediately began to assess the faculty situation. I knew that in the natural and hard sciences I had nigh total faculty and student support. After all, how many medical students stage sit-ins? Our real Achilles' heel was in the social sciences, where, throughout the country, in my judgment, a serious erosion of intellectual rigor and rational discourse was occurring, as now at Brandeis.

I still felt that I could get faculty and student opinion behind my position which eschewed all force. After all, it was the use of force that had galvanized the students at Columbia and Harvard and had divided those faculties. What I proposed was extraordinary for no university president had ever before chosen to ignore a direct invasion of school property. Harvard, Columbia, and others had called in the police. After meeting with some faculty, I received enough encouragement to make an announcement. No further action would be taken unless "the white students who are outside Ford Hall create some terrible incident or unless the students inside Ford Hall commit grievous acts of violence. . . ." It was clear that my strategy enraged the protestors. Being ignored was the last thing they could endure; in fact, at this point most of them began addressing me as "cracker." Some of the white students meanwhile tried to initiate a strike, but it proved ineffective; only 200 of the 2,800 students participated. I then offered to go back to Ford Hall to talk, knowing I'd be alone. The protestors said my offer was "racist," a word which by this time had lost much of its meaning for me. After seven days of siege the *New York Times* reported that I "had impressed observers with [my] flexibility, endurance, and ability to keep the rest of the university functioning smoothly."

Then another contingent from the Roxbury ghetto arrived, this time to confront me rather than assist the students. They entered my office wearing sunglasses and wielding clubs. Despite my impulse to tell them, "Get your asses out of here, this is a Brandeis affair," I merely listened to them, while they said nothing beyond making a few veiled threats. Yet their tactic was not ineffective; I'm sure that many faculty members, fearing violence, were now doubly intimidated. As for me, it was the first time I had personally seen blacks on the inflicting rather than the receiving end of violence. I couldn't believe that this rabble in front of me could share a common goal with the Kings, Randolphs, Jordans, and Rustins with whom I'd worked so many years.

Brandeis produced its own thugs as well. On Wednesday, January 15, five black girls entered the library and scattered 2,500 periodicals. The day before, a number of whites disrupted the class of Professor I. Milton Sacks by blaring recorded music over the classroom public-address system. When the music ended, Sacks invited the students to state their case; Sacks listened and then condemned their behavior as barbarous. No one would identify the culprits involved in either incident as I asked, so I could not discipline them.

As I left to join my family, a faculty member called to me from the shadows just outside the Administration Building. He told me that he had given an examination to his students who were inside Ford Hall. This meant the professor was going in and out of the chained door.

"Don't you know that those kids are under suspension? You have violated a basic rule of this university."

"Yes," he said, "but they have to trust me."

As I stood there staring at that man who looked so much like a priest confessing a sin of the flesh, I was conscious that I was fighting against a tidal wave of mob rule that would hit almost all universities.

There was one more crisis: 150 black students from neighboring colleges arrived on campus, circled Ford Hall, entered it, and then left peacefully, an hour later. Shortly after that, all the occupiers exited by a back fire escape. In the eleven days they had held the building, no one was hurt, and all university property was intact, though some was damaged. The protest had utterly failed in its principal demand that black students be given control over academic functions in Afro-American studies. The plaudits flowed in for the administration; I had won what was described as "a war of nerves," without any compromise of faculty control of academic life, and without bringing police on campus.

I felt an enormous weight had been lifted from my shoulders. If Sachar had founded Brandeis, I had kept intact the principle of faculty control of the academy while preventing violence and bloodshed.

When the blacks emerged, they did so quietly, sullenly, refusing to speak to anyone, not even to their two hundred white sympathizers who were waiting outside. A black named Randy Bailey read the following statement: "We intend to continue our struggle at Brandeis to gain effective control of the Afro-American Studies Department to be established here. In doing so our struggle will take new forms. Our stand," he tersely concluded, "is nonnegotiable."

I wanted to punish the rebels, but every student I consulted and the responsible faculty representatives advised against it. I yielded. The schism between the university and the mind of a lawyer was now at its widest. The law, for me the hallmark of civilized life, would have to be ignored. I remembered Martin King and his respect for the law; if he broke it, he expected to pay the cost. Jail, money, notoriety—he was ready!

Had I flown in the face of university opinion and punished those insurgents, equal justice would have required sanctions against practically every black student and black administrator. Such a black/Jewish confrontation in 1969 was unthinkable. Yet I felt robbed of the capacity to make a moral decision. That abrogation was very much part of these times.

My method of dealing with the takeover without calling in the police, was, however, adopted by other institutions. Edward Levi used it at the University of Chicago. But he was also able to expel a score of white troublemakers. I spoke to him when he was Attorney General and told him how I envied him his courage. He reminded me he had grown up at the University of Chicago, that his roots there gave him distinct advantages. He also pointed out that his school held a unified view of the disruptions; the rioters were really isolated in Chicago as they had not been at Brandeis. Most important, he said, was the fact that his disrupters were not blacks and the university was not Jewish. With a candor to match his talent, Levi went on to say that if the riots had occurred a few months later, he could not have expelled anyone, not even in Chicago; by that time Nixon and the war had divided every rank, his own included.

It cannot be said in my defense that amnesty quieted Brandeis. The blacks continued to complain and demand, while some whites continued to support them, regardless of the issue. Mysterious fires broke out, some classes were disrupted, and a sit-in or two occurred.

As the months passed new student demands centered on quotas for blacks, accompanied by full financial aid. It was, to my mind, their most outrageous demand to date, but, tragically, the most obtainable.

I spoke to the student press, on the school radio, to the representatives of all the campus constituencies warning that the demanded setting aside of scholarship funds for a black quota would sop up the meager resources for needy merit scholars whose presence adds so much to the intellectual life of the university. Though the very word "quota" sends shivers down the spines of Jews, the demands from blacks met little vocal resistance. Those who agreed with my outspoken objection to racial quotas preferred in the main not to challenge what I saw as the then current fad: "If it comes from the blacks, it must be right."

One of the indulgences to which Sachar had consented was the Transitional Year Program, or TYP. The idea was to seek out disadvantaged black students, about twenty-seven each year, bring them to the campus at university expense, and enroll them in a one-year remedial training program. At the conclusion of their studies, those who could meet Brandeis standards would be admitted as freshmen for the following year. The program was first undertaken in the fall of 1968 with more than a score of young people literally lifted out of the slums. A few of them were talented and ambitious. The rest were there to enjoy and exploit the middle-class whites who seemed to feel exposure to the ghetto was in itself educational.

While representing President Kennedy in Dar es Salaam during the independence ceremonies in Tanganyika (now Tanzania), I saw an Episcopal school in the hills where the toilets were trenches, and the food was coarse grain. The students were drawn from the tribal villages where English was only rarely spoken, but so fine was the quality of instruction that many of these natives wound up at Oxford and Cambridge. I reminded my audiences at Brandeis that the English teachers in Tanganyika were not awestruck by the capacity of their pupils to survive.

In contrast, the TYP faculty bent over backward to accommodate illiteracy. They deferred to their immediate and superficial needs. When the day of reckoning came, most of the first-year TYP students could not honestly meet admission requirements. Many nevertheless were admitted by indulgent faculty committee members. Ever afterward I would take with a grain of salt assurances that lowered standards at the starting gate did not mean the same at the finish line.

The TYP program was failing, but, like the black studies department, it was a bad idea whose time had come. However unproductive, however meaningless, it would still be there when I packed my bags and headed for home, and it would be there ten years later despite the efforts of President Marver Bernstein to abolish it. One distinguished Brandeis professor told me in the summer of 1980 that while he vigorously opposed the TYP he had voted against President Bernstein's recent initiatives to get rid of it, "because he had gone about it in the wrong way." I could not resist the observation that the president could not have invented any way that would have brought him the public support of people such as himself.

It is possible that my worst sin at Brandeis was the attempt to use my office as a bully pulpit. Perhaps I should not have tried to stand firm on principles of merit and due process in those times. Perhaps it was outdated to assume that a university president should be anything more than an administrative fund raiser. Did it make any difference, really? The blacks would have revolted in any case. But it might have been much worse had they thought me a simple wheeler-dealer, rather than a man who also believed in something.

Few could honestly doubt that I believed in Brandeis. I communicated my enthusiasm to alumni and supporters across the country. During one month in 1969 I spent but nine nights in the President's House, though I was on the campus practically every day. At night I hunted unceasingly for operating funds to heat the buildings and pay for the programs Sachar had generated. One night I would be in St. Louis, the next in New York, at an endless array of events at which I'd tell the Brandeis story. At the close of 1969 the development people toted up the results of the best year ever despite the student eruptions on campus.

Individually, most Brandeis students were admirable as persons and students. It was the pack psychology and the attendant peer pressures that sometimes skewed, if not the individual's good sense, his manners. It was reassuring, I suppose, but disconcerting to find handwritten notes slipped under my door after a confrontational meeting: "I didn't say anything last night, but I agreed with you. Keep up the dialogue."

Looking back, I do not believe that the campus violence in those days reflected much selfless moral indignation over the Vietnam war. When the most outrageous deed in that sad expedition occurred—the Christmas bombing of Hanoi in 1972, when "peace was at hand"—not a rock was tossed through a single window. For by then the personal concerns that had fueled the long and violent turmoil had been somewhat quelled. The draft was winding down, almost extinguishing the chance of involuntary Vietnam service; the terrible and inexcusable slaughter of the Kent State students had shown that confrontation could bring unacceptable risk; and, perhaps most significant of all, junior faculties, some of whom had supported, led, and even inspired the disruptions, were reining in their activities because of constriction in the academic job market.

Most Brandeis students—a true silent majority—probably agreed with me, for when I occasionally found the time to conduct a seminar, I came away exhilarated by the intellectually provocative but reasonable dialogue. Brandeis was and is something to be proud of.

I did not wish to be a mere administrative time server. I wanted to add dimensions to the university. A case in point was my motive for a law school; the impetus behind my thinking was the image of the law as a bastion of reason. And what an appropriate place for it! Who was Louis Brandeis anyway? I discussed my idea with selected faculty and outside legal educational specialists. As I did so, I won a pledge of nearly three million dollars from a woman to honor her dead husband. She stipulated that the money could be used only for a law school.

The idea evolved in what I thought were innovative and productive directions. The school would not be limited to training practicing lawyers; it would discard much traditional curricula, and aim toward government policy-making. What a boon to society, I thought, and what a feather in the university's cap. I was terribly excited, so much so that I blurted out my dream to whoever would listen. On December 22, 1969 the *New York Times* reported it as if the school were already a *fait-accompli*.

The Brandeis faculty went through the roof. Why had I not gone through channels before making such a statement of intent? Why did Brandeis need another professional school anyway? Some of them even demanded to know why their departments couldn't have the money. They didn't seem to realize that the donor would not give away three million dollars for the discretionary use of the president.

They were, in fact, still upset because I had chosen to prune the luxuriant growth of graduate programs, resist proposals for new ones, and rationalize teaching loads. When I asked for faculty advice, they all suggested reductions in somebody else's backyard. I wanted to bolster the French department, but I was beset instead by demands for a Ph.D. program in economics, requiring econometricians, which I felt would just duplicate the superb program already offered a few miles away at Harvard and MIT. That could hardly serve either Brandeis or the interests of the community.

Finally, in December 1969, I decided to get advice from outside experts on the management function which had developed under Sachar. I hired a team of consultants, Cresap, McCormick & Paget, who would, with trustee approval, report to me on university reorganization. A prime early recommendation was that Clarence Q. Berger's post as executive vice-president be abolished.

In the meantime political forces outside the university were tempting me. Brandeis trustee Hubert Humphrey urged me to seek the Democratic nomination for the Senate in New York; my opponent would be Charles Goodell, an appointed Republican who was falling afoul of the Nixon administration. Cyrus Vance offered me his support, as did Tom Finletter, a former Secretary of the Air Force. I resisted the temptation; I still felt that, given a proper vote of support, I should finish my job at Brandeis.

Blacks continued to press for an increase of set-aside scholarships. Berger was undercutting me and waging a guerrilla war against Squire. At the time I most needed loyal lieutenants, my second in command was courting the shelter of Sachar.

Humphrey then spoke to Larry Wien, arguing my case as a candidate for the Senate. Larry called and strongly urged me to remain at Brandeis. "I don't blame you at all for feeling cheated," he said to me over breakfast. "The job I painted for you is not the one you ended up with. But I still urge you not to quit. It's in your best interest as well as the university's."

"If I stay, Berger must go."

Larry was indebted to Berger and also to Sachar, now Berger's rediscovered ally. He could not agree.

I confess I was not entirely sorry, for beyond Berger there were layers of administrators who reveled in their practiced skills of bureaucratic infighting, a very useful craft which I abhorred and have never mastered. Moreover, Larry, whom I respected, had already announced he would not seek a new term as chairman of the Brandeis board, and neither he nor I had been able to persuade our choice, Robert S. Benjamin, to succeed him. Larry and Bob were both strong board members whom I had known for years and on whose leadership I relied. Now neither was prepared to lead. My responsibilities would be increasing, and my chief administrative officer was scheming to torpedo the Cresap report. Sachar and his allies exuded interest in Humphrey's plans for me. I should have been put on guard, but instead I was flattered.

My expectations had been naive. I was not prepared for my Brandeis experience. I could cope with greed, hypocrisy, and slander when I encountered them in the caucus room or in the marketplace; I could not, however, bear the defilement of my abiding illusion, not to say ideal, that a place of higher learning is sacred, and that Brandeis was symbolic of the Jewish devotion to that ideal. I came to realize that the job of a university president is not equivalent to the role of a Renaissance prince. Unless you have large sums of surplus money to throw at potential troublemakers, unless you have a faculty like Edward Levi's, unless you start off with your own people, unless you have stable times and a popular national president, unless, unless, unless. . . .

By 1970 the principal qualification for the presidency of a distinguished university was not ability as an educational leader, but as a mediator, a keeper of the peace, not through reason or persuasion but by buying off troublemakers.

With the thought of Humphrey's political offer in mind, I went to see Arthur Goldberg and asked him if he were intending to run for either the governor's office or the Senate. If he were, I'd stay away, because our funds would have to be derived from very nearly the same people. Goldberg assured me he wasn't running. Wearied as I was by constant criticism, Humphrey's enthusiasm was extremely flattering.

I resigned, and, in February 1970, declared for the Senate. Soon after, Goldberg capitulated to party pressure and challenged Rockefeller for governor after all. My financial sources dried up, as I anticipated, and my candidacy was stillborn. I returned to New York City, where Lloyd Garrison was too gracious to say, "I told you so."

My attitude toward many issues would be permanently affected. I had always been singularly opposed to quotas of any sort; since Brandeis, however, my opposition has been even firmer, my pas-

194

sion on the subject greater. It was Brandeis that would resonate in me when the *Bakke* case arose at the University of California a decade later.

Quotas—racial, religious, and sexual—were, I now felt, a threat to our constitutional integrity.

As I review these pages, I ask myself: Am I shooting fish in a tank? Isn't it true that the student movement is over, that the furies are quelled? Didn't the great fact of Richard Nixon's reelection in 1972 tell everybody something? Why fight the ancient battles?

The fact is, civilization is no less fragile than it was in 1969. The standards of racial equality I fought for are ever threatened. I first heard the threat from Eugene Talmadge of Georgia. The threat posed by the students of Brandeis was a far more serious one because it was duplicated throughout the world and because it was so damn fashionable. Why, some scholars even fought for the black radicals and furnished them with a semblance of respectability. No, the battle for true human equality is constant, shifting from university to society and back, ever and ever through time.

I felt despondent that I did not stay and fight longer at Brandeis, despite the handicaps. But I resolved never to retreat again.

As I was getting into my car to leave Brandeis, an assistant professor stopped to say goodby: "Mr. President," he said, "I hate to see you leave. I think you're finally beginning to make some of the people on this campus face facts. I wish you would stay." The man had put his finger on my strengths as a university president; I have subsequently reflected long and hard on my weaknesses.

Academia should be my natural home, reveling as I do in the world of ideas, particularly those which relate to the first principles of life and living. I learn and teach by discourse. In the world of the intellect, this is called the Socratic method; but it can also be seen as the lawyer's technique. Admittedly I like to win, but I enjoy the exercise even if I must concede error. I look upon any reluctance to express deep convictions through fear as weakness and treason to the sovereignty of truth. Ideas can become missiles even when expressed with the soft tone and courtesy of my native speech.

Academia is not the courtroom, and contenders on various sides of issues are apt to be personally wounded in a fray that lawyers accept with far more grace. I, the political man to the core, did not relish the diminishing of principles into petty personal quarrels.

Eleven years after my resignation, the *Justice,* the Brandeis newspaper, on February 18, 1981, reported: "University Chancellor Abraham Sachar resigned—following months of pressure from the Chairman of the Board of Trustees—Sachar's action is the culmination of several years of animosity between him and University President Marver Bernstein. . . ."

The paper reported that the Chancellor was reluctant to go, and that President Bernstein felt that there could be only one president of the university. The founding chairman of the Board of Trustees, Norman Rabb, wrapped it all up: "Frankly, it's long overdue."

While I was still nursing my wounds from Brandeis, Vernon Jordan, then the executive director of the United Negro College Fund, which raised money for America's forty-odd predominantly black universities, asked me to become the board chairman. I jumped at this chance to work for another cause in which I believed deeply, and especially to work with Vernon, a man of extraordinary quality. Some black leaders, but more particularly white liberals, tended to dismiss such institutions as segregated relics. However, I knew these colleges had always had integrated faculties, had never barred white students, and as late as 1963 were the only academic places where blacks and whites could freely meet in the Deep South. As a trustee of one of these colleges, Morehouse, I also knew that the majority of outstanding blacks in America, such as Patricia Roberts Harris, Thurgood Marshall, Martin Luther King, Jr., and Vernon Jordan were graduates of these impoverished schools.

I served as the chairman of the United Negro College Fund for nine years, a period in which the annual harvest of contributions doubled and the Fund's slogan, "A Mind is a Terrible Thing to Waste" filtered into the American home.

I was moved by the dignity of the commencement ceremonies at these black colleges, where parents wept openly as the first college graduates, ever, in their families received degrees. I found a marked contrast at a top Eastern college commencement in 1972 where students scorned cap and gown and took degrees mockingly in the name of some North Vietnamese prisoner of war. The comparison drove home, forcefully, the devaluation of education by some who see it as a birthright. Adversity has its compensations.

11

IN THE EARLY 1970s, although I treasured my family and our elegant home in The Dakota, New York's most famous apartment building, there was a growing void between Jane and me. We sidestepped it. Rather, we drew on our store of shared memories and congratulated ourselves that our marriage had held through the turbulence of change. We had developed many common interests—politics, books, early American antiques—and above all, deep love and pride in our five truly decent children. Until a few months before I learned that I was mortally ill, I had taken it for granted that Jane and I had passed the time when our marriage was at maximum risk. Now that we were distinctly middle-aged, calculated by actuarial tables, I assumed we'd coast together to the end. We respected and cared for each other. There would be much too much to leave, too many mutual interests, an investment of too much time.

But in the midst of plenty, I felt a growing emptiness; amidst success, I felt failure. In early 1973, I was, for the first time in my life, constantly tired. I suffered one cold after another. I felt sick to the marrow of my bones. Finally, I could no longer be comforted by happy memories of the past with Jane. I needed present sustenance.

Six weeks before my fifty-fourth birthday, on May 3, I left The Dakota, never to return, save for one fearsome night two months later, on the eve of going to the hospital to join battle with leukemia.

I took a small apartment next door to The Dakota, at The Mayfair—out of the house, but just one building away so that I could be as close as possible to my eleven-year-old son Josh. I had no idea what lay ahead. The separation was the deepest agony I had ever felt; my own hand was severing the life line of my family. I thought continuously of our five children, particularly young Josh, and his great need of me. But how wrong I was to think that separation affects only very young children, that the older ones, and the adults, can take it in their stride. Divorce is the disruption of an organic whole, however imperfect. No part is left untraumatized. Some members may fare better, some worse, but none will ever be part of that whole again.

I had begun to see Carlyn during various business trips to Atlanta. I had known her since 1940, when she was a high school senior and already beautiful, and had courted her until, in 1943, she had told me she had decided to marry not me, whom she found too "overshadowing," but Ted Fisher.

The four of us, the Fishers and the Abrams, continued to live in Atlanta for fifteen years. We dined together, visited each other's homes, and sometimes even entertained together. In those years I never looked back at my early feelings for Carlyn. In fact, it now occurs to me that though I'd easily kiss or embrace other women among our friends, I didn't go near Carlyn. Whatever had led me to write the impassioned letters of 1943 had all been safely repressed. It emerged, if at all, in animated disagreement over the uses and abuses of modern art. Carlyn is a committed painter and sculptor, whose work was, by the 1950s, almost totally abstract. I obstinately preferred the old guard, the Ryders, the Hoppers, and the Wyeths of the world. She got on with Jane better than with me. When Carlyn read *The Second Sex,* the only other woman in Atlanta she felt sure had read it was Jane. She was right. They discussed it for hours on end.

There is, of course, no way for me to predict what would have happened had I not been condemned to death a mere six weeks after I chose to leave Jane. Or whether the heart knows more than the brain can understand and that it was the illness that forced my hand. I gradually became aware that I, for all my attempts at self-knowledge, was very much at the mercy of forces I did not comprehend. Part of me believes that there was a relationship between the tensions in my life and my illness. Four years before the onset of my leukemia, Jane had developed diabetes, a disease which affected two other women in her family. Though we've never discussed it, I am sure she has wondered, too, of the effect of psychological traumas on the weak links in the body.

By the end of the summer, sick with cancer, I asked Jane for a divorce with a resoluteness unprecedented in my past behavior. I was luckier than most patients in my position; I was in love with and loved by Carlyn, who, despite the prognosis of my condition, remained buoyant.

Late that summer, Carlyn and I went to England for three precious weeks. We explored southern Ireland, revisited Oxford, and called on friends in London and Sandwich. I have always loved the British Isles, the most civilized place in the world, and our trip was enhanced by nostalgia and the sweet-sad possibility that I'd never see it again—Oxford's Bodleian Library, the vault of its Divinity School, the extraordinary countryside. I was vouchsafed a last glimpse of life at its greenest. Yet it was guilt, not death, that darkened the landscape, for however justified I felt in my actions, I was still a middle-class person with middle-class values. There could be no escape from the fact that I had lived with one woman for twenty-nine years and I was rapturously traveling with another.

As we drove past the Dean-Drake estate in County Wexford, Ireland, I had recalled that in 1946 Jane and I had visited the lords of this manor, a family descended from Sir Francis Drake. Untouched, seemingly, by war, inflation, and class conflict, they had welcomed us with superb hospitality. On this trip I had wanted so much to knock on their door and reintroduce myself, particularly since I had learned in the village that "Captain" Dean-Drake still lived within. But I was ashamed. I argued with myself, and damned myself for a coward, but I couldn't do it. They'd accept Carlyn—I knew that—but what of the adulterer? Fitzgerald and its landscape of rigid steeples had taught me about sin. Sadly, I had driven away.

Back in New York, I was faced with the painful prospect of telling my children what a few others already knew. I sat on a bench in Central Park with Adam and Morris, Jr. Morris was stoic, but tears welled up in Adam's eyes. They were all still shaken by my separation from their mother. Jane insisted that I keep the news of Carlyn or my illness from Josh until after Labor Day, by which time a therapist would have "cushioned the shock." But the analyst had told me that Josh's primary concern was for my health. That sounded to me like a sign of psychic well-being and lessened my last conflicts about the separation. Oddly enough, I began to see certain signs of relief in Jane, as if she were glad that the unendurable tension between us had been lifted by my leaving. At the same time I knew that she did not believe that my move was final. She might still have been convinced that she could prevent an irreversible mistake I'd regret until I died.

I made another visit to Dr. Louis Wasserman, senior hematologist at Mount Sinai Hospital, in late August 1973, after Carlyn and I returned from England. This stocky, cherubic man, gray-haired and supremely confident, ushered me into his examining room after scanning the preliminary tests. "Take your clothes off," he ordered, "so that Dr. Weinrab can do a bone marrow." The peripheral blood count had apparently shown that the disease was progressing inexorably. The platelets and red cells were being reduced by the rampaging white cells. I lay down, and Weinrab drove his needle through my hip bone until he reached the marrow. Exhausted and scared, I sat and waited an hour for the specimen to dry. The bright memories of England were already fading, and survival was still a fantasy.

"You must report to the hospital within a week to commence chemotherapy."

Morris, Jr. was preparing to enter my college at Oxford in October to study law when he heard the news of the separation and then of my leukemia. He said he had expected the first, and though he reacted to the illness with outward calm, it evidently hit him hard.

His mother and I drove him to Kennedy Airport. It was a very sad moment as this slim, delicate-featured boy departed. My last glimpse of him was his knapsack. My eyes burning, I wondered if

I'd ever see his face again. Perhaps if things went badly in the hospital, he would fly back for another, final farewell.

Before entering Mount Sinai I went to Atlanta to be with Carlyn for the weekend. There I tried to sort out what to do. Should I face the chemotherapy with Jane by my side or with Carlyn? It was a debate that had little to do with the future. In either case, if I recovered, I would leave the hospital and go straight to Carlyn. But I couldn't help imagining the acute embarrassment of a deathbed ringed by five children squirming uncomfortably as their father's lover struggled with her emotions.

Nevertheless, I resolved it should be Carlyn, and she and I decided to visit my psychiatrist, Dr. Feder, together. As I was leaving my office, my secretary handed me a tract written by the former head of the Department of Hematology at Mount Sinai; it discussed my brand of leukemia as an inevitably fatal one. I read it on the subway between Fifty-first and Ninety-sixth Streets, and by the time I reached Feder's office, I was resigned to death. The whole session was submerged in my gloom, and neither Feder, who emphasized that the pamphlet was five years old, nor Carlyn, who pointed out that the language was dramatized and made more alarming the better to raise funds, could dispel it. My resolution to enter the hospital with Carlyn faltered. I felt I needed the familiar—the strong women I knew too well, my mother or Jane—to contend with the world and do battle. Feder agreed with me. He felt that in my situation I should not be called upon to manipulate an awkward extramarital situation. It was an honest, if mistaken judgment on both our parts, and it almost killed me.

Carlyn, it was decided, would go home on Saturday. The next morning, she and I went shopping for hospital accessories. We walked for hours through the Manhattan streets, just walked. Had we been facing the darkness ahead together, we could have treasured those few hours, as we had the meadowlands of England a mere five weeks before. But I had determined otherwise.

I had asked Jane the night before if she'd accompany me to the hospital, making clear that if I achieved a remission, however short, I would return to Carlyn, whom I would wish to marry. She agreed, perhaps doubtful I would emerge from Sinai, or believing, perhaps, that my relationship with Carlyn could not be sustained through so hard an ordeal, or only, perhaps, out of duty or compassion.

201

I put Carlyn in a cab for the airport. There was no kiss, no word, no way to say what I felt; I clung to her, as if to let her know that there were a thousand things I would say if I could. She drove off, and I hurried to my children.

Saturday night, I could not abide my loneliness. I knocked at Jane's door and, like a runaway dog returned, asked if I could spend the night in the maid's room, which had been converted by our children into a private little cave. It was dark and windowless, the air slightly stale. Before retiring I talked with Jane, mainly about the chances of remission. I was clinging desperately to that hope, and frightened that it was only hope. Jane's words were reassuring, but her tone and her lovely eyes were all tragedy and gloom. At eleven o'clock I huddled in the eight-by-twelve-foot cubicle for what would possibly be my last night in the outside world.

Sunday, finally. The leaves were clearly dying; the weather was chilly and wet. This was the same day that Adam, seventeen, our six-foot three-inch, lithe, powerful fencer, was leaving to enroll at Harvard. I went through some personal papers before he left and uncovered a Father's Day greeting he had made for me in the second grade. It was shaped like a covered wagon and read "because you covered me with love." This day I saw the torment in his great brown liquid eyes, which reinforced my own anxieties. I was especially concerned that his worries about my fate would seriously affect his adjustment to Harvard and his studies there. We clasped each other as we said farewell.

On the cab drive to the hospital, Jane and I sat at the opposite ends of the back seat. I reached out and held her hand for the duration of the ride. I needed the warmth of human flesh. When we arrived at the hospital, Ruth, her lawyer husband, and her daughter Anna, three, were already in my assigned room. She knew of my fondness for children and Anna was there to cheer me. The touch of my grandchild's delicious skin and the touch of her long blond hair gave me satisfaction but also sorrow, for I realized I might never see her after this fleeting visit. By evening, dignity seemed a virtue I could no longer afford, and my judgment faltered; I asked Jane to stay with me. With her customary efficiency, she had a cot brought in and set up next to my hospital bed. I shall always deplore the frailty and self-pity which caused me to make such an unfair request of Jane, for it doubtlessly misled her and reinforced her hopes for a reconciliation.

She remained from Sunday to Wednesday, as they subjected me to the whole arsenal of treatment contrived by modern medicine to destroy the major illness of our century. All the while, I had an image of Carlyn in Atlanta walking the suburban roads, head bowed—anxious and lonely. I was glad to receive the first cheering letters from her with cartoons of me in the hospital bed ogling a bevy of comely nurses, undressing them in my mind's eye. Even in her exile, Carlyn saw me as whole, undamaged, and virile. But what was I doing to our relationship? Was I not admitting defeat by estranging myself from her, who embodied my hope of life? And what was I doing to Jane? Wasn't it exploiting her to ask her to look after me when I really intended to go back to Carlyn? If I survived, would my debt to Jane mean soldering the chains I had broken with such effort by leaving home? Incredible as it may seem, I dwelt on my marital problems much more than on the illness. In the end, my most gnawing fear was the thought of losing Carlyn.

Carlyn and I had discussed my leasing of an East Side apartment suitable for both of us. She could move there from Atlanta. As she had often stated, she was content to live with me in New York without the benefit of marriage, but she refused to live with another woman's husband.

During the first three days of chemotherapy, I began to see clearly that I had to rid myself of the emotional tangle that, apart from hurting Jane further, was complicating any chance I had for recovery.

I wondered how I could summon the will to tell Jane. My mind went to the time I had to pull my daughter Anne's foot off a spike, resolutely and without delay. Jane and I faced each other in the hospital room. In my view we were equally uncomfortable. "It was a mistake to have asked you to come with me," I told her. "Worse, it was cowardly."

Jane left the room. Beyond that moment lay only the grinding details of legal matters. Perhaps I couldn't have done it any other way. It was, perhaps, the very fear of death that had helped me to see, in a flash of lucidity, where life lay. I wrote myself a note in the hospital. "I am weaker and hence not able to explain or even make really rational decisions about big matters; however, I feel I need Carlyn's sustenance to get well—even for a while—and if I don't, then what's the use of thinking about it."

Jane was gone, but there was no assurance Carlyn would come to me. Now I was wholly bereft of a woman's devotion—a lifelong need, but which I needed then, most sorely.

On September 27 Carlyn returned to New York. As she entered my hospital room she said, "It's Rosh Hashanah—the beginning of the New Year."

12

"I have set before thee life and death,
the blessing and the curse; therefore,
choose life."   —Deuteronomy 30:19

CANCER IS SELDOM AMBIGUOUS. But according to Dr. Louis Wasserman I was suffering from myelocytic leukemia, and its form was
"subacute." Acute myelocytic leukemia, the worst form of the disease, rapidly wipes out the white blood corpuscles that ward off
bacteria. The first streptococcus that creeps in from an infected
drinking glass can be deadly. By calling the disease "subacute"
Dr. Wasserman hedged his bet. He was an optimist, but every subsequent chart designated my illness as "acute myelocytic leukemia."

I had entered Mount Sinai on September 16, a remarkable research and teaching hospital, but where, as in similar centers, personal service has declined. There, I immediately began to fight
against any carelessness that—considering the potential hazard of a
single cold germ—I knew could kill me. I was outraged when ele-
mentary principles of hygiene and nursing care were violated. I
never surrendered to the system. After the first week, I expressed
my independence by telephone, calling every responsible person
within its reach to find out why special requests for blood were not

joined to the routine, and why certain of Wasserman's orders were not fulfilled. I even eventually succeeded in moving to a more efficient floor.

I had allies, too; one, in Dr. James F. Holland, a consultant Wasserman had called in. Holland, a confident, aggressive man, attacked my illness as if it were a personal enemy, as if the mere existence of leukemia were an affront to his power. He was as insistent on proper hygiene as I, and finally posted a sign on my door that read, "Do not touch this patient without washing up." Even so, I had to watch the attendants like a hawk.

The idea underlying the new protocol was to murder my disease without murdering me. I was informed about the probable and possible side effects of the drugs employed and had to sign bundles of consents. Not one of the organs in my body would be out of jeopardy. The first drug I received was daunomycin, recently developed in Italy. In chemotherapy, the drug must wash directly into the bloodstream. I soon felt the power of daunomycin when a few drops failed to flush through my veins and leaked into the tissues instead where it burned like pure fire, scarring my right arm permanently. Three times they loaded me with daunomycin; three times I eyed the dark red liquid and was haunted by its uncanny resemblance to the clay soil of southern Georgia.

Every time doctors prepared the injection by dissolving the orange and red powder in distilled water I contemplated the warning that this drug has a "peculiar cardiac toxicity" to the degree that limits must be established for the total amount administered over a period of time. Each injection was preceded by an electrocardiogram examination. Daunomycin's other side effects are more routine. It is merely incidental that it would turn my urine red for two days. But its power for good is as great as a knife in the hand of a good surgeon.

Then there was cytosar. They dripped it through my veins for seven continuous days and nights, interrupted only when the needle or connecting line got clogged. After a day the irritation was so bad they had to stick a new needle in a new vein, and soon the supply of veins was drying up. I began to run a fever and a powerful antibiotic was now administered to take care of the presumed, unidentified infection. My fever did not abate. At this point the physicians faced one of many hard choices in six years of treatment.

My white cells, the defense against infection, and the platelets, the protection against bleeding, had been almost wiped out. After some hesitation the doctors decided to try an extraordinary antibiotic, carbenicillin, which can itself produce a qualitative platelet disorder. The fever disappeared in two days. They pumped one arm full of wonder drugs while the cytosar continued to flow through the other. The doctors meanwhile tried to identify the bacteria that had caused the fever, but none was ever cultured.

It was at this low point that I inexplicably experienced the certainty that I was going to survive. It may have been out of pure spite. One day my brother Lewis, who sat at my bedside, discussed with an attending junior hematologist the questionable wisdom of keeping patients alive through all these chemotherapeutic horrors when the chances of survival were so slim. Lewis thought that I was asleep. The conversation at first frightened me: Had I been duped by the hopes aroused by Wasserman and Holland? Then rage and fierce determination surged in me.

Everyone seemed to assume there was no greater torture than the effects of daunomycin. Yet I thought the bone marrow taps were worse. And if the taps were the worst they could throw at me, I'd be glad to take them in exchange for a shot at life.

At least once every few days they penetrated my hip where the bone was thickest and hardest. I'd lie face down and feel the deep plunge of the anesthetizing needle as it brought novocaine to the bone lining. Despite the anesthesia, I knew when the metal met the bone, for the doctor had to force the steel through to the center. And there was always an awful moment, before the great sucking extraction, when several fears converged. Would the needle break? Was it a "dry well," in which case we would have to start all over again? Would the pain of the extraction be unbearable? And what would the doctor see when he examined the marrow?

When it was over, the weariness that ensued was close to death itself. I'd lie motionless and watch the autumn leaves in Central Park, visible from my window. Josh was eleven years old, and I wanted to be outside playing ball with him. It was a need that helped keep me alive. Josh came by to see me almost every day. He would look from the mass of bottles and bandages to me and then to the park. He felt the same need. He was then a curly-haired blond, whose beauty made him seem so vulnerable that I worried as he traversed the Park from the Dakota to the hospital. At first the separation had hit him harder than the illness, since we had not told him it was cancer. "I have a shortage of red cells which carry oxygen," I said. That was true, but Josh did not ask and no one volunteered the reason for the shortage.

As the third week approached, I was near death. My fever intensified, I was very weak, and there were innumerable sores around my gums. I was bleeding profusely, and my hair fell out in large clumps. Members of my family, anticipating the end, came from all parts of the country. I received massive transfusions of both red cells and platelets. I was still alive, ninety-eight days after the initial diagnosis, because I was full of other people's blood cells.

There were more miracles as well—the antibiotics, for one. No rampaging infection had broken the lines of defense. My optimism increased even as my condition worsened. Now I had something even stronger than anger to bolster my spirits; the conviction that my treatment was theoretically sound. The physicians could wipe out the bone marrow with chemotherapy while keeping me free of infection through artificial means. But would the marrow then regenerate in a healthy state? It was a tall order, to be sure. The bases of my optimism were two extraordinary support systems.

The first was the new capacity to transfuse red cells and platelets separately and in great quantities, a technique that made it possible to sustain life until the entire system regenerated. A transfusion of whole blood substances would have destroyed other delicate and vital balances; I would have blown up like a helium balloon. The second support system was the antibiotics, without which the chemotherapeutical attacks on the marrow would have posed too great a hazard.

Today, support systems are even further advanced. Laminar flow chambers maintain defenseless patients in germ-free environments. Even white blood cells can now be transfused, an absolutely momentous achievement—though I have no intention of testing it!

In my case, the support systems worked. My gums bled, so they brought in platelets. The loss of red cells was nigh total, so they replaced them. I ran a vicious fever, and a deadly infection might be around the corner, so they flooded me with antibiotics. The red cells had to be matched: AB positive to AB positive. It was not, however, essential that the platelets be of the same blood type;

the body will accept any type but with chills and fever as a side effect. I asked for protection against these reactions, and they gave me antihistamines, which proved somewhat effective, though as the cells, which look like liquified pork, dripped into my veins, I'd shudder with chills. On a few occasions the floor staff would forget to bring the antihistamines and I would refuse the platelets.

I kept fighting through all the fevers and transfusions. I felt I could only survive it by insisting on control. And there would be plenty of chances to test my resolve. The personnel assigned to monitor various functions never coordinated their blood sample requirements on a given day, so they'd come two or three times to leech my tender, collapsing veins. I finally put my foot down.

"You're not going to take more blood," I shouted. "You take it once a day. Get together and find out how much you want and for what purpose, and, goddam it, in the absence of an emergency, don't you touch my veins. Also, no one's going to draw blood except the intravenous nurse team," I said, "because that's all they do, and they know how to do it."

I got my way in both instances, thereby saving myself considerable pain. I was doing everything I could to avoid being an invalid, or a good patient. I knew, for example, that muscle tone was vital to recovery, yet nobody had prescribed exercise for me, a man with a tube full of cytosar in one arm and an i.v. of antibiotics in the other. So I prescribed my own. I sprinted down the hospital corridors, lugging my bottles and needles with me—an unusual sight in the cancer ward.

Eight years after this first stay in the hospital, a medical administrator confessed: "It's a wonder they didn't kill you with a dagger. You pushed them to the limits of their endurance. Now you are a patient whom they respect and they are proud of their success."

I never regarded myself as a bad patient. I was always willing to try any experimental procedure, to take any risk, and undergo any test. I only insisted on knowing what was going on, its rational basis, and on the strict compliance of the nursing staff to the prescribed regime.

The doctor whose visits I relished was Feder, my psychiatrist, who'd come a few minutes each day. We wouldn't talk much about leukemia; we'd assume recovery and discuss Jane and Carlyn. Yet

209

it was comforting to realize that he had trained in hematology and understood precisely what was happening to my body. Feder was a superb link between psyche and soma; indeed, with him there, it was perhaps inevitable that I would perceive that vital connection between my life and my disease, and I doubt I could have survived without making the connection and acting accordingly. By a remarkable and totally appropriate coincidence, Feder's training in hematology had been under Dr. Louis Wasserman.

There was, however, another doctor besides Feder who became very important to me, a woman named Janet Cuttner. She was bright, of my own generation, precise, direct, realistic, and, as everyone kept pointing out, the best chemotherapist in the business. Logic told me that a woman had to be nearly superhuman to get as far up the greasy ladder as she had. When Wasserman later suffered a heart attack, Cuttner joined Holland in supervising my treatment.

It was Dr. Cuttner who read an early October bone marrow and almost danced into my room the next day. "The megakaryocites are back," she said. I learned that megakaryocites are the huge cells that produce platelets, and the fact that I was producing them despite the chemotherapy indicated remission and regeneration. I wanted to cry out with joy.

The next day I was sober again. Though the doctors were prepared to release me from the hospital, they advised that I return in ten days for the first of a continuous series of "maintenance therapies." These would entail chemotherapeutic drugs, but they would be administered in less radical dosages. The idea, of course, was to extend remission for as long as possible. The drugs would be given in rotation. For the first five days I would receive intravenous dosages of cytosine arabinoside along with thioguanine, the latter in pill form. The cytosar would thereafter be continued once a month, again for five-day periods; it would be alternated with cytoxan, thioguanine, CCNU, and then more daunomycin. No time limit was set for the program. And no time limit was possible. For when I checked out of the hospital on October 10, ten to fifteen percent of my white cells were still cancerous. The pathologists believed they were degenerating. I had so far gained a technical knockout of the disease.

Despite the success, I was chastened by the rigor of the chemotherapy, and an awareness of the cancer's great malignity. This was not despair; I was simply being realistic. But I could now play that game of baseball with Josh, go with him to Pawling, New York, to visit friends and enjoy some touch football. This was the reprieve that I had struggled for, and now, as I savored it, I sensed my mortality all the more keenly. I was not confident I'd survive very long but I was extraordinarily happy.

Ten days raced by and I returned for maintenance therapy. To start, there were the inevitable bone marrows—the first to show a complete remission. Mornings and evenings were spent at the hospital. I also slept there, but each morning I'd check out about eleven and go to my office. I'd return by eight at night for the next round of chemotherapy. The thioguanine was administered three tablets at a time; the drug, I was told, bears some generic kinship to nitrogen mustard, the usefulness of which was discovered accidentally during World War II when the effects of leaking mustard gas were observed. But I had no idea what it would do, and, even though I was able to continue working, I worried that the therapy would debilitate me and possibly affect my relationship with Carlyn. Yet I was delighted when, at the end of the week of the first cycle, I wasn't nauseated, and I felt only vaguely tired.

I spent six hundred dollars on a wig because I wanted to look as good as I could for however many months were left. But I didn't want to waste money on a new suit, though I had lost weight and the suits I had were too ample. Nor did I look for a new apartment. My happiness had nothing to do with a long-term future. When I returned to the hospital to begin maintenance, I felt like a soldier coming off leave and returning to the front.

In December I was able to be treated outside the hospital. The mornings were spent with hematologists who did the blood tests and intravenous therapy. At night the doctor or a nurse would come to my apartment. But when this cycle ended, I felt exhausted, and I soon knew why. The red cells were way down, and the whites were at six hundred; normal is around six thousand. The maintenance, far from maintaining me, had nearly wiped me out.

I asked Wasserman if I'd be returning to Mount Sinai. "Oh no," he said, "that's the worst place for you. There are too many germs there. Go wherever you like." Apparently my office and the New York subway would be safer than the hospital; that at least was Wasserman's opinion, and he was probably right, because I did indeed stay cold-free and infection-free for the next few weeks. My blood count rose again.

"We really clobbered you," said Wasserman. "It wasn't intentional, believe me. You're just more sensitive to those drugs than we thought, and we have to learn to regulate the dosage." Wasserman went on to explain that I had endured what amounted to a second remission-induction, without the transfusions, antibiotics, and sterilized environment to serve as support systems. Nothing in the history of my struggle with leukemia astounds me more than this extraordinary luck, together with Wasserman's candor and the instinctive clinical sense with which he works his way through a medical problem.

As my condition improved, I visited Atlanta, and my mood was once again exuberant. Carlyn and I enjoyed a round of cocktail parties thrown on our behalf. At one, Jean Ferst, an old friend came up, clasped me, and teasingly pulled my hair. Off came the wig, exposing my bald pate. Jean was visibly embarrassed but I was so glad to be alive and partying that I roared with laughter as shock spread through the room.

I drove to Fitzgerald to see my mother, who did not know I had been ill. My sisters and brother thought that at her age, eighty-three, living alone, and suffering from arterial disease, the news would add to her burdens while relieving none of mine. At least the latter judgment was wrong. Mother noticed my new "hairdo," which I dismissed as "citified." I yearned to tell her about my still desperate condition. I visited no one in town, but I reviewed every scene of childhood, absorbing each detail in the fear that this was the last opportunity. When time came to say goodby to mother, I feasted on her strong, dignified features. She was as tall as ever, but now slightly bent.

On the way back to Atlanta I felt suddenly weak again and my urine turned an orange color. I immediately returned to New York and asked one of Wasserman's junior physicians if I had hepatitis. He examined my eyes and poked around my abdomen. "I can't find anything wrong," he said. "Nothing to indicate hepatitis."

I asked him to wait while I stepped into the bathroom. I emerged with a sample that was as orange as a sunset. "What the hell do you think of that urine," I barked.

"Gee, I think you're right," he said.

Hepatitis would pose the greatest struggle yet, for it would necessitate a total cessation of maintenance chemotherapy. Yet without it, I might soon be back to where I was at the beginning of the year. There was nothing to do but rest, eat well, and hope against hope that it would not be long before we could resume the treatments.

During all the years of treatment, particularly in periods when it was suspended because of hepatitis and I felt defenseless, I trudged to Mount Sinai Hospital and gazed on that edifice, thinking: At least I am one person who knows where my end will come, for in this building I'll slip away, not in some gigantic trauma or after long excruciating pain, but silently, a victim of some infection that will bring a halt to breathing.

Over the Christmas holiday season of 1973 I was laid up in the cheerless apartment I had furnished at Seventy-second Street and Third Avenue. I searched for knowledge about the state of the art in leukemia therapy. Suddenly I noticed a review of a book by the journalist Stewart Alsop entitled *Stay of Execution,* the story of his battle with leukemia. I couldn't wait for the book to be delivered. After all, Alsop had remained alive long enough to write what he described as "a sort of memoir." I thought that the title was foreboding, but I was avid to read the book, to compare every symptom and every therapy. As I flipped the pages to find out how Alsop was doing now, I saw these words: "Actually, I'm not sure what I would do if it turned out I had acute leukemia, after all, and had to choose between chemotherapy and sleeping pills. I think I'd choose the pills, but when you're near death you grasp for life. Perhaps I'd simply refuse to take chemotherapy and then let nature in the shape of infection take its course." I put the book away. I had acute leukemia; I'd been through massive chemotherapy and expected to continue it perhaps until I died. At the moment I was chafing because hepatitis was holding up my chemotherapy.

Alsop did have a form of my disease. I was shaken when he died.

The new year of 1974 now lay grimly ahead. And I felt burdened with a particular responsibility. I had been working on an important tax case, *Textron* v. *United States*, for two years; when I went into remission, I assured Paul, Weiss that I would be there to try it. As a result, no substitute attorney had been scheduled. If I withdrew

213

from the case, whatever the reason, the client might be badly hurt.

The trial was scheduled for January 8 in cold, snowy Providence. There was no way to postpone it. The judge was old—even I might outlive him—and Textron was itching for an immediate hearing. As the day approached when we'd have to either force a postponement or send in a less prepared partner, Dr. Cuttner grasped my dilemma. Realizing that incessant fretting might hurt me more than hepatitis, she told me to go. For four days I corralled every ounce of fortitude within me, and I won the case.

The return trip to New York was a nightmare. Planes were grounded by a snow storm, and I couldn't even find a taxi to get me to the Providence train station. I trudged despondently through the streets, and finally slumped into the seat of a turboliner, wondering how much the human body could take. Worse news awaited me in New York. Carlyn had left for Atlanta, disgusted with my reckless trip to Providence, and disheartened by my inability to complete arrangements for my divorce.

During this tough period in my physical and emotional life, I leaned heavily on Ann, my second child, who was now twenty-five. She had worked in a halfway house for runaways in Washington, D.C. Ann gathers friends like a magnet, and the bonding holds. She possesses an innate capacity to give and receive confidences and to confer comfort—the natural resource of an effective psychiatric social worker, which she has become. She was always less involved in my political activities than my other children. When I was stricken, she became a rock on which I leaned. It was only later that I learned how torn she was. As she put it, "It was the blind leading the blind." Ann constantly undervalued herself. Though she had the gift of relating to people and as much intelligence as any of her siblings, she had never felt challenged to sharpen her mind. We had a straight talk about this during the worst phase of my chemotherapy regime. I urged her to enroll for another graduate degree at a distinguished university, preferably Chicago, arguing that she needed the theoretical underpinning for the social work in which she was already engaged. She dismissed the idea: "I'll never get in—anyway, it's too late for admission this fall." I pressed; she demurred. Finally, she went to the University of Chicago to see for herself. Admitted, she graduated with flying colors two years later. I felt that my illness had brought us closer to one another.

My sister Ruthanne was also a great support when Carlyn despaired that I'd ever be free. I was at Ruthanne's, in Washington, when Carlyn called to say, "Morris, I just can't take it anymore. I think we'd better call it quits." I returned to New York more depressed than ever to take care of Josh in the Dakota, since Jane was away on holiday. He had a good time. He loved my being there, for he was almost young enough to believe that the past could be renewed.

Yet what was this hunger in me to return to my family? Hadn't I already understood that divorce meant rebirth and that my emotional bankruptcy had to be redeemed if I were to survive? And what was hepatitis doing to me? I was sliding back and only the right combination of circumstances could break the fall. That combination began when Carlyn called me from Sarasota in mid-January 1974. She was utterly exhausted and had gone there to rest.

"Why don't I join you?" I asked.

"Please do," she said.

My rebirth was assured in early spring when blood tests showed that the hepatitis was finally receding. And it also may be that the hepatitis, which would return twice more, was a blessing in disguise. There are some scientists who believe that the disease naturally recharges the body's cancer-immunity system. No one thinks that hepatitis alone can bring leukemia under control, but it may produce interferon, which snipes at the bad cells missed during chemotherapy. Even so, I would hardly recommend it as a deliberate course of treatment, for it, too, can be fatal.

My blood count finally rose to a point where resumption of chemotherapy was possible. There never was a patient more anxious for the strenuous ordeal of cytosar. Dr. Cuttner also told me that this cycle would emphasize CCNU, a drug that is supposed to have a particularly long-lasting effect on the marrow.

At this point, however, my therapy took on a new dimension, largely by my own instigation. When I first began my treatment I learned, through a friend from Brandeis, Zmira Goodman, of a new immunological agent, Methanol Extract Residue, or MER. It had been developed by Dr. David Weiss of the Hebrew University-

215

Hadassah Medical School in Jerusalem but was not then available in the United States. On my behalf my friend approached Weiss, who reported extended remissions with MER without systemic side effects, except localized ulcers, which left healing scars. At the time, the prospect of ulcers could hardly dampen my enthusiasm.

Zmira had also learned of another new immunology, which consisted of radiation-treated leukemia cells. It was being administered to patients in remission at St. Bartholomew's Hospital in London. I had asked my physicians about both therapies when I first went into remission in October 1973, but they said, "We'll see—not for now." Dr. Holland did tell me, however, about still another immunotherapy with which he and Dr. George Bekesi had experimented in Buffalo at the Roswell Park Memorial Institute a year before. They used leukemia cells treated with an enzyme, neuraminidase, in the same way that the British physicians used the radiation-treated cells. But Holland was waiting for the equipment and the personnel to institute his program at Sinai.

We went ahead with the chemotherapy in March 1974. The first dose of cytosar was fine, but the second nauseated me; it was the first really intense nausea that I had suffered since submitting to chemotherapy. My temperature shot up to 101° and I began to shake with chills. For the next three years I would suffer from "Tuesday sickness" on every second day of chemotherapy. It was a clockwork agony to which, alas, I never grew inured.

Until Carlyn moved to New York in January 1975, I sometimes went through the week of maintenance without her. On those occasions, Josh usually slept over at my apartment. In August 1974, I wrote Carlyn: "I didn't do well in maintenance. I was sicker than usual. My temperature went up to 103.6. I warned Josh that should I become delirious, he was to get Janet." By chance, Dr. Janet Cuttner lived in the same building as I.

By the time Carlyn came to live in New York, the cytosar dosages were changed from intravenous to subcutaneous and she was able to give them to me. She armed herself with needles, vials, bottles, and swabs, and the nightly visits of the nurses or physicians were thus dispensed with. I thought of the paradox that Carlyn was administering poisons out of love. The only palpable change in my physical reactions was that "Tuesday sickness" now came on Monday. By subcutaneous injection I was absorbing the drugs over a longer period of time, which meant that more white cells were critically affected at their most vulnerable time.

I had, however, been long worried about the efficacy of the whole maintenance program, that we were not always on schedule, and that the dosages were too small. My knowledge of medicine, though naive, was the only real defense I had, and, as I pondered the information I'd been given about MER and the immunizing leukemic cells, I knew I'd have to contest my doctors once again. I simply could not believe that remission would continue under the present regime.

In the meantime, Dr. Weiss in Jerusalem had been receiving constant reports of my condition from Zmira Goodman. "A perfect case for MER," he said. But the FDA hadn't released it yet, not even for clinical trials, and my physicians were still not convinced that it was indicated. By the middle of May, I was ready to take things in my own hands and fly to Israel.

Dr. Cuttner intervened and agreed to try MER if somehow I could get it released to her. Senator Henry "Scoop" Jackson had called several times to inquire about my condition, first as I was undergoing remission-induction chemotherapy in Mount Sinai. One day Scoop asked if there were anything he could do, and I replied, "Yes, perhaps you might get a drug (MER) released for clinical trials in this country." He teamed up with Hubert Humphrey and the vials were soon delivered to Mount Sinai. Also I was delighted to learn that Dr. Holland was within months of testing his own immunotherapy with leukemic cells. I could foresee a remission stretching way into the future. My expectations were much higher than they had been upon my initial remission in October 1973. I began to think that, as long as I avoided a head-on collision with a moving vehicle, I might well live several more years.

I wanted, however, very much to live out my normal life. In August 1974, when Carlyn was still living in Atlanta, I wrote her: "I would like to say something about how I feel about life. I love it. I do not feel fulfilled. In this past year I poured more than ever before into my children. . . . Leukemia has provided a sense of urgency. I feel I have meant a lot to all these children this year and I have a lot more to give. I am productive in my work, enjoy my friends, and take quite some pride in the implicit admiration I sense as people see me move ahead despite leukemia, divorce, and some

217

disappointments. There is in me a will to live, one which is borne by pure zest for life, but also buttressed in the highest degree by my love of five children, my friends, and now by a supreme and unmatched love for a woman."

I must add something else at this point. Yes, I had the will to seize my own life, and I had the understanding to comprehend the fine points of my own condition. But I was surviving also because I had access to the institutions and practitioners at the frontier of cancer research and therapy. What about someone who doesn't know where the best doctors are, or who does not have the comprehension and the will to see that others carry out and coordinate the doctors' orders? The issue is not money, for anyone who gets to the right doctors in the progressive centers and is prepared to sign the waivers and take the risks, can receive experimental treatment. And wealthy cancer patients have continued to pay far more for outdated treatments.

When I reported to Dr. Cuttner for my first dosage of MER, she told me that Holland wanted it administered in tandem with his new immunotherapy. If I started MER before he was ready with his therapy, he would simply refuse to include me in his program.

Dr. Holland was not my physician; he was technically a consultant, called an investigator. His primary duty was to science. If we chose not to take his advice and submit to his experiments, well and good. This was what my daughter Ruthie learned when she tried to find out why he insisted on the delay.

We went to Holland's office together:

"Is MER potentially helpful in daddy's condition?" Ruth asked.

"Yes."

"Why do you object to his taking it before your cell therapy is ready?"

"Because I wish to do both treatments at the same time."

"Do you believe that the prior use of MER will have an adverse effect on the benefits of your treatment?"

"I doubt it."

"Then why do you insist on his waiting?"

"Because I wish to do both treatments at the same time."

"Is there any evidence that this is the better course?"

"No, it's all experimental."

218

"Then why don't you just let daddy go ahead and take the MER now?"

"Because I do not wish to adopt that protocol."

"But it's daddy's body. Why can't he have control over it?"

"He can."

"No, he can't. You're forcing him to make a choice. Your duty . . ."

"My duty is to advise. You must bear in mind that I am not your father's physician; I am an investigator."

I respected Holland's firmness then and even more now, heading as I do the President's Commission for the Study of Ethical Problems in Medicine and Biomedical and Behavioral Research.

Medicine's advance against disease requires controlled experiments. Inevitably, some lives may be expended, a necessary price if knowledge is to be expanded.

Hard choices for Holland and his colleagues mean easier lives for humanity. I knew for sure after this conference that I was a soldier in the battle against leukemia, and I had not been conscripted.

The dilemma became academic when Holland called me one day in June and said, "Let's go. Meet me in my office at three."

When I arrived, he told me to strip for a bone marrow. The thought of his doing one terrified me, though I had to realize that he was not going to start treatment without having proof that I was still in remission. But here was a very senior physician about to undertake a technical procedure performed routinely by younger persons. So I could not resist asking, "Do you know how to do a bone marrow?" He took no offense, and, laughing, replied that he never asked a member of his team to do what he could not do himself.

The test would reveal that I was still in remission, and that we could proceed with the experimental protocol. I had enormous faith in Holland; however intense my confrontations with him and his colleagues, I knew that I had been treated with immense care and skill.

The immunized cells were injected in about fifty lymph glands, the punctures forming a kind of necklace around my collar. They were also administered in the groin and the arms. Each one produced an intense burning pain. At one point they were injected into the sternum, and that was just unbearable. Each red-hot pin of pain represented millions of cancer cells. Later, the anguish was, mercifully, submerged in demerol.

The MER was injected in five, and then ten, spots across my chest and legs. There was no particular pain during the administration, but Weiss wasn't kidding when he talked about ulcers! Some of them, particularly along my legs, were as big as quarters. In order to heal they needed air, and that posed a problem since I always returned to work directly after treatment. But I did what I could to keep my clothes from touching the sores, and tried to expose them at every opportunity. Salt water was especially healing, so I went to the beach whenever possible. Carlyn eventually contrived a veritable wall of Dr. Scholl's bunion pads to protect the sores from my trouser legs. My doctors admired the contraption and soon began recommending it to other patients.

The early rounds of immunotherapy were administered in a ward where I was curtained off from a husky nineteen-year-old lad, T.J. Martel. Sometimes he'd go first, and his outcries assured me that my threshold of pain was not unduly low. T.J., his mother, Carlyn, and I joked about our "social occasions." Then after one Christmas, I no longer saw T.J. I was afraid to inquire.

I endured another two years, two more bouts of hepatitis, two liver biopsies.

I was, of course, still also receiving chemotherapy, a fact which came to trouble me. I didn't want to argue with success, but weren't the two systems acting in theoretical opposition? They were filling me full of diseased cells in order to immunize me against a recurrence. The immunization included components that were both general (the MER) and specific (the enzyme-treated cells). But the cytosar and the others—weren't they supposed to be wiping out the cancer cells? Weren't they killing the immunizing agents? I was incredulous and the fact that I was by now utterly weary of the chemotherapy contributed to my discomfort.

I tried and generally succeeded in not feeling sorry for myself. Still, sometimes, riding a subway through the Bowery I would see a drunk with glazed eyes, uncertain gait, and a bottle in a brown paper bag. Momentarily, I might catch myself saying, "Why can't

I have his normal bone marrow, which he puts to such poor use?'' But I don't think I brooded excessively.

In September 1976, I wrote Dr. Cuttner a letter that clearly, and respectfully, outlined the issues involved and my considerable perplexity regarding them:

"To what extent has maintenance damaged my immune system?

"What are the benefits of continuing maintenance?

"Are the bad cells increasing between maintenance treatments? If so, can the immunizing agents handle them?

"Is there hard evidence that the chemotherapy is destroying the bad cell formations?

"What are the dangers of combining the two therapies? If chemotherapy is damaging the immune system, what sense is there in continuing it?

"What sort of time limit do you now foresee on the chemotherapy?''

Dr. Cuttner's reply was most responsive. Apparently my letter had indeed persuaded the doctors to meet and fully discuss my condition. Their decision was that I should continue maintenance until remission hit the five-year mark. That meant two more years.

When I reported for immunotherapy in January 1977, Dr. Bekesi said they were stopping MER but continuing with the neuraminidase cells. His monitoring system had picked up indications that I was being made auto-immune—my immune system was overcharged and its effectiveness was diminishing. Bekesi and Holland were operating in an uncharted field with no texts or even monographs to guide them. Two years later, Dr. Weiss praised the Sinai team for superb clinical judgment in stopping the MER in the nick of time. The other treatments proceeded.

Far from settling into complacency, however, my good fortune made me suspicious, particularly when I considered the antithetical purposes of the two therapies. Part of me worried that some unanticipated disaster, some sort of a volcanic explosion of cancer cells, would end my remission and kill me in a month or two.

As the time approached for the termination of maintenance, I became more and more restive. I had come so far; the thought of losing it all after much struggle was unendurable. Bone marrows became an emotionally, as well as a physically, draining experience. I couldn't bear to leave the doctor's office without knowing the results. If there was bad news, I didn't want it on the phone.

In reality, nothing less than the enthusiasm of Dr. Cuttner's "the megakaryocites are back" would satisfy me. In the meantime, however, I was growing more robust with each new day. The immunotherapy was making me resistant to even the slightest sniffle. After so many years, I had regained a physical muscle tone, color, and exhilarating bounce. I could look at my own flesh and not see the vile contours of decomposition. I was finally taken off chemotherapy in December 1977, because of the third attack of hepatitis. I was then freed of the cycle of gut-wrenching pain, and my energies were no longer sapped by the devastating drugs. The cell injections would continue for another year.

One incident concludes the tale.

It occurred in January 1979. I went to Holland's office for my fifty shots, expecting the nurse, who usually administered them, to greet me. Instead, I found Holland himself, his lips pursed in a strange smile. A whole assemblage of doctors was gathered around, including Bekesi, with whom he had first tried his therapy in Buffalo. It was ominous.

"What's going on?" I asked.

"These are your last shots," he said.

"Why?" I asked.

"Because you're cured."

Why have I now survived? Why have I been free of disease for more than seven years, out of chemotherapy for three and immunotherapy for two? Why are scores of others who received the same treatment dead, some after a few months, others after several years?

Without my doctors, who were aware of the newest drugs and anxious to try them, I never would have had a chance. The rampaging immature cancer cells would have multiplied in legions, crowding out the healthy cells.

I know that I owe my life to the experimental, aggressive chemotherapy that destroyed my hair and took a toll on every fiber of my body. The tendency of the cancer to recur was held at bay or perhaps even wiped out by my will to live, by a new love and new interests, by immunotherapy, maybe by hepatitis, maybe by good fortune, maybe by God.

I feel the connection between physical and emotional health is

222

indivisible. The channels by which the mind and body interact will, I suppose, some day be uncovered. Then, scientists will be able to identify the agents and agencies through which these causes and effects work. Data from controlled experiments will be collected, collated, and interpreted. The original investigators will publish their results and invite their peers to repeat their work for verification, concurrence, or criticism.

It was through this tradition of medical research that the drugs that induced my remission from myelocytic leukemia were developed. The reasons why remission has been sustained are not clear at all. My doctors will readily admit this. I certainly do not underestimate the power of the mind and spirit, and the joys of work and love. But I give respectable scientific methods the credit due and reserve for the unknown factors the awesome name of the mystery which I refuse to confuse with science.

The good physician acknowledges the mystery of the healing process.

Recently, Dr. Cuttner called to say that she had a patient in Mount Sinai with my disease about to undergo remission-induction therapy. He was frightened and very depressed. She asked if I would speak to him, saying, "I don't know whether he can survive the therapy or go into remission, but he certainly won't if his mood doesn't improve."

"Good morning, doctor, this is Morris Abram. Dr. Cuttner suggested I call you . . ."

There was a long silence—then a small voice, hollowed by despair, said, "Yeah, she said you would. . . ."

"Listen," I said, "I was exactly where you're at eight years ago. Same diagnosis. Everything. The only difference now is that Sinai didn't have the isolation equipment. I was wide open for anything coming at me. They didn't have the white cell packs either. . . ."

More silence. I wondered if I was boring him, "Doctor . . ."

"It can't be worth the agony," he said finally.

"It can! It was! I've got a good life again. I've gotten married again. I swim every day. I've never worked harder, and I'm working well—you're a physician, aren't you?"

"Yep. That's precisely the problem. Look, I know all about these chemicals, they're dreadful, terrible poisons."

"They poison leukemia, too, doctor. You've got to fight fire with fire. Fight, doctor! I'm sure you've fought plenty for the lives of others."

There was another interminable silence and then he said, a shade stronger, I thought, "Oh, yes, I did do that."

Ten days later I visited him at the hospital. He had begun his therapy. When the buxom young nurse bent over him to plump his pillows, he turned to her as if to apologize, "This therapy has aged me, you know."

"We can't make you any younger, doctor," she said cheerily.

"I'm not here to get younger," he joked with her, "I'm here to get older."

Of one thing I am sure: Cancer is a battle between a disease and its host. The host wants to live. The cancer never discloses its final intentions. I am content to leave the contest in status quo.

13

CANCER CREATES many psychological ramifications. For me there was first the question of whether to mask the nature of my illness from friends and clients. My family, except for Josh and mother, immediately were told the whole truth. Then there was the question of whether to restrict, so far as possible, knowledge of my predicament to those with "a need to know." I decided early that secrecy would be just one additional burden; that caution, evasion, and the false front needed to carry off such a policy would be a psychic and physical strain. That course would also deny me the support of people outside the family, though there would be some who would withdraw in a way I came to understand as self-protection. There are people who become anxious in the presence of the dying and even a few who actually feel, against all credible evidence, that cancer is contagious.

Independent of the decision to disclose my condition to associates, was the decision to go public with the startling success of my somewhat novel treatment. This was prompted by a mixture of motives. By the fall of 1975 I was already in an unusually long remission. I recall my anxiety and original doubt that any real remission was possible, or that life could be extended for a sufficient length and of such quality as to make the heroic effort worthwhile. I knew that in the hinterlands and even in the metropolises, the advanced treatment which seemed to be working for me was not merely unavailable but unheard of. Friends were calling regularly, on behalf of relatives afflicted with leukemia, to inquire about the place and nature of my therapy. I realized that the story of my so far successful struggle might be more significant to more people than any political or educational effort I had attempted.

Paradoxically I felt that the hardest blow I had yet received might afford the opportunity for the greatest service I could now bestow.

So when the remission seemed consolidated, I cooperated with a *New York Times* reporter, a former student at Brandeis, in a sensitive story of my illness. I was astounded when I saw the story featured on the front page. There was indeed a thirst for good news and especially some even tentative success with the therapy for acute myelocytic leukemia. Phone calls, letters, requests for more information poured in from all over the country and from abroad. The American Cancer Society effectively worked to inform, enlighten, and encourage its vast constituency with the lessons from my case.

The loss of some privacy is insignificant compared to my gratification when I see or hear a fellow victim rally as I relate my story. "The loss of hair doesn't matter—it will come back; the drugs are bad, but certainly endurable; and life can be good when in treatment and for me it's been wonderful afterwards."

I always urge that the caller get his doctor in touch with a top treatment center for newest information, closing with the advice, "Never stop fighting for information about your condition. Work with your doctor; but make sure he works with you, and if you want life you've got to affirmatively choose it."

The taping sessions with Eli served as a diary during the fifteen months I served as chairman of the New York State Moreland Act Commission on Nursing Homes, which brought me into collision with a variety of actors in a scandal that greeted Governor Hugh Carey in the first days of office. When the governor, who knew I was a leukemic patient, called me in early January 1975, I was receiving five varieties of chemotherapy and two immunotherapies. Some treatments were very debilitating and others painful. The governor didn't mention my illness. I appreciated his leaving that issue up to me. I was determined to continue an active life and I missed only a few days' work. Major events such as hearings, which were televised on the New York State Public Television network, were fitted around a rigorous medical schedule.

When the Moreland Commission was convened, New York State was infested with rat-trap proprietary nursing homes that grew on the landscape like sores. Service was indifferent at best and abusive at worst. Hygienic conditions were deplorable, and the old people unfortunate enough to be trapped within were left alone to decay and die. The politicians of New York State were grossly implicated in these conditions; indeed, they reaped enormous benefits, political and otherwise, mainly by looking the other way.

The cast of characters ranged from a heartless and grizzled old rabbi named Bernard Bergman to a vastly wealthy former governor who happened to have become vice-president of the United States by the time the Commission was ready to question him. I suppose that I, too, helped make it a colorful cast, for I was a southern liberal Jew dying of leukemia. I was appointed to the Commission by Governor Carey partly because I was a Jew; Carey knew that a number of prominent Jews might be disgraced, maybe imprisoned. I, also, knew that I'd eventually be going after a rabbi or two. Many nursing homes in New York City must keep kosher to succeed. Carey, a consummate politician, wished to have a thorough investigation, but naturally wanted to limit his political risks in the inevitable exposure of businessmen with religious titles, which they would flaunt. Without exacting any promise or even mentioning the subject, Carey knew that I would not be deterred from pursuing whomever was responsible, and if a rabbi became a target, no one would suggest that discrimination was among my motives.

When Al Smith was governor, he created a Moreland Commission and was its only member. In my situation I recommended that four others be added, who would reflect different segments of the community. Carey approved my selections: Dr. Isadore Rossman, one of the finest geriatricians in the country; Peter Berle, the incorruptible son of Adolph and Beatrice Berle; Amanda Wilkins, who was Roy's wife, and an extremely able social worker; and, finally, Dorothy Wadsworth, an upstate Republican appointed by Rockefeller to his Attica Commission to investigate the riots at that prison.

The extent of Rockefeller's responsibility in the nursing home scandal was rather hazy to me as we began, but I felt the failure to examine him had flawed the so-called "Stein Commission," which had investigated nursing homes under the aegis of legislator Andrew Stein.

We built our case block by block, and there was soon no doubt about it. The deplorable conditions had developed under Rockefeller's fourteen-year reign, but to go after that man was always a very dangerous enterprise. In New York State there was no power base that Rockefeller's Yankee imperialism had not helped to build.

I felt he had squandered power badly. With almost the whole system in his pocket, he had still failed to administer the state frugally and efficiently. He had expended the treasury for the Albany Mall, and had broken the downtown Manhattan real estate market in the early 1970s with the World Trade Center. He had established a system of state-guaranteed loans which permitted voluntary nursing homes to sprout like mushrooms. As I put it to the press: "Anytime the government makes funds available which do not come directly from the person paying, there will always be enough hands to hold the gush of money."

A Jewish Republican in New York State could collect Jewish votes in New York City, and if he was part of the Rockefeller machine, like Javits or Keating, he would win upstate. But a Gentile Republican, even Rockefeller himself, had to erode the conventional Democratic voting blocs if he were to succeed. One of those blocs is, obviously, labor. The key to New York labor was the building unions and the numerous trades that attend the construction of a skyscraper, a mall, a university, or a nursing home. By emptying the public coffers to erect buildings, Rockefeller bought their support. For fifteen years it was economically advantageous for the important construction unions of the AFL-CIO to support their Republican benefactor or to put up only a token resistance. Of course, it's against the law for a man to buy votes out of his own pocket, but it's an enduring irony of American politics that, if he

228

does it out of the taxpayers' pockets, he may be handsomely re-elected. The Commission found that the voluntary nursing homes Rockefeller had built would lay on the New York taxpayer one-half billion dollars of unnecessary costs.

Once Rockefeller had enough unions, he only needed to woo one more bloc and that was, of course, the Jews. They were more stubbornly Democratic than labor, for the Jews maintained their essentially liberal attitudes throughout the 1960s, whereas many labor unions were more than happy to join the great white backlash. Rockefeller courted the Jewish community by public consumption of knishes and by assisting Jewish charitable campaigns. His chief political contact to the community was a generous Jewish businessman, Samuel Hausman, who had become mixed up with a target of our investigation, a nursing home profiteer, Bernard Bergman.

The Moreland Commission waited six months before summoning Rockefeller. We had to build a case, and the nursing home business is complicated. Our move came just after our hearings on a Bergman facility called The Danube, a filth-hole on Staten Island that Bergman had been kept from opening for three years because a bad press had forced the state to withhold approval. But Bergman had built it anyway, confident that he would get his approval eventually from Rockefeller, or his hand-picked successor, Malcolm Wilson. Bergman was right. Wilson did indeed approve it, and, as we concluded the hearings on The Danube, it seemed reasonable to ask why. That meant Rockefeller.

It meant Rockefeller for many reasons. His Chief-of-Staff, T. Norman Hurd, had communicated with Bernard Bergman at least a dozen times through Samuel Hausman, who described himself as the governor's "eyes and ears to the Jewish community." Bergman contacted Hausman through a rabbi named Twersky, who was a public relations man for the Mizrachi, an Orthodox Zionist movement. Twersky said that Bergman was being discriminated against by the State Department of Health, and Hausman took the tale directly to Rockefeller.

Initially we suspected that Bergman had personally met with Rockefeller, but Rockefeller contended that he had never seen him, an assertion we never disproved. From the very beginning of the hearings, Bernard Bergman was pinpointed as the chief villain. He was a prince of darkness that none of us who ever saw him is likely to forget. His was a presence that exuded power, the unharnessed force of evil.

Getting Nelson Rockefeller to testify was no easy matter. Even the decision to call him came hard. He was now the vice president of the United States, recently nominated by President Ford and confirmed by the Senate. When serving as governor, he had not been sworn as a witness and examined in public concerning his pivotal role in the Attica uprising, in which men lost their lives. Rockefeller's influence ran wide and deep. I recalled how contributors to Arthur Goldberg's campaign against him for governor in 1970 had trembled lest a check to Goldberg's chest come to the attention of the loan department at the Rockefellers' bank.

Rockefeller's personal fortune had tied legions of "independent" and influential figures to his political fortune. Large "loans" to such men were made only to be converted at the appropriate time to gifts on which Rockefeller had even paid the resulting taxes. The amounts totalled well over one million dollars and the list of recipients included the following: Judson Morehouse, former New York State Republican Chairman; Henry A. Kissinger, National Security Adviser to Rockefeller's foe, Richard M. Nixon; William J. Ronan, Chairman of the Port Authority of New York and New Jersey (which built the World Trade Towers); Edward J. Logue, Head of Rockefeller's pet building octopus, the Urban Development Corporation; Emmet J. Hughes, Aide to President Eisenhower and a political pundit; James W. Gaynor, State Commissioner of Housing and Community Renewal; Henry L. Diamond, Head of the Department of Environment and Conservation; Victor Bordella, labor "expert"; and William F. Miller, Barry Goldwater's running mate and Republican National Chairman, and even at the time of the loan Rockefeller's bitter political foe.

From the outset I determined that if the trail of responsibility or a whiff of political influence led to Rockefeller's door, we should follow him even though he was vice president and obviously anxious to run with Ford in 1976.

I have thought a lot about my willing assumption of what I knew was the risk of crossing Rockefeller. I am not a physically brave man; my childhood fear of the fist fight survives, offset by determination to stand by what I believe is a principle, especially one invested with civic responsibility. As others had retreated or compromised in the face of Rockefeller power, I was inclined to confront it if need be. My illness and the possibility that this might be my last public service gave me added strength. I preferred to be remembered as a man of courage rather than of expedience. Then there was the memory of my father, Sam, hounded by the pigmy bankers of Fitzgerald during my childhood. Those "Rockefellers" had in the penny currency of that small realm tethered the power centers in "perfectly legal" ways.

I would never unjustly oppress a Rockefeller or a Bergman, but neither would I exempt the one or the other. Rockefeller, the bipartisan Commission decided unanimously, must be examined as any other witness having relevant information. So soon after Watergate, we were determined that not even a sitting vice president would be beyond the reach of accountability under oath and in public for his actions.

That decided, I had to spar with William E. Jackson, a Chase Manhattan lawyer, the son of the Justice Jackson with whom I had served at Nuremberg. They were expecting me to accept a letter from the vice president or his answer to written-out interrogatories. That had been the procedure with the Stein Committee, but I wouldn't buy it.

"Well," said Jackson, "the vice president is a very busy man. I don't know what we should do."

"We should examine him on the same basis as everyone else," I said.

Jackson was startled. "Can he be examined in private?"

"The vice president may choose to be examined like everyone else, in executive session first," I replied. "But," I continued, "if the Commission decides it is necessary, he will then have to be examined, like everyone else, in public."

Jackson, choosing to limit the times of examination, waived the executive session. And he asked, as the law provides, to have broadcast media excluded from any public session, which meant the print media would have a monopoly. But that was a political mistake; television and radio broadcasters were outraged and even threatened a lawsuit. Rockefeller had no choice but to let all the media in. His staff tried to compromise us by setting the date too early, before we had collected and examined Rockefeller's files.

231

We'd look stupid, while he'd seem in total command of the facts. So I insisted on a date that afforded us a full month to prepare.

We had discovered that there was a labyrinth of intermediaries between Rockefeller and Bergman. Hurd and Hausman were only the major links. If there was no question of legal culpability, what did we prove, then, by interrogating Rockefeller? First and foremost, we proved to anyone willing to watch and listen that the vice president and former governor had known of those conditions in the nursing homes and never once tried to do anything about them. We showed letters of complaint asking him for help that had been sitting in his office for years, one bearing a notation in his own hand. We reminded him that he had failed to keep a campaign pledge to monitor nursing homes, a pledge for which no funds were ever allocated or personnel assigned. His excuse was only that he was a very busy man.

And besides, he claimed, there were budget crunches that had prevented him from funding an ombudsman for nursing homes. We reminded him that the federal government had offered to set up and pay for an ombudsman and his own State Health Department had advised him to accept the offer; it was the kind of federal giveaway that few governors would ever turn down. Why had he? The unmistakable conclusion was that Rockefeller didn't want anyone looking over his shoulder, particularly someone whose power would originate two hundred miles away, in Washington, D.C.

Nelson Rockefeller took wealth for granted. It was power he coveted and exercised with extraordinary zest. We never expected to find a smoking gun of legal corruption—only political use of medical funds, personal callousness, and the slippery evasiveness he amply displayed in the day-long cross-examination of him.

In the face of his poor record in policing nursing home fraud, estimated to have cost the state four hundred million dollars, Rockefeller persistently chose to brag about his building programs, financed by state-backed loans, repaid out of operating funds. Of the billion dollar nursing home construction he had proudly proclaimed: "And this . . . will cost the taxpayers absolutely nothing." Since the funds to repay these construction loans came largely from public Medicaid appropriations, it was difficult to understand Rockefeller's boast that the taxpayer didn't foot one penny of the bill. So I asked him:

How could it be that it costs the taxpayers nothing, the fact that it is borrowed money doesn't mean that it cost the taxpayers nothing, does it, sir?

THE VICE PRESIDENT: Indirectly, you are correct, but directly, you are not.

.   .   .   .   .

CHAIRMAN ABRAM: Governor, you seem to have the view that if you use borrowed money for the construction of nursing homes, that the building costs the taxpayers nothing, even though the funds must be repaid, and the interest thereon repaid out of tax revenues. How can this be?

Finally, the vice president conceded that his characterization was "excessive."

The most crushing indication of the man's flinty disdain for human welfare came when we questioned his program for removing the chronically ill from state mental asylums. The idea, with which my Commission did not disagree, was to reserve mental hospitals for acute cases. Thus, the Rockefeller administration had unloosed thirty-four thousand disoriented and incurably senile patients on communities unprepared to receive them. I asked the vice president: "And [these communities] resisted vigorously?"

"That's right," he replied.

"And what happened was that the old people got caught in the middle of a crunch . . . isn't that what happened?"

"Yes," Rockefeller replied, "and this happens very often in a democracy."

When the examination turned to Rockefeller's office's connection to the notorious Bergman through Rockefeller's friend and political ally, Sam Hausman, the vice president became testy. I referred to his statement filed with the Commission in which he claimed that Bergman's request for his help originated with Hausman, who said that Bergman was "being discriminated against in connection with his license application for proprietary nursing home facilities." After that, there were the following exchanges:

CHAIRMAN ABRAM: So he [Samuel Hausman] told you that Bergman was a friend of his.

THE VICE PRESIDENT: That's my memory.

CHAIRMAN ABRAM: Did he ever tell you that a relative of his, that is Sam, had an interest in a proposed Bergman nursing home?

THE VICE PRESIDENT: No, sir.

233

CHAIRMAN ABRAM: Does that shock you?

THE VICE PRESIDENT: Frankly, I thought myself that he had been pretty well taken in by Mr. Bergman, but if you tell me that he had an investment in there— —Did Mr. Hausman know it?

CHAIRMAN ABRAM: Yes, according to the testimony. Does that shock you, sir?

THE VICE PRESIDENT: I am listening.

CHAIRMAN ABRAM: I am asking you, does it shock you?

THE VICE PRESIDENT: I am waiting to see what you are coming to.

CHAIRMAN ABRAM: Well, I have finished on that. Does it shock you, sir?

THE VICE PRESIDENT: No, it doesn't shock me, and I will tell you why, because anybody has a legitimate right, if they feel they are discriminated against to ask somebody on behalf of somebody, and if it is a member of the family, fine, they ask—they say they are being discriminated against. I would have to ask you, have you never asked for anything from somebody in public office where your family was involved or had an interest?

CHAIRMAN ABRAM: I am asking the questions, not answering them.

THE VICE PRESIDENT: I don't blame you.

Rockefeller told a high state official that at this very moment he had been on the verge of pulling from his inside jacket pocket a "damning piece of evidence," to explode in my face. His sleuths had acquired a letter I had written before I had accepted my post, proposing relatives of mine as bidders on a Port Authority concession in New York. Though this could not possibly have represented a conflict of interests, in an excess of caution I had withdrawn my suggestion, in writing, as soon as I had accepted my post. Rockefeller's defensive move showed the significance he attached to the Moreland investigation at a time his Republican enemies were trying to pry him off the Ford reelection ticket. Aware of the stakes for him and of the resourcefulness of his huge staff, I assumed he had his letter, so I was armed with mine. If he had pulled the pin in his grenade in front of the television cameras, the thing would have blown up in his face.

Rockefeller claimed that his Chief of Staff's intense interest in Bergman's problem arose out of the rabbi's claim he was being discriminated against by the State Health Department. So I inquired:

What did the discrimination involve?

THE VICE PRESIDENT: He didn't get the license he asked for.

CHAIRMAN ABRAM: Was there any implication that there was religious discrimination?

THE VICE PRESIDENT: I couldn't say, I don't remember.

I then advised the vice president that, the day before, the Commission had unanimously decided, on the basis of three days of public hearings on the Bergman matter, there was absolutely no basis for Hausman's contention that his friend Bergman had been the victim of discrimination. I therefore asked:

Now, did [Dr. Hurd] ever tell you that he found no discrimination?

THE VICE PRESIDENT: No, sir, I didn't follow up on it.

. . . .

CHAIRMAN ABRAM: Well, isn't it rather strange, Governor, that your Chief-of-Staff as busy as he is could have found an opportunity to meet during your administration with Bergman or Hausman on Bergman's problems about eight times?

THE VICE PRESIDENT: Well, I asked him to look into it, and because I asked him to look into it, he looked into it. If these gentlemen were persistent, which I have to assume they were based on the number of telephone calls I used to get and take—

CHAIRMAN ABRAM: From whom?

THE VICE PRESIDENT: Mr. Hausman.

CHAIRMAN ABRAM: Go ahead.

THE VICE PRESIDENT: That's what I said right along. I already had made that statement earlier.

CHAIRMAN ABRAM: Well, the Commission has had testimony that Dr. Hurd soon found out that there was no discrimination and he soon found out that Bergman had been turned down, not because of discrimination, but because of a willingness to deceive your Public Health Council. Yet he persisted for two and a half years.

Is this what you would call, to use your words, Governor, "Appropriate action according to established policies.''?

THE VICE PRESIDENT: I won't—yes, because there was no action taken except the courtesy extended to see someone.

CHAIRMAN ABRAM: In other words, you feel that as long as no improper action was taken, this kind of use of your Chief-of-Staff not to correct the situation which was wrong, but to keep trying to change a situation was proper?

THE VICE PRESIDENT: Yes, but I don't think that he was necessarily trying to change the situation during that period. My hunch is he was courteous in seeing a friend of a friend of mine.

. . . .

235

CHAIRMAN ABRAM: We are very much aware of the fact that in this instance Dr. Hurd was meeting many times with Dr. Bergman on the basis of the private interests of a private entrepreneur, and nothing involving a basic policy decision of New York.

THE VICE PRESIDENT: That's correct. He is a very courteous gentleman.

CHAIRMAN ABRAM: Are you suggesting that almost anyone with a problem could walk into his office and have meetings eight times with the Chief-of-Staff—

THE VICE PRESIDENT: Not almost anyone.

CHAIRMAN ABRAM: Who could?

THE VICE PRESIDENT: Anybody that I asked him to see.

Rockefeller had put on a jaunty performance. He was petulant, testy, arrogant, and threatening. However, the instincts of the political animal prevailed as he profusely thanked the Commission as his day on the stand came to an end:

I would like to say that this Commission has done an extraordinary job. . . . I thought the discussion this morning brought out some points that were extremely valuable . . . and I would like to congratulate all of you on the job you have done and the care and thought with which you have gone into it. . . .

Despite Governor Rockefeller's ultimate responsibility for the nursing home debacle at every level—patient abuse, fraud, extravagant waste—all laid out in detail, the press never laid the blame where it had to rest and where the Commission really placed it, at the door to the governor's office.

Rockefeller was in many ways a remarkable man, dazzling the public by his energy, zest, hubris, and money, but most of all by the paradox that the head of a billionaire family seemed actually to enjoy campaigning in the streets, rubbing shoulders with the hoi polloi. His power and spirit infected the press, and though I had a duty to discharge in exposing his responsibility in a great human tragedy, even I admired what he himself would have called his "chutzpah."

In a curious way the Moreland Commission service, while draining my limited energies, helped me through a critical period of my treatment. Statistically I was at a time of maximum risk. Sometimes I had to drag myself into the Moreland Commission office.

236

In the days I was being infused with cytosar and daunomycin, I was either nauseous or on the verge. Yet I knew I could make it through to the next hearing and after that the next, and again, and again. My will to survive was fortified by the determination to complete the task.

Whatever I knew about health care in the United States was confirmed by my experience as Moreland Commissioner. Underlying New York State's tolerance of the shabby treatment of old people were two serious flaws in American society. The first has been stated often enough. We just don't care to look at old folks. In this country, whatever isn't young is dubious.

Second, there is extremely limited housing space in the American city. There is no place for old people, and no one in the family to care for them, for as spatial relationships change, so too do personal relationships. The Bernard Bergmans of the world feed on this gargantuan change.

Though the Moreland Commission couldn't begin to solve such a massive social problem, its achievements were nonetheless considerable. Because of our investigation, class action suits were authorized so that one healthy resident of a Bergman rat-trap could sue for all the helpless ones.

The Commission was also responsible for the Controlling Persons Bill. This law makes the financial operator of a nursing home responsible for the quality of care. Before the bill was passed, the realtor, someone in Bergman's position, was no more than a stockholder in a large corporation, reaping all the profits, but uninvolved with whatever went on inside.

The work of the Commission provided personal satisfaction to me at several levels. I could now, for example, put to rest the old phantom of regretting my decision to choose law over medicine. Had I become a doctor, I could not possibly have made a more satisfying contribution to health care than I did here, for I was able to attack a peculiarly extensive insult to human dignity.

Finally, after Brandeis I had felt robbed of the chance to do the moral deed. The Moreland Commission was a dynamic palliative.

I was disappointed that a secondary achievement of the Commission went unnoticed: When we commenced our work, the state's financial condition, after years of Rockefeller excesses, was tottering. We had been given an appropriation of nine hundred thousand dollars for a nine months' term. I announced to my staff that no matter what, we were never to ask for further funding and that as an example to a shaky state and a now bankrupt city government we would return some of the nine hundred thousand dollars. Members of the staff, experienced in the ways of the bureaucracy, and cynical too, chided me as the nine months extended into twelve.

They counseled me to ask for more money for further studies and against turning any sum back to the state.

"But," I said, "we can finish the job and return one hundred thousand dollars, even if it takes fifteen months."

"You're naive. We can do other fruitful work and what we give back will only be gobbled up by lesser men and in frivolous work."

I persisted: "No, the *Daily News* and the *Times* will trumpet our example and will demand other government agencies take heed."

"They'll do nothing of the sort; if the Commission turns money back, other government heads will be angry, not embarrassed, and the papers will neither note nor remember."

In March 1976 I delivered the six-volume report containing the ten Moreland Commission Bills, now the law of New York, to the governor, together with the one hundred thousand dollars unspent. Carey thanked me, the bureaucracy stood mute, and no editorial writer lifted a pen to comment on our frugality.

I warned that given the sums of money involved, the vulnerability of the aged, and the cupidity of providers, another Moreland Commission would be needed within five to ten years.

Except for the year spent with the Moreland Commission, I continued to practice law almost as I had before my illness. After my determination to handle the Textron tax case in 1974 despite hepatitis, my physicians never discouraged me from work. Even during the two subsequent bouts of hepatitis, I carried on at my own pace. In 1977, though jaundiced and accompanied by a stand-in should I have faltered, I appeared for an hour on the live public television show "The Advocates," as the attorney arguing against a Palestinian state.

Hepatitis is known to cause psychological depression, and during my third encounter with this ailment I brooded on the "reforms" adopted in 1938, known as the New Rules of Federal Civil Procedure, and on every expensive pretrial practice in which I had been engaged since coming North. My secretary, Rose Gioeli, trundled scores of books to my apartment while I lay in bed tracing the course by which this well-intentioned and badly needed reform had in some instances been permitted to run amok.

The *National Law Journal* published my findings. As I wrote, the heavily jowled face of my University of Chicago Professor, Crosskey, seemed to materialize, repeating his conviction, "Law comes from the belly of judges." I cited as a classic instance of emotional jurisprudence the case of *Adickes* v. *Kress*. There the Supreme Court, in 1969, possibly because of understandable sympathy with a northern white civil rights worker arrested in Mississippi, had undermined the power of the lower federal courts to dismiss cases without trial when there was no "genuine issue" for trial.

The plaintiff school teacher had accompanied six young black students to a Kress lunch counter in Hattiesburg during "freedom summer" of 1964. The blacks were served; the plaintiff, as their leader, was refused service, and when she left the store she was arrested for "vagrancy." The heart of the plaintiff's case was a charge of conspiracy between Kress and the arresting police, but the plaintiff admitted she had no knowledge of any agreement and based her entire damage suit on surmise from the mere sequence of events. The Federal District Court summarily dismissed the case, a decision which the Federal Circuit Court of Appeals upheld. The Supreme Court, obviously believing that there was more to the case than met the eye—and this was reflected in the record—reversed the dismissal. This Supreme Court decision, I argued, was compassionately decided, but its legacy became a precedent which has discouraged lower federal courts from getting rid of hundreds of cases based on surmise, costing litigants millions in legal fees and clogging court calendars.

Professor Crosskey was right—the harder the case, the more disposed the judges are to bend the law "to do justice" in the one case. But society is the loser when the legal system, based as it is on precedent, is distorted.

By the time my piece was published, I was back in the courtrooms, too busy to brood but embarrassed by the growing cost of

litigation under rules adopted "to promote simplicity . . . [to elim-
inate] unjustifiable expense and delay."

From 1977 on, I worked in the courtroom more than at any time
since I had moved North. New York clients tended to be very different, but the techniques I had developed in the rough and tumble
of the Georgia courtroom sometimes proved as useful as the pains-
taking preparation done by super-sharp legal staffs.

In Atlanta in the 1950s, even major cases were meagerly staffed.
We didn't take endless depositions before trial and consequently the
trial was often full of surprises, the courtroom frequently a place of
ambush. In major New York law firms, every important litigation
is well-staffed and intensive preparation is the rule. Little is left to
spontaneous courtroom response.

The extraordinary legal talent undergirding a senior partner at
Paul, Weiss, Rifkind, Wharton & Garrison bears the major brunt
of the research and the tedium of litigation. In complicated cases,
legal assistants keep papers and exhibits in order, responding within
seconds to calls for critical documents. I preferred the Atlanta type
practice, at least that of the 1950s, in which more was left to chance
and surprise, where clients were poorer and the stakes less high.
When in the early 1950s I was offered a partnership in a prosperous
labor law firm in Atlanta representing management, I turned it down
because my heart was on the other side. My choice was not based
on morality, for I believe that every side must be represented if our
adversary system of justice is to work. I simply preferred not to
make my living working solely for management against labor, which
was just getting a foothold in the South.

The major New York law firm could not subsist on the catch-as-
catch-can plaintiff-type practice, such as Justice Black had known
in Birmingham, and which constituted much of my practice in Atlanta, where it proved very prosperous.

In 1976, when I was still undergoing chemotherapy, my legal
docket included suits pending in five cities against the building
cleaning arm of the National Kinney Corporation. The United States
Department of Labor contended that the lesser wage scale paid for
cleaners, sometimes called matrons, as compared to those called
janitors constituted sex discrimination in violation of the Equal Pay
Act. Claims for back wages ran into the millions, and the injunctive

relief the government sought against our client could put it at a competitive disadvantage in the cities where Kinney's wage practice was the same as that of other companies, though it alone was sued.

These facts and the government's absolute confidence, based on repeated victories elsewhere in similar circumstances, made compromise impossible.

The first case was to be tried in Hartford, Connecticut, and the outlook was dismal. I went to a leading cleaning consulting firm, hoping to get an expert who would say in court that the duties of the "heavy duty" cleaners required more skill and effort and were performed under more onerous working conditions than those of the "light duty" cleaners. The president of the company said his analysis came to precisely the opposite conclusion, and he reminded me needlessly that repeated court decisions supported his view.

On a cold winter day in 1976, I drove with a young associate to Hartford to have a look at the premises and interview some of the hordes of Kinney workers toiling through the night with mops, pails, brushes, vacuums, buffers, and various scrubbers. Suddenly I turned to my associate and asked, "Do you know of a single case where the cleaning tools and machinery have been trundled as exhibits into the courtroom?"

"No."

"Well, if the judge could see the difference in weight alone between what some men, as opposed to women, have to handle, at least he'll know that there is a difference in the effort exerted."

Then I came upon Maria Perez, a spunky woman of Cuban origin, now the supervisor of all the cleaning crews in the huge Hartford National Bank building.

"Is it different?" she repeated, as if astounded by my naivete. "Look, I started as a matron, worked up to the higher paying heavy jobs, and now I run the whole operation. I tell you the jobs held mostly by men are harder."

"Mostly?" I questioned.

"Of course," she said, "nobody keeps these women from taking these higher-paying jobs, cleaning public rest rooms, hauling these drums of cleaning materials, holding down these rambunctious scrubbing machines." I believed Maria.

"We're going to win in Hartford," I said to my associate, "with Maria on the stand and every piece of this machinery in the courtroom."

The trial in Hartford commenced in spring 1977. My team of associates had been on the scene for a week interviewing witnesses, assembling the exhibits as I underwent chemotherapy in New York. The day I arrived in Hartford, I surveyed the courtroom, now crammed with cleaning equipment and supplies from dusters to giant floor scrubbers. I noticed that this federal building had cleaning crews in which males and females appeared to do different types of work. I dispatched a legal assistant to inquire if the government of the United States was per chance engaged, in this very building, in the same practice for which it was suing National Kinney. The government attorneys got wind of what we were up to and put up roadblocks. We nevertheless obtained the relevant job classifications and wage scales which paralleled those of our client.

In court the government made the ultimate effort to close off this terrible damaging fact, claiming that even if the General Services Administration of the United States was doing wrong, that did not excuse National Kinney.

I rose very slowly, exhibiting, I am certain, a delicious self-satisfaction, and said:

"I offer the comparison between what Kinney and the government do, not to show that they are equally wrong but that they are equally right. The personnel officials of the United States government are presumed to be nondiscriminatory in attitude and expert in job classification—and they agree with our client."

When Maria Perez took the stand, the government lawyer attempted to discredit her testimony that the men who operated the electric floor waxers had a hard and responsible job. The lawyer, trying to show that Maria and I had cooked up a collusive story, inquired if I had ever talked to her before trial.

"He visited my building once," she answered. "He tried to run the machine [the floor waxer] one night and he almost kicked the wall down. It's true."

Maria had now wiped the courtroom floor, using my opponent as her mop. Then the preparatory work done by my associate team demolished whatever remained of the government's case: a careful analysis of accident reports for years showed that heavy duty cleaners

242

were injured more times and more seriously than light duty cleaners.

The judgment in Kinney's favor in Hartford was duplicated in a trial in Philadelphia. The government conceded in St. Louis and settled on terms favorable to Kinney in Newark and Chicago. As I argued in Philadelphia:

"To Gertrude Stein, 'a rose is a rose is a rose'; but it cannot be said as a matter of law that a cleaner is a cleaner is a cleaner." I savored these victories because of the odds against me at the beginning; and because they were won through the technique of combining typically thorough Paul, Weiss pretrial preparation with the element of courtroom surprise. As I said to my senior associate when we finished at Hartford, contrary to academic wisdom, surprise is often not the enemy but the friend of truth. Nor was I troubled in the slightest by my representation of management in these cleaning cases. I felt my client was absolutely right, and in any event, the plaintiffs had the United States government on their side.

14

In January 1976, while I was still under full-scale treatment, Carlyn and I were married. The following July, Eli and I spent a few days at Cape Cod tying up the loose ends of my oral history. We had already recorded my tenure at Brandeis as history and the Moreland Commission investigation as it was occurring. We had not discussed other post-1970 events, and at that very moment delegates to the Democratic National Convention were assembled in Madison Square Garden to nominate Jimmy Carter.

When I began to tape the story of my life, Jimmy Carter was still governor of Georgia. I had first laid eyes on him in 1971 when, as we sat on an Atlanta dais together, he handed me his card with a friendly note, "Call me when you are in Atlanta, Jimmy." I had known a Carter from Plains since 1933, when Jimmy's first cousin, Don, bested me in an essay contest. I had driven from Fitzgerald to Americus certain I would receive first prize for my informed and pungent prose. When Don, even runtier than I, went up on the stage at the Martin Theatre to get the medal, I despised him in-

244

stantly. Later he showed up at Athens, where I came to respect his good mind and literary style.

In 1974, I met Jimmy again at a large Atlanta dinner where I introduced Ted Kennedy, then testing the waters for 1976. Speaking after Carter, I referred to his address as one of "quiet eloquence." Spontaneously he asked Carlyn and me to breakfast the next morning at the mansion:

"What do you like to eat?" he asked us.

"Anything with grits."

When Carlyn and I drove up, Carter was pacing the driveway in jeans and plaid shirt. We had grits, eggs, bacon, sausages, and biscuits. Carter told me he was running for president in 1976 and asked for my help. I replied that I was pledged to become Scoop Jackson's cochairman in New York, out of due respect for him and a little, I confess, because he had managed to obtain a prohibited drug for use in the treatment of my leukemia.

But Carter persisted. "I don't know many Jews outside of Georgia. Could you help me to meet them?"

It seemed an honorable enough ambition, one with which I could comply. I arranged immediately for him to address a meeting of the Einstein College of Medicine patrons in Palm Beach in February.

I later heard that Rose Kennedy, who attended, had remarked that Carter's looks reminded her of her son Jack. That brought to mind the first occasion on which I'd ever heard of Carter. Bobby Troutman had touted him to me during Carter's unsuccessful race for governor in 1966, noting the same physical resemblance Mrs. Kennedy had commented upon.

My link to Carter should have been very strong. He played as I did—as an outsider, and it drew me to him. True, we were radically different sorts of outsiders, but both of us had felt disenchanted with Georgia conventions, and both wanted to be taken seriously. Then, too, there was the land that linked us. Much more than the velvet-gloved power brokers of Atlanta, Carter and I had the dusty, gnat-ridden summers in our blood. We had both endured the interminable heat, yet were glad that the beating sun would keep the boll weevils from eating the cotton crop. Carter knew those cold flowing springs I used to swim in, and he knew how the first flushes of autumn felt in Georgia—more welcome than anywhere else I've ever been.

Since we were so near in age and background and since he staked his claim as a liberal southerner, I found it strange that I had never met Jimmy Carter until after he became governor in 1970. For eighteen years prior to that he was living in Plains. Until 1963 I was engaged in three burning issues which affected his county and on which some of his neighbors and I were firmly allied. Yet, I never heard the name of Jimmy Carter either during the county unit struggle or when the Koinonia cooperative interracial farm, only eight miles from his home, was fire-bombed, boycotted, and interdicted; nor in 1963 when I represented Martin Luther King's youthful disciples, charged with the capital crime of sedition in Americus. During this unjust incarceration and acrimonious trial, State Senator Jimmy Carter was inaudible and invisible.

I was not unaware of all this after Scoop Jackson withdrew from the presidential contest in 1976 and I found myself uncommitted. I had long been tempered in the slow fires of southern gradualism and I reasoned that you don't hang a man for getting there late if you're glad to have him there at all. Besides, I could not help but feel proud that my victory over the county unit system had helped to prepare the way for the national candidacy of a Georgian. Senator Richard B. Russell, Jr., a much admired man, had tried for the presidency in 1952, but foundered on the racial politics which affected all southern politicians. Russell, dependent on unit votes, was hobbled more than most because Georgia's better enlightened cities had almost no political influence. Thus, for thirty years he was held political hostage to the redneck vote. On the other hand, in 1973, Jimmy Carter could safely place Martin Luther King's picture in the State House because others, I for one, had paved the road on which he would march to the presidency. I saw him as a logical candidate to erase McGovern's insipid interlude as party leader.

Here was a southerner with his feet on the ground, who had cleansed himself of the stain of race bias and who, at his inauguration as governor, had declared the end of segregation.

He must be strong, I thought, wishfully; certainly he was bold. Everyone knew how he had started the race with a two percent recognition factor—an obscure former Georgia governor. I was very impressed that while governor he had appointed as chairman of the Board of Regents of the university system of Georgia a Jewish friend who lived ten miles from Fitzgerald. It was an office I had wistfully coveted.

My mind was made up. I announced for Carter.

I knew Carter was surrounded by a weak and provincial staff, for that was the best a sure loser could enlist when he started his run for the Presidency. Hamilton Jordan and Jody Powell were carriers of his sedan chair when no others were willing to shoulder the poles. Still, he had adopted the slogan "Why not the best?" and if he made it, he would certainly have available and would draw upon, I reasoned, the talent bank of the nation. As a Jew, who knew about prejudice, I was outraged that he should be attacked for his Christian fundamentalism just as Al Smith was for his Catholicism. I went to his defense on the stump and on the op-ed page of *The New York Times*.

"Of course Jimmy Carter is a Baptist and I know Baptists well. They are among the best and some of the worst people I have ever known—substitute any other religion and the same statement holds. . . . I understand the suspicions that many northern liberals have of southern Baptists. They are like the suspicions of the southern Protestant towards the Catholic Al Smith. As with all generalization, this one falls apart under specific scrutiny."

During that campaign, on another editorial page, I conceded there were myriad strands of tradition and interest in the Democratic party that were not part of his experience, but I thought he had the political skills to reach out beyond the coterie "of friends and advisers who guide him . . . through the thickets of Georgia politics where ambush was always possible."

The traditional liberal "vital center" of the Democratic party had been fractured in the mid-sixties and early-seventies. I had hopes that Carter would tie together this coalition that I had watched disintegrate in the Brandeis period. I didn't think this impossible, for I conceived the politics of the time as a manifestation of the aberrent thinking of a special breed of liberal Democrat. Liberal Democrats in the real world, I reassured myself, were still moored to the principles of FDR, Harry Truman, and JFK.

I myself had strayed somewhat from the "vital center." Early in the year of McGovern's success, I was enlisted as the chief of a task force on domestic matters in the campaign of Edmund Muskie for the Democratic presidential nomination. I was shaken when a friend on the task force challenged a background paper I had prepared for Muskie, which reflected my dark mood after the Brandeis period. I sounded like President Carter six years later in his much criticized "national malaise" speech, in which he attributed the ills of the country to the mood of the people. I had put it to Muskie this way:

"The major crisis of America today is that of its soul. Far too many of our best people, especially the young, live as if there were no tomorrow, convinced that there is no honorable or acceptable work for them in America, mesmerized by our constantly expressed fear that the world is about to end in nuclear holocaust or environmental poisoning. They believe that the nation's problems cannot be solved by existing governmental structures. Indeed, they believe that these structures are themselves problems and that vast military-industrial complexes and nameless bureaucracies are beyond their influence or appeal. They exude hopelessness.

". . . there is a considerable distortion in such apocalyptic viewpoints."

The friend retorted in a letter, "No doubt this is how many members of the upper-middle-class feel, and it is also what large numbers of college students think. But my impression is that the vast majority of Americans still have to struggle to make ends meet, and that most of them are still largely worried about achieving or maintaining or improving their material circumstances. It is to these people and their problems that the Democratic party ought in my judgment mainly to address itself."

I soon realized that my critic was right. While I had advocated to Muskie not a single program that deviated from my rooted beliefs, I was falling into the temper which led to the capture of the Democratic party by its more extreme elements, which downplayed America's virtues and magnified its flaws. This was the mood that resulted in the nomination of McGovern and the reelection of Richard Nixon. Eventually it became the pervasive climate of the Carter administration.

Looking back, I do not understand how I was ever persuaded for a moment that the 1960s and early 1970s were a bad period of our history. Within a few years the civil rights movement, working

248

through the courts, the president, and Congress, had overturned every legal vestige of discrimination. The women's movement had shaken cultural perceptions of the role of women. Speech, the press, and the right of petition were never freer; and the nation's productivity was at an all-time peak. In three miraculous years—1964, 1965, and 1966—President Johnson had declared his war on poverty, the omnibus civil rights and voting rights bills were enacted, and other programs were developed. The number of black families with incomes of over ten thousand dollars had more than doubled in the eight years before 1967 and the number of black youths in college had grown from something over two hundred fifty thousand in 1960 to more than one million by 1972. It was understandable that young people with limited personal histories could be upset by their country's shortcomings but it is astounding that so many of their parents, surviving as they did segregation, world depression, and war, should have adopted their despair.

By June 1972, I had rescued my political soul. I redefined myself as an American liberal, one who loves his country, believes in its ideals and processes, and strives continually to make them more effective. True liberals from Roosevelt to Kennedy were committed to democratic means and humane ends and understood the inextricable connection of the one to the other.

Those who had captured the voice of the Democratic party in 1972 seemed to have lost faith in America. They denigrated American institutions and maligned many of them as frauds. They saw the society as racist, exploitative, and imperialist. They equated America's faults with evil intent and American defense postures with aggressive purpose. Much domestic violence was soft-pedaled as a natural result of economic and racial injustice while international terrorism was selectively excused as "liberation movements." Israel was perceived, not as the practicing democracy it is, but as a satellite of the contemptible Western world, whereas neighboring Mideast societies, even the most authoritarian, commanded sympathy.

I remember the point at which I returned to the sentiments that had guided my political stance. It was when I was invited to give the commencement speech at Emory University in Atlanta. I asked my son Morris Jr., who had earlier graduated from Harvard, for an appropriate subject. He replied, "Dad, why don't you tell them what you have learned since you graduated from college?'' I said that the period involved was thirty-four years, and the time assigned was thirty minutes. He said he was serious.

The more I considered his suggestion, the more sense it made. The period 1938–1972 had spanned depression, war, political and cultural revolutions, the civil rights revolution, the development of the United Nations, the growth of megalopolis, the degradation of our cities, the emergence of a persistent and growing American underclass, and the challenge to conventional mores and institutions. I had in some small way been connected with several of these changes and touched by all.

I delivered a commencement address that, in retrospect, marked a reexamination of my views and of the priorities of my life. I spoke of what I had both learned and unlearned.

In 1938 my science professors taught that the ''atom is the smallest indivisible particle of matter,'' a truth discredited at the University of Chicago four years later in an experiment that led to the atomic bomb. Social and political beliefs had to be revised, too. The civil service, originally adopted to curb the evils of patronage, now shielded the slothful worker from discipline. In my Atlanta years I had enraged wealthy factory owners and potential clients by my open support for labor unions. Now I was critical of restrictive practices, featherbedding, and downright corruption in some unions. As a young man I thought that the surest and fastest route to the truths of human experience lay in biography. Now I knew that fiction was often more enlightening and truthful to life.

''I've become leery of easy solutions to complex problems,'' I summed up my commencement address. ''Indeed, reforms in which I have deeply believed have sometimes impaired the capacities of government and society to function effectively. . . . Don't be too damned certain about anything; but with this exception: Love is the only thing in life which seems to be an unmixed blessing; in the case of children, it is as necessary as food and water.''

Looking back, I see that I did not mention the love of man and woman. It was a curious omission, but significant in light of my ensuing divorce. I realize now it was perhaps too painful then to articulate what I well knew; that the greatest gift a man can give his children is to love their mother.

Still, in the warm sunshine of that outdoor commencement, joined by old Georgia friends, I savored the realization that, whatever my shortcomings, disappointments, and failures, I did have the capacity to bestow and receive affection. And I was pleased that at this midpoint in life I was sufficiently flexible to carefully reexamine the beliefs which had guided me for years. I was not content with slogans, nor could I uncritically adopt the fads of political associates. During the long illness which soon followed, I further refined my core beliefs and priorities.

During his presidency, Jimmy Carter's policies in international human rights, race relations, and foreign affairs at first drifted and then moved, so it seemed to me, with gathering momentum away from the liberal center to which I adhere.

During the 1976 campaign I had urged Carter to distinguish himself from Gerald Ford in significant ways, specifically by making a commitment to international human rights. In October 1976, at the New York Hilton, I handed him a memorandum which said, "Urge you announce that one of your first acts would be speech on the subject to the United Nations General Assembly." I described the UN as being in "shambles and disarray—to use one of your favorite descriptions: 'It is a disgrace,' " referring to the absurd voting patterns in the United Nations General Assembly and its outrageous assertion in 1975 that "Zionism is Racism."

I urged Carter to advocate use of America's record in domestic human rights as a foreign policy asset and as a challenge to the rest of the world to live up to standards of the Declaration of Human Rights, trumpeting our liberty and creativity, inviting criticism, and pointedly reserving to ourselves the right to criticize others, friend and foe alike. If, I argued, the world understands that America's devotion to human rights is a part of our tradition, we can brandish human rights principles without endangering alliances vital to our national security. Some governments, I added, may regard our dedication to freedom as quirky, but our example and a little coercion could filter through the borders of oppressive states and eventually improve somewhat the lot of the afflicted.

In early 1977, President Carter, inviting me as his guest, went before the United Nations General Assembly and outlined initiatives which later became his international human rights policy. This redounded to the credit of the United States and certainly lifted the hope, if not the condition, of the oppressed throughout the world.

251

At last we had proclaimed our serious commitment to human rights on an international scale. He had articulated the principle that under the UN charter the rights of citizens of any country were not to be considered strictly a domestic concern. As I had put it a decade earlier in the Human Rights Commission of the United Nations, "no state since the adoption of the Universal Declaration of Human Rights has a sovereign right to torture its own citizens."

While I listened to Carter that night at the UN, I realized that the deployment of this issue in foreign affairs would require extraordinary sophistication. Distinctions would have to be made in dealing with countries that are open to the press and those that are not. A vast police state may give the appearance of a peaceful society, while an open democracy is often seen as turbulent. I was very aware that any flaw in internal Israeli affairs would receive worldwide attention, whereas the most medieval conditions in other states of the Third World would as likely go ignored or even excused. In late 1981, the director of the UN Division of Human Rights referred to the extensive black slavery by the Arabs in the Islamic Republic of Mauritania as a "tradition and social custom that can't be done away with overnight."

Since our allies were more receptive to the Western press, we would have to be careful not to hold friends more severely accountable than enemies. Finally, since a nation's foreign policy has as its primary goal the protection of its sovereignty, its positions will inevitably be tainted with expediency and never wholly altruistic.

I could not have dreamed that the implementation of so sensitive and delicate a program would be placed in the hands of those totally inexperienced in foreign affairs and I was dumbfounded, for example, when a newly created post of Assistant Secretary of State for Human Rights was bestowed upon one Pat Derian, a civil rights activist from Mississippi whose dedication, though laudable, hardly qualified her for the sophisticated complexities of international human rights. The Carter administration commendably brought strong pressures on the USSR to abide by the human rights terms of the Helsinki Accords; on the other hand, it harried autocratic governments where we might have some diplomatic leverage to bring about reforms, though affecting scarcely, if at all, infinitely more despotic and intractable regimes. Carter's policy, for example, made it virtually impossible for us to continue our support of the Pahlavi regime in Iran, even after reforms had been initiated by American prodding. Instead, that country was delivered into the hands of a fanatic, lawless Ayatollah hopelessly beyond reasoning or influence. An admittedly despotic monarchy which was nevertheless susceptible to a degree of American persuasion was overthrown by an even more despotic theocracy, venemously hostile to Western interests.

At the time I was surprised by the duplicity of the attacks on the Shah's oppressive rule by the so-called Third World countries. My mind flashed back to the time ten years earlier when I was a member of the American delegation to the twentieth anniversary celebration of the Universal Declaration of Human Rights held in Iran. The UN, without a single dissent, had elected the Shah's twin sister, the Princess Ashraf, as the chairman of this auspicious convention! The hundreds of delegates to this international human rights conference were not innocent of the nature of the Pahlavi regime. The blatant corruption of the royal family was as notorious then as a decade later. Still, in 1968, the delegations of the countries that later spoke in outrage against the Shah had poured torrents of appreciation upon him as host and praise of his sister for her work on behalf of women and education in Iran. The UN establishment accepted the lavish hospitality of the Pahlavis on that occasion and turned on them when the tides of fortune shifted. Even President and Mrs. Carter chose to celebrate the 1978 New Year in the Shah's palace, where Carter toasted his host as "beloved" by his people and as a leader who "deeply shared" the cause of human rights.

Carter may not have understood that a nation's vital interest must take precedence over its commitment to foreign human rights. This, alas, has always been so.

Carter deserves credit, though, in maintaining that conscience must be quickened in the international arena through consistent proclamation of human rights even when it antagonizes allies. A case in point was America's intervention in the freeing of Jacobo Timerman from an Argentine prison. Yet such effective, moral, and timely acts must not be escalated into campaigns to alienate nonhostile regimes that might yet be responsive to diplomatic pressure after years of destabilizing internal terrorism, of the right or left. This is particularly true when the insurgents already in the wings are anti-American, antidemocratic, and, even at best, unpredictable.

Carter made many foreign policy mistakes, which may have stemmed from his adoption of George McGovern's values and the appointment of McGovern's men, without, I suspect, the slightest idea of what he was doing.

His appointment of Andrew Young to the United Nations turned out to be a mistake. I was elated when Young was elected to the seat I had sought in Congress. I had known and helped him during his lieutenancy in the ranks of Martin Luther King. When Martin King, Jr. was slain, I immediately helped organize and cochaired a New York event that raised several hundred thousand dollars to help sustain the Southern Christian Leadership Conference. Young, still in shock, spoke without changing from denims after he arrived at the meeting from Atlanta.

In the UN, Young, schooled in the same domestic civil rights struggle as Pat Derian, damned his own country for "its thousands of political prisoners," supported USSR-supplied Cuban forces as a "stabilizing influence in Africa," and praised the Ayatollah Khomeini as a possible saint. The fact that he was not dismissed for his conduct created confusion over United States policy and doubts about Carter's willingness or ability to control his administration. I watched in amazement as the president of the United States appeared to be held as a hostage by a member of his own administration who behaved as if he were the ambassador of the Third World to the United States.

As for domestic affairs, I was increasingly worried and rankled by Carter's refusal to speak out against the public anti-Semitic remarks of his close friend Bert Lance and his brother, Billy. The most telling failure occurred a few days after Ambassador Young was dismissed for deceiving the Secretary of State about an unauthorized meeting between him and a PLO representative.

Two hundred New York City black leaders, called together to discuss Young's resignation, according to a *New York Times* correspondent, "widened their session into a discussion of black grievances against American Jews." Vicious sentiments erupted which Vernon Jordan and Bayard Rustin tried unsuccessfully to allay. Rustin then was condemned by Reverend William Jones, president of a Baptist convention, for ". . . having an organized relationship with Jews." I was first appalled and then frightened that this eruption of blatant anti-Semitism in a convocation of American black leaders evoked no significant public rebuke within their ranks or outside. I detected that the fair-minded were being intimidated by pack pressures—precisely as decent southerners had been by white racists in the 1950s.

When the National Broadcasting Company called me to offer an hour on network television to untangle these volatile issues in a "quiet conversation between two old friends, yourself and Ambassador Young," I instantly accepted. As requested, I called Young, who agreed, and we set tentative dates for the studio taping, fitting his schedule. Thereafter, Andy and his staff evaded me and network representatives until the project had to be abandoned.

President Carter was also urged to set the record straight, to state his reasons for requesting Young's resignation, but he never did, and the dispute roiled on, poisoning the relations between old allies in the struggle against bigotry.

I was dumfounded when Andrew Young, a disciple of Martin Luther King, Jr., did not denounce anti-Semitism. This was in sorry contrast to the position unambiguously asserted in a letter from King to me, dated September 20, 1967. In it, the Nobel laureate, responding to my plea that he repudiate anti-Semitic statements that had been made by one of his workers, wrote:

"SCLC has expressly, frequently and vigorously denounced anti-Semitism and will continue to do so. It is not only that anti-Semitism is immoral—though that alone is enough. It is used to divide Negro and Jew, who have effectively collaborated in the struggle for justice. It injures Negroes because it upholds the doctrine of racism which they have the greatest stake in destroying. . . . There has never been an instance of articulated Negro anti-Semitism that was not swiftly condemned by virtually all Negro leaders with the support of the overwhelming majority."

These developments after Young's firing reflected a wider, and, for me, painful, political chasm between American Jews and former allies. For many years it was taken for granted by most American Jews that their own dreams coincided with a common liberal agenda. But now this axiom was being called into question by both the indifference of many and the hostility of a few to a resolute

America, a secure Israel, and a racially neutral public policy.

By the beginning of the presidential election campaign of 1980, I knew that many of the positions of the Carter administration were alien to my own. In the racial area, Carter had permitted a coterie of black leaders to define the agenda for the improvement of the lot of Afro-Americans in terms I could not rationally or morally accept.

The statistics of 1980 conclusively showed a dramatically expanding black middle class, with more to come from a college population now proportionately distributed between blacks and whites. Yet it was undeniable that the overall condition of black America was not improving because of a vast increase in the impoverished female-headed single parent households with young children from ten percent of the black population in the 1960s to 47 percent by 1980, despite the increase of federal social programs during the two decades. This one fact had caused the overall gap between black and white income to widen when otherwise it would have substantially narrowed. Black intellectuals such as Professors William Wilson and Thomas Sowell, who deigned to address these facts, even from chairs in universities as distinguished as Harvard, Chicago, or UCLA, were ignored or roundly attacked as apologists for America's racism or as practitioners of self-hatred.

Some black writers were hardly alarmed by the geometric growth of these impoverished black households, frequently headed by a teenage mother. Professor Martin Kilson of Harvard disapprovingly summed up the views of Joyce Ladner of Hunter College thus: "[She] argued for an uncritical relativity of values and norms, and asserted that the woman-child life-style among lower-class black teenagers—heavy premarital sex and unwed motherhood—constitutes as valid a life-style as any other, cannot be held worse, and indeed just might be better."

I had invested too much in the civil rights struggle to join in this romanticized celebration of the desperate plight of the black poor. Many allies in the civil rights movement, especially black administrators of federal programs, and whites who take their cues from them, are not critical of views such as Ms. Ladner expressed. Indeed, she became a member of the board of The Field Foundation.

Although I was as sensitive as I had been two decades before to the needs of the disadvantaged, I had always understood that absolute equality cannot be achieved—certainly not by government—and that equal opportunity will not produce equal results. I have always supported affirmative action as an effort designed to seek out, to train, and to educate (often by remedial means) disadvantaged persons who would not otherwise acquire the qualifications necessary to make equality of opportunity a reality. This was the clear purpose of the Civil Rights Act of 1964 and the EEOC when President Johnson offered me its first chairmanship. I have come to deplore the skewing of the laudable purpose of equal opportunity and nondiscrimination into a program of racial preferences and quotas to enforce equality of result. Affirmative action has been transformed into racial favoritism enforced by law, mainly for the benefit of minority middle-class persons already on the economic and social escalator. In the 1950s and early 1960s, the only persons who argued in favor of the constitutionality of racial preferences were the white supremacists.

When Justice Thurgood Marshall argued the school desegregation cases in the Supreme Court in 1952/53, he pled for a color-blind interpretation of the Constitution, the removal of the race line from our governmental systems.

I was astounded when the civil rights leadership reversed field a few years later and demanded compensatory racial preferential treatment. I saw this as racist, an inverted form of an evil I had fought for forty years. I could not comprehend why a movement based on the equality of man before the law could now, after five decades, espouse a legal theory that some races should be specially treated. I saw the terrible risk in a constitutional construction that would permit the government of the moment to legislate on racial or ethnic grounds to advance some "public good." It was precisely this argument that led to the shameful Supreme Court decision during World War II which upheld the internment in concentration camps of every United States citizen of Japanese ancestry.

I myself certainly could not ignore the fact that Jews, as well as blacks, Japanese, and Chinese-Americans, had experienced the curse of "special legislation" based on ethnic distinctions. I was not about to experiment with the renewal of this dismal practice which had been extirpated from American constitutional law after so titanic an effort. Racial preferences and quotas, sometimes euphemistically coded as goals and timetables, were now becoming a hallmark of

257

the Carter administration, which, predictably, was getting further and further ensnared in the competing demands for preference by Hispanics, Indians, and a variety of other ethnic groups, all of whom saw themselves as having been aggrieved. There would not be enough of America to satisfy the insatiable grievances, real or imagined, in this country whose first and last settlers were refugees.

In March 1980, Andrew Young's successor, Donald McHenry, cast America's vote in the Security Council on a resolution referring to Jerusalem as Israeli "occupied territory." President Carter claimed there had been a mix-up in instructions—that the reference to Jerusalem was a "mistake." I had served too long at the United Nations to be misled by this apologetic revision. The ploy, I thought, was the administration's attempt to divert attention from the most significant and portentous part of the resolution, one charging that Israel had violated the Fourth Geneva Convention— that is, was guilty of monstrous inhumanity on the West Bank in terms in which Hitler's genocidal occupation of Poland and the USSR had been appropriately described at the Nuremberg trials. Moreover, I noted that the preamble of the resolutions for which McHenry had voted had curiously omitted any reference to UN Security Council Resolutions 242 and 338, by which Israel's withdrawal from the West Bank was made contingent on the agreement of safe and secure boundaries. These two resolutions had been a cornerstone of United States and Security Council policies since 1967. President Carter did not suggest that either of these dramatic shifts in the American course at the United Nations were part of the "mistake." Soon after this American vote in the Security Council, I and other New York Jewish Democrats voted four to one for Ted Kennedy in the New York presidential primary, in which the senator shellacked the president.

Carter's persistence in hammering out the Camp David accords between Egypt and Israel was undeniable, but he received less than deserved credit, because it was his previous bumbling of Middle East peace negotiations that had sent President Sadat scurrying to Jerusalem to seek an Israeli/Egyptian settlement. The Nobel Committee gave its peace prize to Sadat and Begin.

The security of Israel was certainly not a new concern for me, but my views of Israeli policy positions were compatible with the stances of neither Prime Minister Begin nor the nervous American newspaper pundits and editorial writers, many Jewish, who from the safe distance of five thousand miles tediously attacked Israel for defending itself against enemies avowed to destroy the Jewish state.

On a visit to Israel in 1980 I was speaking with a former Israeli diplomat, an Oxford graduate, and surely one of the most urbane and civilized of men. I put a puzzling question to him: "Why is Israel—the one democracy in the Middle East, the one stable and reliable friend of the West, the one state which has created a humane society out of desert scrubland—treated like a leper in the United Nations and judged by its faults rather than its virtues?" In reply, he cited papers on Middle East affairs which had recently come to light from certain West European foreign ministries. Many of these documents, which routinely passed from the lowest functionaries on up to foreign ministers, prime ministers, and occasionally even heads of state, contained handwritten in their margins anti-Semitic slurs from the lowliest officials. Those who scribbled the anti-Semitic comments had had to assume that such views would hardly impair their careers no matter who saw them in the upward spiral of distribution.

On my return from Israel to the United States, I picked up the *Times* and saw a picture of a grinning Yassar Arafat being hailed by the Olympic games officials in Moscow. Incredible that this conspirator in the murder of the Israeli Olympic athletes at Munich in 1972 was receiving the plaudits at the Olympic games of 1980.

By August 1980, I was so disenchanted with President Carter that I began to doubt whether I could support him for reelection. I was particularly offended by the president's employment of his brother, Billy Carter, as a contact with Libya, one of the world's most vicious anti-Semitic and terrorist regimes.

In September, Arthur Schlesinger, Jr. called me to ask me to join him in an endorsement of the presidential aspirant, John Anderson. My reply was, "Arthur, you're a smart man. You know, of course, that John Anderson is not going to get elected and that every vote for Anderson reduces Carter's chances." Arthur agreed. Then I said, "You must have decided that you prefer Reagan to Carter and if so, the forthright thing to do is to vote for Reagan." Schlesinger was not persuaded nor was I ready to follow my own logic. It was so easy and respectable in many political and social circles to vote for Anderson—though he had three times sponsored constitutional amendments to declare America a Christian nation. Reagan, on the other hand, was the totemic ogre of the liberal Democrats, replacing Goldwater, whose once fierce reputation had been sanitized by time. His defeat by LBJ had soon displaced him in the catalogue of fiends and warmongers.

There were pressing personal reasons for me either to support Carter or to remain silent. He had in 1979 appointed me chairman of the President's Commission for the Study of Ethical Problems in Medicine and Biomedical and Behavioral Research. There were professional reasons for me to avoid taking a stand against him. I was then presenting a major case before a public body consisting entirely of his appointees. But I was abashed at the thought that personal or professional considerations should influence me. I checked with law partners directly concerned, who responded without a moment's hesitation, "We are free men in this firm, we practice law on the merits. Act on your own beliefs."

By mid-September I had decided I could not vote for Carter. I ticked off the reasons: I could not vote for him if I asked myself his own perennial question, "Why not the best?" His inner circle from Georgia was a mélange of bright youngsters and tired hacks. I concluded the deficits could not be offset. They were greater than I had imagined. The bright young men whose sole experience was in his service were way out of their depth. The old boys that surrounded him had no depth at all. The innermost phalanx of Carter's White House—Jordan, Powell, and Lance—at best served the president's insecurities more than the country's needs. Only at the last did Carter replace his counsel, an old Georgia friend, Bob Lipschutz, with Lloyd Cutler, a superb Washington lawyer. But the circle of which Jordan was the linchpin held through the final days.

True, I think Carter had truly worked diligently and he was doubtless intelligent. He drilled deeply into every problem with a sharp but narrow bit. He had hopelessly confused our allies and pandered to potential enemies by his irresolute foreign policies. I thought how Europe had stumbled into World War II by failing, in the early 1930s, to call Hitler's bluff when he invaded the Rhineland. Carter's wheedling pleas for the release of the hostages, followed by a rescue mission which seemed to have been planned by a Catch-22 Commander-in-Chief, evinced a lack of will. Such flabbiness was as likely to get us into an unintended war as was absurd bellicosity, for a world in which American power is respected will be a more peaceful world in the long run.

Nor had I any confidence whatsoever in Carter's profession of "friendship" for Israel. One of the cogs in his campaign was the Reverend Jesse Jackson, who on Sunday, September 16, 1980, bared his teeth and his soul on television's *Sixty Minutes*, declaring that Jews, while willing to share morality with blacks, were unwilling to share "power," which he itemized stereotypically as banks, the media, and so on. Jackson did not mention any obligation of Protestants or Catholics to share Chase Manhattan, IBM, the railroads, steel, insurance, coal, timber, and other resources. I wholly believe that the "mistaken" UN vote cast by the Carter administration against Israel in an election year would have become unmistakable administration policy in a second term.

In late September I began to experience real jitters that Carter might be reelected. I saw him now as a 1980 reincarnation of George McGovern, whose adherents were salted into the important middle echelon of Carter's foreign and domestic policy apparatus. Now I felt Carter must be defeated before the Democratic party could be returned to the vital center from which it had slithered. But I hesitated to publicly bolt the party. My agonizing apparently reached the notice of the White House. Bob Straus called my office while I was in court. Ann Wexler, another Carter aide, reached me:

"Will you join Diplomats for Carter?"

"No, I am not going to vote for him."

"What! You're not supporting the president?"

"No."

With that, she curtly terminated the conversation.

A few nights later I was called by Alfred Moses, an old friend from the leadership of the American Jewish Committee, a Washington lawyer, then on assignment to the White House.

"I understand you have reservations about supporting the president."

"I certainly do, Al."

"Could I arrange a meeting with the president so that he may answer your concerns?"

"No, Al, it would be a waste of his time and mine."

I had now burned my bridges with Carter but I was still within the circle of those Democrats who felt Carter had failed, freeing them to endorse John Anderson. I began to debate with myself. If I felt these increasing anxieties for my country, as I contemplated Carter's reelection (in a race now believed neck and neck), didn't I have a responsibility to use whatever influence I had against him? To abstain or to vote for Anderson amounted to an oblique vote for Reagan. Why not follow the logic I had advanced to Arthur Schlesinger, doing the forthright thing—declaring for Reagan? I put this dilemma to at least a dozen liberal Democrats disenchanted with Carter. "Vote for Reagan but keep silent," several, who intended to do just that, advised. "Your life has been devoted to too many people and too many liberal causes to which Ronald Reagan is anathema."

A few days later I was in the Washington office of an academic who was supporting Reagan. He had on display an old lifesized poster of movie actor Ronald Reagan in a cowboy costume. I thought, "I can't do it."

I called a chronicler of presidential elections. He said, "Ronald Reagan is a decent human being who ran a good administration in California. I am not advising you what to do, but if you decide to support him, you shouldn't feel personal embarrassment." I still wavered. My law partner, Eddie Costikyan, former leader of Tammany Hall and author of two acclaimed political books, called and asked, "Are you thinking of voting for Reagan?"

"Yes."

"So am I. Let's announce it together."

I agreed to draft a joint statement which I sent to Eddie. He called back in an hour:

"The statement is OK. You and I have simply got to do everything we can to prevent Carter from carrying New York, which could be the swing state."

"Fine, Eddie . . ."

He interrupted. "Morris, there's a photograph of Jim Farley hanging on my wall. I swear there are tears in his eyes. . . ."

As I announced for Ronald Reagan I felt that Carter's feckless administration had caused the country to lose faith in itself. He was leading the country into a dangerous psychological depression. He had to be swept out of the White House. Ronald Reagan was the only broom at hand. My vote against Carter was exactly that, not an endorsement of the personalities or the platform of the Republican ticket. I believed that Carter's was a failed first term, and that if relieved of political constraints, in a second term he would continue to retreat from his commitment to Israel and other allies and meekly accept further erosions of the principle of equal treatment of all Americans.

As I watched Carter concede to Reagan on election night and observed Jesse Jackson, the friend of Arafat, standing beside him, I believed I had done right, though I was then and am increasingly concerned about the cluster of single issue constituencies and greedy interests around Mr. Reagan. I shared the common view that he is a decent man, but the President of the United States is symbolically the moral leader of a country which has no Archbishop of Canterbury. He himself must thus face down all manifestations of bigotry, racial or religious, lest such forces, which I suspect lurk in the shadow of his tall figure, do damage to his reputation and that of the country.

Even before Reagan's victory, old friends, many of them black, had begun to say, "Morris is going conservative." When challenged I asked to be shown the text book or decalogue for liberals. None could point to any betrayal of my basic political philosophy.

Since Reagan's election I have testified before the United States Commission on Civil Rights and the Senate Judiciary Committee in opposition to preferential treatment of Americans by race, ethnic, or gender classification. I have opposed the litigation stance of the Lawyers' Committee for Civil Rights Under Law contesting merit system examinations in the Federal Civil Service on the sole grounds that proportionately fewer blacks and Hispanics pass than whites.

In the political and philanthropic mansion in which I have resided, these and similar views and actions have aroused not a little resentment. In the face of such reaction I would be a case-hardened fool to refuse to examine my views. I owe it to myself to take a compass reading of my present course in relation to the causes for which I have worked: civil rights, civil liberties, intergroup relations, international cooperation, and academia.

I joined the civil rights movement to remove the hideous stain of racial discrimination in American society. When I urged Atlanta Mayor Ivan Allen, Jr. to support the Civil Rights legislation of

President Johnson, the key word "desegregation" was explicitly defined as ending racial preferences, not instituting new ones. The legislation enacted made it unlawful "to discriminate against any individual . . . because of . . . race, color, religion, sex, or national origin. . . ."

I have relished the close association of blacks and Jews in the struggle to make America better, but I never intended to embrace, as some liberals have, a Third World ideology which excoriates Western nations and ennobles leftwing dictators.

I have always acknowledged the necessity of intergovernmental organs in a world of increasing interdependence, but I discern no moral authority in the bloc votes of a mass of UN members that apply double standards not only in the General Assembly but in many of the important UN specialized agencies. I hear the increasingly vocal demands of undeveloped UN members for a "new economic order," meaning a redistribution of benefits from the developed Northern hemisphere to the South. But I wonder why these demands are not addressed stridently to fellow Third World nations in OPEC, awash in wealth extracted from the West and their own people, much of which is being squandered?

I have always believed in a rational American defense posture, one in which the military is held to strict civilian accountability for its spending and its operations. But I do not assume a benignity in a Soviet military build-up. I believe a capable and accountable national intelligence service lessens the risk of war.

I hold academia in esteem, to such a degree that I am appalled that distinguished institutions (Amherst is one such) in the cause of liberalism are willing to accept money for endowed chairs with strings attached which make race the element in the appointment of the occupant. I believe it is a disservice to the university and all of its community for different academic standards to be applied on a basis of race, religion, or gender.

I joined the Lawyers' Committee for Civil Rights Under Law to work for the legal equation of black skins and white, not, as I now perceive the Committee's thrust, to throw all blacks into one group and all whites in another, apportioning social and political benefits by the number in each group. I find the oft used argument that we suspend the constitutional equal protection for a limited period no more acceptable than a plea to temporarily abridge free speech or habeas corpus.

I joined the American Civil Liberties Union and have supported its defense of civil liberties of the Nazis in Skokie, Illinois, and the Klan in Alabama. Freedom of peaceful expression is necessary for the full development of humaneness and it is the best corrective for private, public, and intellectual error. I deplore the latter-day reluctance among civil libertarians to discuss the pathologies of the black ghetto ("racist"), radical leftwing politics ("McCarthyism"), or the Soviet threat ("cold war politics"). I did not support the cause of civil liberties to advance certain ideas while throttling others.

I hope it can be truly said that I adhere to the tradition of American liberalism, in which certain individual moral rights are basic— free speech is one—and in which lesser claims for public services, such as for schools and parks, are settled by majority vote. Such claims are not rights like free speech. In the tradition I espouse, the general welfare is advanced by the strict enforcement of basic individual rights and by the freeing of individual initiative in a society of equal opportunity. Poverty does not have a legal claim on society on a par with free speech; but neither may society assign any person to a condition or status of poverty.

Thus, liberalism for me means that, while men differ in their natural endowments, they must be treated as equal citizens in the eyes of the law; that they should possess equality of opportunity and be afforded some minimum of social benefits. These principles, which united American liberals for generations, now divide me from some who seek equality of result and who sanction the preferences imposed by government to attain it.

In 1962, when I applied for admission to the Bar of the State of New York, I was required to state my understanding of the principles that underlie the form of government of the United States. I then said:

"While the government legislates and administers generally by representative majorities, not even these may affect certain rights of the people, including those to equal protection and due process of law. . . . I conceive ours as a government designed to achieve and safeguard the maximum possible liberty of conscience, expression, and human effort. This liberty is contained within the framework of law which I regard as the source of liberty for man living in society.''

Obviously I would give the same response today.

I believe that this definition of liberalism—this combination of egalitarianism and individualism—was the basis of the Democratic coalition which Franklin Delano Roosevelt forged and which Lyndon B. Johnson mobilized to transform our society. Those who now argue the case for ''benign'' discrimination betray that great tradition of liberalism and weaken the political coalition that makes social and economic progress possible, in that they set group against group in competition for preferences.

Elements of the Democratic coalition had, since McGovern, succeeded in changing the direction of the party. New rules governing the Democratic National Convention had structurally transformed the body that nominates its presidential candidates and legislates its platform. The Convention was then somewhat apportioned by race, gender, and even age. The Democratic party was becoming the ''quota'' party.

Hubert Humphrey in 1968 was the last Democratic candidate nominated by the political mechanics that placed successively Franklin Delano Roosevelt, Harry S. Truman, Adlai Stevenson, John F. Kennedy, and Lyndon B. Johnson at the top of the ticket. I felt very much at home in the Democratic coalition from Franklin D. Roosevelt to Hubert H. Humphrey. But now I was at odds with many present leaders and themes of the Democratic party as defined by its Conventions.

When my friend, Shirley Williams, former Minister of Education in the Labor Government of Great Britain, joined other labor ministers in forming a new party, I understood why. She could not abide the sharp left turn of Labor under my Oxford classmate Anthony Wedgwood Benn, and she could not affiliate with the Conservatives led by Margaret Thatcher.

Shirley Williams made a lonely decision. I hope her new party will work. For myself, I can only wish that in a rigidly two-party America, new leadership will restore the Democratic party to the vital center. The American left is a legitimate and sizeable voice, but I do not believe it embodies the traditions of the Democratic party. I hope my party will return to its traditional centrist liberal moorings.

266

I was well aware that the public positions I adopted in the Carter/Reagan contest and afterwards would strain old comradeships. I knew the risk I ran. Already my opposition to racial quotas and my public condemnation of Andrew Young's conduct at the UN had marked me as a deviant by some colleagues from previous political wars. I revel in the opportunity to discuss the points of difference, especially with old friends, asking always, "How have my views changed?"

Frequently I am told that I overemphasize preferential treatment. "Why do you make it such a cause?" The reason is the transcendent importance I assign to a racially and religiously neutral public polity. My battle for one man, one vote was but one of the many stages in the fight for the principle that every person by law possesses in America the same bundle of constitutional rights—no more, no less.

It is also contended that I've grown too vehement, too combative. I concede there is no more determined advocate than I and that on issues of principle I will not be budged. I cannot deny that I enjoy—yes, relish—debate, which has been one of my greatest pleasures; nor will I conceal that I like to score and, if possible, win. Conversation in which agreement is rampant soon bores me. I like the sparks of contest between peers.

Since I was a sixteen-year-old freshman at Georgia, I have tended to consider a stand-up position on a core belief as a mark of good character, and failure to defend a belief as cowardice. It is unlikely I shall rid myself of this trait, especially as I have reveled in it so long.

Still, I grieve the unnecessary chill in old and valued friendships, simply because of honest political differences. It is a sad paradox that in almost every instance where the ties of friendship have been severed, it was done by one who professes devotion to the principle of freedom of expression, to the promotion of difference of opinion, in the search for truth.

Sometimes I lie awake at night wondering whether my public bolt from the Democratic candidate was worth the personal cost. As it turned out, neither my voice nor that of Eddie Costikyan was needed to dethrone Jimmy Carter, our sole reason for announcing for Reagan. Yet I was schooled that it is a civic duty to act as if one's vote would make the difference. My principal regret is that the real choice of November 1980 was limited to Ronald Reagan and Jimmy Carter.

My vote for Reagan caused deep rumblings within The Field Foundation, from which I resigned as president at a special meeting on October 12, 1981. It was ironic that my separation from the Foundation came about in part because of my efforts to bring other than a monolithic view to the board on the issue of racial preferences, a subject on which I had been invited to lecture at All Souls College, Oxford, and for which I was leaving that very day.

Other differences had developed within the Field board since my old friend from Atlanta, Leslie Dunbar, had resigned as executive director in 1980 because the Foundation, under my leadership, had rejected his recommendation for a grant to an umbrella organization opposed to all CIA covert activity abroad. After Dunbar's departure, I was unsuccessful in opposing a grant to the Institute for Policy Studies, established in the turbulent 1960s. There had been a history of Field support of IPS but now there was credible evidence that it or its "fellows" were negative to the United States and its allies and sympathetic toward revolutionary and terrorist movements, including the PLO.

When I was outvoted, I did not resign, as did one director who called the IPS activities "disgusting," for I hoped to reverse the Foundation's drift away from its primary concerns of race relations, child welfare, and poverty. However, I became increasingly isolated from the majority of the board when I tried to direct attention to the hard-core poverty in the growing numbers of single-family female-headed households. This raised the resistance of blacks and others on the board akin to that which met Daniel P. Moynihan's paper identifying the same problem—then much smaller—in 1965. I was unwilling to resign before meeting with the board, for, as I said to my colleagues on October 12, "I could not leave ambiguously assigning any reason except the sad circumstances which exist." I acknowledged that, after twenty-two years on the board and sixteen years as president, it hurt to leave; "Ruth Field, Adlai Stevenson, and Lloyd Garrison of this Foundation had a lot to do with the decision of my then young family to move from Georgia to New York, where I joined giants on the board, among whom were notably Ralph Bunche and Clarence Pickett (each a recipient of a Nobel Prize), to continue on a larger stage and with more resources the civil rights and civil liberties struggles I had pursued in Georgia.'' I felt I must make clear to my associates my continued commitment to the purposes of the Foundation, recalling "milestones of our common effort, the massive drive for black voter registration in the South, exposure of the terrible secret of hunger in America; the pioneering efforts of early childhood education . . . [and] perhaps the most contentious—and some of our best thrusts—to preserve civil liberties and the rule of law.''

I then opened a magnum of champagne and in a voice which unashamedly revealed my sorrow, toasted the Foundation, and Ruth Field. I had to leave the meeting at once to catch the plane for England.

15

IT IS NOW NINE YEARS since I was stricken with fatal illness and restored to the living. I carry as full a load in my legal practice as before and now spend considerable time as chairman of the President's Commission for the Study of Ethical Problems in Medicine. In this post my interest in law and medicine intersect, intensified by my personal experience as a patient in an advanced medical research program. Once again I trust somehow that I will be spared long enough to complete that task.

Useful, interesting work and love possess healing properties. All my doctors give ample credit to the powers of the spirit. One day I thanked Dr. Holland for his unstinted efforts. He pointed to Carlyn and said, "Thank her." Challenges add to my well-being. I became physically ill at a period when I was depressed; I never felt *as* depressed during the illness itself.

My illness and the breakup of my marriage have left their marks on my entire family. Although the children continue to see Jane and me separately, out of some intuition they tend to shield us from each other. Josh, who was more afraid of losing our close relationship than of losing me through death, said recently, "Divorce has been at the center of my life for nine years—almost half of my life." When my marital ties were being severed, it never occurred to me that practically all the ties of a thirty-year relationship would be severed as well. As Josh put it, "How can there be a successful amputation? You never can have what you used to have."

I suppose it is human nature to think that you can. At least I felt myself constantly stretching over the chasm for contact with Jane, though on a different basis. I discovered, however, as have legions of others before me, that this cannot be. I do not easily surrender friends to time, distance, or even death. Yet I find myself cut off from the woman who was my closest friend for most of my life and whom I respect for her character and intelligence and as the mother of my children. We have learned how to deal openly with the problems of alcoholism, sexuality, and even cancer, but we have still to develop humane ways to convert a failed marriage into something different, fruitful, and ongoing.

In the past nine years I have reflected greatly on death. I cannot say that I ever accepted the prognosis in June 1973, though all the evidence confirmed it. I did not resist out of fear; it is just that I have always enjoyed life, and in accordance with the primary obligation of my tradition, I choose it, embrace it. I regard the spirit that burns in every person as holy, never to be extinguished—not even by death—for it shines in the lives of others.

True, when I left Dr. Ashman's office on that June night, I was devastated. My first thought was that my illness was the dramatization of a metaphor. For years since Brandeis I had been hurting. My spiritual malaise was deep—to the very marrow of my bones, and now in the marrow of my bones, a disease was threatening to snuff me out.

Whether the disease would have its way was not the primary question that came to me. I was instead preoccupied by the thought, why now, why at this time, when my children are still so young, when I need to test myself again, and when I am once again in love?

In the days following the diagnosis, I always found relief in the contemplation that if death were the end of existence, it also had a curious and even magnetic fascination for me. A painting on a canvas of infinite size, worked on forever, would be without focus or

271

meaning and probably without beauty. A painting, like life, needs limits. Since I have an almost insatiable craving for knowledge, I found some comfort, too, in the possibility that death may be the greatest as well as the final, teacher, the one that provides the key to the ultimate questions life has never answered.

Much has changed for me in the last nine years. I have worked hard, realizing that the frame of the picture is closing in. I have tried to focus on what is important. The ceaseless dinners, receptions, and other public functions, have been curbed. The list of acquaintances called friends has been trimmed while real friendships have been intensified. I give more of myself to fewer. I am more open to my children and I have come to know them at a deeper level. I've wanted to make up for time spent away from them. As I said to Eli: "My needs now are closer to theirs; but they always knew what I did not." Cancer can bring balance and its own kind of wisdom.

Too late I realize that I could never be a political man, for I could never invest my interests in the exhausting banalities demanded of a successful politician. I know that he has to blot out, as I never could, the face of his small child pressed against the car window as he leaves for a tour of kissing other people's children. Nor could I ever have adopted positions incongruent with my beliefs. I have been freed, in a way that few men are, by living for almost a decade under the present threat of extinction.

Still, the worry that I might fall out of remission never ceases. Each day I examine my fingers and palms to be reassured by the rosy flush from healthy blood cells, nervous that some day I'll flunk a bone marrow examination and be promptly sentenced to chemotherapy or worse.

Dr. Cuttner told me years ago, "Every day you remain in remission improves your chances, not arithmetically but geometrically." But I do not relish advancing age, for I know there are only so many grains in the hourglass. I must, therefore, be one of the few happy men who greets birthdays with distinctly mixed feelings. Although I do not dwell unduly on death, I now read obituary pages in a different way. Of what did each neomort die and at what age— and if from cancer, under what circumstances? And how advanced was the medicine available at the place of treatment? I am, of course,

272

always saddened at the death of friends, but I feel a special stake if cancer is the cause.

I had been most concerned that I would predecease my mother, whom I visited several times each year, always departing Fitzgerald with the fear that the farewell meant something entirely different to her than to me, she believing herself, of course, the earlier candidate for the grave. I knew, however, that in spite of her age, she was in better health than I.

My mother died in November 1979, at the age of eighty-seven, still without knowledge that I had been ill for years. My brother and sisters and I assembled in Fitzgerald, where the services were conducted by a rabbi imported from Valdosta. He had never met my mother. I did not intend to speak, but as the rabbi delivered the usually effusive eulogy in which the deceased is totally misrepresented, I felt I had to set the record straight for the fifty people or so who had assembled. I described "a strong, proud, intelligent woman who inculcated independence and a sense of worth in her four surviving children, who love one another . . . not an easy person to know . . . she admired people of independence and intelligence, appreciated the common people and their ordinary ways, but she could not abide fraud, pretense, or hypocrisy." My voice broke as I continued, "Irene Cohen Abram was a woman of quality and principle. She will live on as a force in the lives of those whom she nurtured."

Of course I could not then speak of my psychic isolation from her since my marriage to Jane; how, once I had connected with a woman of far greater vision and experience, I found very few chords other than those of duty and memory which would tie me emotionally to my strong but closed-off mother. For years my visits to Fitzgerald had been perfunctory. Once the topics of childhood and local news were exhausted, we had little to say to each other. Sadly, the wider my horizons became, the more mother and I lived in separate worlds. I felt guilty that my parents' struggles in my behalf had created a gulf. I comforted myself with the thought that they would still have wanted each of their children to succeed. I found satisfaction, too, in the belief that my relations with my own children were different. At least we inhabited the same world of educated men and women.

Mother spent her last year shuttling between a nursing home and a hospital. She had lived past the point when life was pleasant. It has given me food for contemplation.

As much as I relish life, I realize that there may come a time for me also when it is no longer enjoyable, when death is near. Then I wish to extend the usefulness of my life, by offering myself as a candidate for high risk therapy. Human subjects are a rare resource for research medicine and can leave an incalculable legacy to succeeding generations.

This is not entirely an altruistic choice for me. It is partially a reflection of my disposition. I have never been a cautious man, and in a good cause, I would be more willing than ever to take risks. As my remission continues, I notice that I am more inclined to consider the long-term consequence of actions. But I know that time is limited, and I tend to be in a hurry. I am daily reminded of an ancient Hebrew text that says, "The day is short, the work is great. . . . It is not thy duty to complete the work, but neither art thou free to desist from it."

Index

277